Nov 1/17

De[ar]

Congratulations
on an excellent
semester in Grade 10
Frodo you were
truly a ray of
sunshine!
Best wishes for a
great school year.

Ms. Murray

Better Homes and Gardens®

CHRISTMAS COOKING

FROM THE HEART™

Simple to Sensational

Meredith® Books
Des Moines, Iowa

Test Kitchen

Our seal assures you that every recipe in *Christmas Cooking from the Heart* has been tested in the Better Homes and Gardens® Test Kitchen. This means that each recipe is practical and reliable, and meets our high standards of taste appeal. We guarantee your satisfaction with this book for as long as you own it.

All of us at Meredith® Books are dedicated to providing you with information and ideas to enhance your home. We welcome your comments and suggestions. Write to us at: Meredith Books Editorial Department, 1716 Locust St., Des Moines, IA 50309-3023.
Christmas Cooking from the Heart is available by mail. To order editions from past years, call 800/627-5490.

Cover Photograph:
Blaine Moats
Pictured: Crustless Cheesecake, page 104; Peanut Butter Cup Fudge, page 91; and Christmas Sugar Cookies, page 74

Back Cover Photograph:
Southern-Style Pork Loin Roast, page 19

Better Homes and Gardens®
CHRISTMAS COOKING
FROM THE HEART™

Editor: Jessica Saari
Contributing Editors: Carrie Holcomb, Joyce Trollope
Contributing Recipe Developers: Juli Hale, Shelli McConnell, Jennifer Peterson, Colleen Weeden
Associate Art Director: Todd Emerson Hanson
Copy Chief: Terri Fredrickson
Copy Editor: Kevin Cox
Publishing Operations Manager: Karen Schirm
Senior Editor, Asset and Information Manager: Phillip Morgan
Edit and Design Production Coordinator: Mary Lee Gavin
Editorial Assistant: Cheryl Eckert
Art and Editorial Sourcing Coordinator: Kathy Stevens
Book Production Managers: Pam Kvitne, Marjorie J. Schenkelberg, Rick von Holdt, Mark Weaver
Contributing Copy Editor: Carol DeMasters
Contributing Proofreaders: Karen Fraley, Judy Friedman, Jody Speer
Contributing Indexer: Elizabeth T. Parson
Test Kitchen Director: Lynn Blanchard
Test Kitchen Product Supervisor: Jill Moberly

Meredith® Books
Editor in Chief: Gregory H. Kayko
Executive Director, Design: Matt Strelecki
Managing Editor: Amy Tincher-Durik
Executive Editor: Jennifer Darling
Senior Editor/Group Manager: Jan Miller
Senior Associate Design Director: Ken Carlson
Marketing Product Manager: Toye Guinn Cody

Executive Director, Marketing and New Business: Kevin Kacere
Editorial Director: Linda Raglan Cunningham
Executive Director, New Business Development: Todd M. Davis
Director, Marketing and Publicity: Amy Nichols
Executive Director, Sales: Ken Zagor
Director, Operations: George A. Susral
Director, Production: Douglas M. Johnston
Business Director: Jim Leonard

Vice President and General Manager: Douglas J. Guendel

Better Homes and Gardens® Magazine
Editor in Chief: Gayle Goodson Butler
Deputy Editor, Home Design: Oma Blaise Ford
Deputy Editor, Food and Entertaining: Nancy Wall Hopkins

Meredith Publishing Group
President: Jack Griffin
Senior Vice President: Karla Jeffries
Vice President, Corporate Solutions: Michael Brownstein
Vice President, Creative Services: Ellen de Lathouder
Vice President, Manufacturing: Bruce Heston
Vice President, Consumer Marketing: David Ball
Consumer Product Associate Marketing Director: Steve Swanson
Consumer Product Marketing Manager: Wendy Merical
Business Manager: Darren Tollefson

Meredith Corporation
Chairman of the Board: William T. Kerr
President and Chief Executive Officer: Steve Lacy

In Memoriam: E.T. Meredith III (1933–2003)

Copyright © 2007 by Meredith Corporation. Des Moines, Iowa. First Edition.
All rights reserved. Printed in the United States of America.
ISSN: 1540-5478   ISBN: 978-0-696-23558-0

Table of Contents

French Toast, page 48

How much time do you want to spend in the kitchen this holiday?

Whether you crave the chance to create the most fabulous holiday feast ever, or simply hope to put together the easiest (yet utterly delicious) Christmas spread possible so you can join in the fun—*Christmas Cooking from the Heart* has you covered. Throughout this book, you can find a simple and sensational version of every recipe—from turkey, pork, and beef dishes for the big Christmas feast, to sinfully sweet nibbles for cookie trays and gifts. Depending on how much time and energy you want to put into holiday goodies, there's both an easier and a fancier version to help you out.

Traditionally, Christmastime is a chance for home cooks to pull out the stops and prepare all the tempting foods they desire. From golden roasted turkey and creamy mashed potatoes to sweet pies and irresistible cookies, there is no end to the fabulous foods that often only make an appearance during the holiday season. Can anyone really prepare it all? In order to enjoy the spirit of the season, finding time to spend with family and friends is equally important. This year, cook the practical way by simplifying some of the cooking and sensationalizing other parts. That way, you'll have a fabulous spread, but you'll deliver it in a fraction of the time! Each recipe in this book has a simple version and sensational version, so you can pick and choose what holiday foods you want to highlight. If you love desserts, in that chapter you'll find a chocolate cake that melts in the mouth and is decked out with rich homemade frosting and garnishes galore. If you want a great dessert, but don't want to spend extra time on that part of the meal, you'll find a simplified chocolate cake that can be made in half the time. This holiday season, choose which foods you want to simplify and which you want to sensationalize!

The "Simple" icon indicates that a recipe is the easier version—it takes less time to prepare and has fewer steps and ingredients. The "Sensational" icon symbolizes that a dish is the fancier, more involved version with all the bells and whistles. For each type of recipe in this book, there is a simple and sensational version—generally the simple version appears first.

Molasses-Spice Gravy, page 26

Snow Angel Cake, page 100; Christmas Sugar Cookies, page 74; Easy Bittersweet Chocolate-Orange Fudge, page 91; and Peanut Butter Cup Fudge, page 91

Special Christmas Feasts

Christmas dinner is the culmination of the holiday season! To make this celebration the best it can be, prepare a combination of simple and sensational dishes. The simple dishes can be just as fantastic as the sensational! For example, three-ingredient Orange-Glazed Baby Carrots boasts a windfall of flavors, and no one will ever guess that Cream Cheese Mashed Potatoes is based on instant mashed potato flakes. On the flipside, for many, the holidays bring a yearning to spend time in the kitchen, cooking with family and friends. For those times, try Pear-Glazed Roast Turkey, a culinary masterpiece packed with an array of spices and herbs, or Holiday Cranberry Salsa, which brings a freshness to the table that will tantalize tastebuds. Whatever the recipe, remember that togetherness is the heart of every feast!

Pear-Glazed Roast Turkey, page 16

Insalata Mista

This Italian mixed greens salad is flavored with fresh mozzarella, a specialty cheese worth seeking for its distinctive sweet flavor and soft texture. Look for it at specialty Italian markets, cheese shops, and many supermarkets.

Start to Finish: 15 minutes **Makes:** 8 servings

 8 cups torn mixed salad greens
 2 cups cherry tomatoes, halved
 1 cup tiny yellow pear-shaped tomatoes
 1 cup Greek black olives and green olives
 ½ cup snipped fresh basil
 1 recipe Italian Vinaigrette
 6 ounces sliced fresh mozzarella cheese

1. Toss together greens, tomatoes, olives, and basil. Drizzle with Italian Vinaigrette; toss to coat. Add cheese.

Italian Vinaigrette: In screw-top jar combine ¼ cup olive oil, ¼ cup balsamic vinegar, 4 teaspoons snipped fresh basil, ¼ teaspoon salt, and ¼ teaspoon ground black pepper. Cover and shake well.

Per serving: 168 cal., 13 g total fat (4 g sat. fat), 15 mg chol., 296 mg sodium, 7 g carbo., 2 g fiber, 5 g pro.
Daily Values: 21% vit. A, 16% vit. C, 18% calcium, 7% iron

Beet Salad with Orange-Balsamic Dressing

Using the hollowed beet to hold tender baby greens is just one more way to add an unexpected—and beautiful—presentation to the holiday table.

Prep: 30 minutes **Cook:** 35 minutes
Chill: 4 hours **Makes:** 8 servings

Beet Salad with Orange-Balsamic Dressing

8 medium beets (about 2½ pounds)
12 baby golden beets, untrimmed with tops
1 pound fresh green beans, trimmed
¼ cup orange juice
¼ cup olive oil
2 tablespoons balsamic vinegar
1 small shallot, finely chopped
2 teaspoons Dijon-style mustard
¼ teaspoon kosher salt or sea salt
8 cups loosely packed arugula or
   mixed baby salad greens (mesclun)
   Freshly ground black pepper

1. For medium beets, cut off all but 1 inch of the fresh beet stems and roots; wash. Do not peel beets. In a large saucepan cook the medium beets, covered, in boiling salted water to cover for 35 to 45 minutes or until tender; drain. Cool; slip off skins. Use an apple corer to cut a hole through the center of each medium beet. If necessary, cut a thin slice from bottoms of medium beets so they stand upright. Cover and chill thoroughly. In a medium saucepan cook baby beets, covered, in boiling salted water to cover for 8 to 10 minutes or until tender; drain. Cool. Slip off skins and halve the beets. Cover and chill thoroughly.

2. In a large saucepan cook green beans, covered, in a small amount of lightly salted boiling water for 10 to 15 minutes or until crisp-tender. Drain and transfer beans to a bowl of ice water to chill; drain again.

3. Meanwhile, for dressing, in a screw-top jar combine orange juice, oil, vinegar, shallot, mustard, and salt. Cover; shake well.

4. Stand a medium beet upright on each of eight salad plates. Fill center of each beet with some of the greens. Arrange remaining greens, beans, and 3 baby beet halves around the larger beets. Drizzle with dressing. Sprinkle with pepper.

Per serving: 149 cal., 7 g total fat (1 g sat. fat), 0 mg chol., 195 mg sodium, 20 g carbo., 6 g fiber, 4 g pro.
Daily Values: 18% vit. A, 29% vit. C, 7% calcium, 11% iron

Tomato Soup

This scrumptious soup tastes like it's made with fresh-from-the-garden tomatoes—but since it uses the canned variety as its base, it can be made any time of the year!

Prep: 20 minutes **Cook:** 25 minutes
Makes: 4 side-dish servings

1 14.5-ounce can diced tomatoes,
   undrained
1½ cups water
½ cup chopped onion (1 medium)
½ cup chopped celery (1 stalk)
½ of a 6-ounce can (⅓ cup) tomato paste
1 tablespoon snipped fresh parsley
2 teaspoons instant chicken
   bouillon granules
2 teaspoons lime juice or lemon juice
1 teaspoon sugar
   Few dashes bottled hot pepper sauce
   Snipped fresh parsley (optional)

1. In a medium saucepan combine undrained tomatoes, water, onion, celery, tomato paste, parsley, bouillon, lime juice, sugar, and hot pepper sauce. Bring to boiling; reduce heat. Simmer, covered, about 20 minutes or until celery and onion are very tender. Cool mixture slightly.

2. Place half of the mixture in a blender or food processor. Cover; blend or process until smooth. Repeat with remaining mixture. Return all of the pureed mixture to the same saucepan. Cook and stir over medium heat until heated through. If desired, garnish with additional parsley.

Per serving: 61 cal., 0 g total fat (0 g sat. fat), 0 mg chol., 795 mg sodium, 13 g carbo., 2 g fiber, 2 g pro.
Daily Values: 10% vit. A, 35% vit. C, 6% calcium, 7% iron

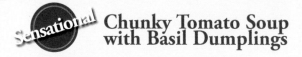 ## Chunky Tomato Soup with Basil Dumplings

Dainty basil-flavored dumplings set this delicious soup apart from other versions.

Prep: 30 minutes **Cook:** 40 minutes
Makes: 6 side-dish servings

- 1 cup coarsely chopped onion (1 large)
- 2 tablespoons chopped shallot (1 medium)
- 2 cloves garlic, minced
- 2 tablespoons olive oil
- 1 14-ounce can reduced-sodium chicken broth
- ½ cup coarsely chopped carrot (1 medium)
- ½ cup coarsely chopped celery (1 stalk)
- ½ cup coarsely chopped red sweet pepper (1 small)
- 1 tablespoon lemon juice
- ½ teaspoon sugar
- 1 14.5-ounce can diced tomatoes, undrained
    Dash cayenne pepper
- 1 recipe Basil Dumplings
    Salt
    Freshly ground black pepper
    Fresh basil sprigs (optional)

1. In a large saucepan cook onion, shallot, and garlic in hot oil over medium heat about 5 minutes or until onion is tender, stirring frequently. Add the broth, carrot, celery, sweet pepper, lemon juice, and sugar. Bring to boiling; reduce heat. Cover; simmer for 20 to 25 minutes or until vegetables are very tender. Cool slightly; do not drain.

2. Place half of the mixture into a blender or food processor; cover and blend or process until smooth. Repeat with remaining mixture.

3. Return all of the pureed mixture to the same saucepan. Stir in undrained tomatoes and cayenne pepper. Cook, uncovered, over low heat about 10 minutes or until heated through, stirring often.

4. Meanwhile, fill a pot half-full with water; bring to boiling. Drop Basil Dumplings dough from a slightly rounded ½ teaspoon measuring spoon into boiling water. Cook for 4 to 5 minutes (start timing after dough rises to the surface) or until dumplings are cooked through, turning once. To test for doneness, remove a dumpling and check the center, mak-ing sure it is cooked through. Using a slotted spoon, remove the dumplings; drain in a colander. Rinse dumplings under cold running water; drain again.

5. Add half of the dumplings to soup in saucepan; heat through. Season soup to taste with salt and black pepper. Ladle into soup bowls or cups. Top with remaining dumplings. If desired, garnish individual servings with basil sprigs.

Basil Dumplings: In a small bowl combine ⅓ cup all-purpose flour, 1 tablespoon snipped fresh basil, ¼ teaspoon baking powder, and ½ teaspoon salt. In a small bowl stir together 1 beaten egg and 2 teaspoons cooking oil; pour all at once into flour mixture. Using a wooden spoon beat until a soft, sticky dough forms.

Per serving: 137 cal., 7 g total fat (1 g sat. fat), 35 mg chol., 549 mg sodium, 15 g carbo., 2 g fiber, 4 g pro.
Daily Values: 45% vit. A, 61% vit. C, 5% calcium, 6% iron

 ## Oyster Soup

For many people, a holiday dinner is only complete with a starter of steaming oyster soup—and this classic version is sure to please.

Prep: 10 minutes **Cook:** 8 minutes
Makes: 4 main-dish servings

- 1 pint shucked oysters
- ¼ cup finely chopped onion or sliced leek
- 2 teaspoons butter or margarine
- ½ teaspoon salt
- 2 cups milk
- 1 cup half-and-half or light cream
- 1 tablespoon snipped fresh parsley
- 1 tablespoon chopped pimiento (optional)
- ¼ teaspoon ground white pepper
    Butter or margarine (optional)

1. Drain oysters reserving 2 tablespoons of the liquid; set aside. Discard any remaining liquid. In a medium saucepan cook and stir onion in 2 teaspoons butter over medium heat about 5 minutes until onion is tender but not brown. Add the oysters, 2 tablespoons reserved liquid, and salt. Cook and stir over medium heat for 5 minutes or until oysters curl around the edges.

2. Stir in milk, half-and-half, parsley, pimiento (if desired), and pepper. Cook and stir until heated through. If desired, garnish each serving with a pat of butter.

Per serving: 238 cal., 14 g total fat (8 g sat. fat), 97 mg chol., 619 mg sodium, 14 g carbo., 0 g fiber, 14 g pro.
Daily Values: 14% vit. A, 12% vit. C, 26% calcium, 43% iron

Oyster and Corn Chowder

Shucked oysters should be used as soon as possible after purchase. As long as they are fresh-looking and fresh-smelling, they can be refrigerated for up to two days.

Start to Finish: 45 minutes
Makes: 3 main-dish servings

- 1 **cup chopped onion (1 large)**
- ½ **cup chopped red sweet pepper**
- 1 **clove garlic, minced**
- 2 **teaspoons olive oil**
- 1 **14-ounce can reduced-sodium chicken broth**
- 1½ **cups coarsely chopped potato**
- 1 **fresh jalapeño chile pepper, seeded and finely chopped***
- ¼ **teaspoon salt**
  Dash ground black pepper
- 8 **ounces shucked oysters with their liquid**
- 1 **cup fresh or frozen whole kernel corn**
- 1 **tablespoon snipped fresh oregano**
- ½ **cup half-and-half or light cream**
  Fresh oregano sprigs (optional)

1. In a medium saucepan cook and stir onion, sweet pepper, and garlic in hot oil over medium heat until tender.

2. Carefully stir chicken broth, potato, jalapeño pepper, salt, and black pepper into vegetable mixture in saucepan. Bring to boiling; reduce heat. Simmer, covered, about 10 minutes or until potato is nearly tender. Stir in undrained oysters, corn, and oregano. Return to boiling; reduce heat.

Oyster and Corn Chowder

3. Cover; simmer about 5 minutes or until oysters are plump and opaque. Stir in half-and-half; heat through. If desired, garnish with oregano sprigs.

*Note: Because hot chile peppers, such as jalapeños, contain oils that can burn skin and eyes, avoid direct contact with chiles as much as possible. When working with chile peppers, wear plastic or rubber gloves. If your bare hands do touch the chile peppers, wash them well with soap and water.

Per serving: 276 cal., 10 g total fat (4 g sat. fat), 55 mg chol., 728 mg sodium, 36 g carbo., 4 g fiber, 13 g pro.
Daily Values: 36% vit. A, 107% vit. C, 10% calcium, 37% iron

Simple

Potato-Bean Soup

Standard potato soup goes upscale when dillweed and sour cream are included.

Prep: 15 minutes **Cook:** 25 minutes
Makes: 6 side-dish servings

- 1   cup shredded carrot (2 medium)
- ½   cup sliced celery (1 stalk)
- 1   clove garlic, minced
- 1   tablespoon butter
- 4   cups chicken broth
- 3   cups cubed, peeled potato
- 2   tablespoons snipped fresh dillweed or
     2 teaspoons dried dillweed
- 1   15-ounce can cannellini beans
     (white kidney beans) or Great Northern
     beans, rinsed and drained
- ½   cup dairy sour cream
- 1   tablespoon all-purpose flour
- ⅛   teaspoon ground black pepper
     Dash salt (optional)

1. In a large saucepan cook and stir carrot, celery, and garlic in hot butter over medium heat for 4 minutes or until tender. Carefully stir in chicken broth, potato, and dillweed. Bring to boiling; reduce heat. Simmer, covered, for 20 to 25 minutes or until potato is tender. With the back of spoon, lightly mash about half of the potato in the broth. Stir the drained beans into the potato mixture.

Curried Bean and Pepper Soup

2. In a small bowl stir together sour cream, flour, pepper, and salt (if using); stir into soup mixture. Cook and stir for 1 minute more.

Per serving: 175 cal., 6 g total fat (3 g sat. fat), 14 mg chol., 799 mg sodium, 28 g carbo., 5 g fiber, 7 g pro.
Daily Values: 72% vit. A, 27% vit. C, 5% calcium, 8% iron

 ## Curried Bean and Pepper Soup

Even without meat, this well-seasoned soup boasts plenty of satisfying flavor. Serve the colorful mixture over hot cooked rice, if desired.

Prep: 25 minutes **Cook:** 20 minutes
Makes: 4 to 6 servings

- 1 medium onion, cut into wedges
- 4 cloves garlic, minced
- 1 tablespoon olive oil
- 1 15-ounce can tomato sauce
- ½ teaspoon curry powder
- ¼ teaspoon salt (optional)
- ¼ teaspoon ground allspice
- ¼ teaspoon ground ginger
- ⅛ to ¼ teaspoon cayenne pepper
- 3 medium yellow, red, and/or green sweet peppers, cut into bite-size strips
- 1 15-ounce can red kidney beans, rinsed and drained
- 1 15-ounce can garbanzo beans (chickpeas), rinsed and drained
- 1½ cups water
  Hot cooked basmati or brown rice (optional)
- 1 medium mango, peeled, seeded, and sliced (optional)

1. In a large saucepan cook and stir onion and garlic in hot oil over medium heat about 5 minutes or until tender. Add tomato sauce, curry powder, salt (if desired), allspice, ginger, and cayenne pepper. Cook and stir for 1 minute.

2. Add sweet peppers, drained kidney beans, garbanzo beans, and water to the soup mixture. Bring to boiling; reduce heat. Cover; simmer about 20 minutes or until sweet peppers are tender, stirring occasionally. If desired, serve over hot cooked rice and top with mango.

Per serving: 290 cal., 6 g total fat (1 g sat. fat), 0 mg chol., 1,114 mg sodium, 53 g carbo., 13 g fiber, 15 g pro.
Daily Values: 14% vit. A, 444% vit. C, 9% calcium, 23% iron

 ## Pumpkin Soup

Curry, cumin, and coriander add a terrific flavor to this seasonal soup. Serve as a starter to an elegant meal.

Start to Finish: 25 minutes
Makes: 6 to 8 side-dish servings

- 2 tablespoons finely chopped onion
- ½ teaspoon curry powder
- ¼ teaspoon salt
- ¼ teaspoon ground cumin
- ¼ teaspoon ground coriander
- 1 tablespoon butter or margarine
- 2 15-ounce cans pumpkin
- 2 14-ounce cans chicken broth
- 1 tablespoon packed brown sugar or maple syrup (optional)
- 1 cup half-and-half, light cream, or milk
  Dairy sour cream or purchased crème fraîche (optional)
  Fresh sage leaves (optional)

1. In a large saucepan cook and stir onion, curry powder, salt, cumin, and coriander in hot butter over medium heat until onion is tender. Whisk in pumpkin, chicken broth, and brown sugar (if desired) until well combined.

2. Bring mixture just to boiling; reduce heat. Stir in half-and-half and heat through. If desired, garnish with sour cream and sage leaves.

Per serving: 127 cal., 7 g total fat (4 g sat. fat), 21 mg chol., 663 mg sodium, 14 g carbo., 4 g fiber, 3 g pro.
Daily Values: 445% vit. A, 11% vit. C, 8% calcium, 11% iron

 **Pumpkin-Pear Bisque
with Crème Fraîche**

*One way to serve leftover poached pears is to fill
warm pear halves with ice cream or whipped cream.*

Prep: 35 minutes **Cook:** 40 minutes
Makes: 8 to 10 side-dish servings

- 2 leeks (white part only), thinly sliced (⅔ cup)
- ½ cup chopped sweet onion (1 medium)
- 2 tablespoons butter or margarine
- 3 tablespoons all-purpose flour
- 3 14-ounce cans chicken broth
- 1 15-ounce can pumpkin
- ½ of a vanilla bean, split lengthwise, or
    1 teaspoon vanilla
- ¼ teaspoon salt
- ¼ teaspoon ground white pepper
- ¼ teaspoon ground nutmeg
- 3 Poached Pear Halves plus 1 cup
    poaching liquid
- ½ cup half-and-half, light cream, or milk
  Purchased crème fraîche or
    dairy sour cream
  Ground nutmeg (optional)

1. In a 4-quart Dutch oven cook and stir leeks and onion in hot butter over medium heat until tender. Stir in flour. Carefully add chicken broth all at once. Cook and stir over medium heat until slightly thickened and bubbly. Stir in pumpkin, vanilla bean (if using), salt, pepper, and the ¼ teaspoon nutmeg. Return to boiling; reduce heat. Simmer, covered, for 20 minutes. Remove from heat. Cool slightly. Remove vanilla bean; discard. Add Poached Pear Halves and poaching liquid to Dutch oven.

2. In a food processor or blender cover and process or blend mixture in three or four batches until smooth. Return mixture to Dutch oven. Stir in half-and-half and vanilla (if using).

3. Heat through, but do not boil. To serve, ladle soup into bowls. Drizzle with a spoonful of crème fraîche; swirl to make a design. If desired, sprinkle with additional nutmeg.

Poached Pear Halves: In a large skillet bring 1 cup sweet white wine, such as Sauternes or Riesling; 1 cup water; ½ cup sugar; and 3 whole star anise to boiling. Peel 3 firm, ripe pears; halve lengthwise and core. Add to wine mixture in skillet. Return to boiling; reduce heat. Simmer, covered, for 10 to 15 minutes or until pears are tender. Remove pears from skillet with a slotted spoon. Bring liquid in skillet to boiling; cook, uncovered, about 8 minutes or until reduced to about 1 cup. Discard star anise. (Cover and refrigerate remaining pears for up to one day.) Makes 6 pear halves.

Per cup: 258 cal., 11 g total fat (7 g sat. fat), 35 mg chol., 708 mg sodium, 31 g carbo., 3 g fiber, 2 g pro.
Daily Values: 178% vit. A, 8% vit. C, 4% calcium, 7% iron

Pumpkin-Pear Bisque with Crème Fraîche

Blended Soups

Blended or pureed soups are quite lovely—but take care when you're processing hot soup or you could have a dangerous mess on your hands! Before transferring hot soup to a blender or food processor, be sure to allow it to cool slightly. When you put the lid on the blender or processor, the hot steam from the soup can expand under pressure and cause the mixture to literally explode. Also, be sure to blend or puree in batches so as to not overfill the blender or processor.

Filet Mignon with Cognac Sauce

Easy Beef Tenderloin

Meat lovers appreciate beef tenderloin for its amazing flavor. Serve this decadent dish with a zippy horseradish sauce for extra pizzazz.

Prep: 15 minutes **Roast:** 50 minutes
Stand: 15 minutes **Marinate:** 8 hours
Oven: 425°F **Makes:** 12 to 16 servings

- 1 tablespoon dried thyme, crushed
- 1 teaspoon ground white pepper
- 1 teaspoon garlic salt
- 1 teaspoon seasoned salt
- ¼ teaspoon dried oregano, crushed
- 1 4- to 6-pound beef tenderloin roast
- 2 tablespoons Worcestershire sauce

1. In a small bowl combine thyme, pepper, garlic salt, seasoned salt, and oregano; rub over all sides of meat. Place meat in a large resealable plastic bag; seal bag. Place in refrigerator for 8 to 24 hours.

2. Preheat oven to 425°F. Remove meat from bag and place meat on a rack in a foil-lined roasting pan. Drizzle meat with Worcestershire sauce. Roast for 50 to 60 minutes or until an instant-read thermometer inserted in center of meat registers 135°F for medium rare. (Or roast for 60 to 70 minutes or until thermometer registers 150°F for medium.) Cover meat with foil and let stand 15 minutes before slicing. The temperature of the meat after standing should be 145°F for medium rare or 160°F for medium.

Per serving: 237 cal., 11 g total fat (4 g sat. fat), 92 mg chol., 304 mg sodium, 1 g carbo., 0 g fiber, 31 g pro.
Daily Values: 2% vit. A, 1% vit. C, 2% calcium, 25% iron

Filet Mignon with Cognac Sauce

Be sure to use quality cognac or brandy when preparing this special dish. Inexpensive brands can impart a bitter taste.

Prep: 10 minutes **Grill:** 16 minutes
Stand: 15 minutes **Makes:** 4 servings

- 4 beef tenderloin steaks, cut 1 inch thick (about 1 pound total)
- 3 tablespoons cognac or brandy
- ½ teaspoon coarsely ground black pepper
- 1 cup sliced fresh mushrooms
- 1 tablespoon finely chopped shallot
- 1 tablespoon butter or margarine
- ½ cup beef broth
- ¼ cup half-and-half or light cream
- 2 tablespoons Dijon-style mustard
- 1 tablespoon all-purpose flour

1. Trim fat from steaks. Place in a shallow dish. Pour 2 tablespoons of the cognac over the steaks. Cover and let stand at room temperature for 15 minutes, turning once. Drain steaks, discarding cognac in dish. Sprinkle pepper over both sides of each steak.

2. Place steaks on the rack of an uncovered grill directly over medium coals. Grill to desired doneness, turning once. (Allow 16 to 20 minutes for medium-rare [145°F] or 20 to 24 minutes for medium [160°F].)

3. Meanwhile, in a small saucepan cook mushrooms and shallot in butter for 3 to 4 minutes or until tender. Stir in beef broth and remaining 1 tablespoon cognac. Bring to boiling; reduce heat. Boil gently, uncovered, for 5 minutes.

4. In a small bowl stir together half-and-half, mustard, and flour until smooth. Stir into broth mixture. Cook and stir until thickened and bubbly. Cook and stir for 1 minute more. Serve sauce over steaks.

Per serving: 281 cal., 14 g total fat (7 g sat. fat), 83 mg chol., 372 mg sodium, 4 g carbo., 0 g fiber, 25 g pro.
Daily Values: 3% vit. A, 1% vit. C, 3% calcium, 18% iron

Turkey Breast with Raspberry Salsa

Everyone will rave about this five ingredient recipe.

Prep: 15 minutes **Roast:** 1¼ hours
Stand: 15 minutes **Oven:** 325°F
Makes: 8 servings

⅓ cup seedless raspberry jam
1 tablespoon Dijon-style mustard
1 teaspoon finely shredded orange peel
½ cup bottled mild salsa
1 2- to 2½-pound turkey breast half with bone
 Orange peel strips (optional)

1. Preheat oven to 325°F. In a small bowl stir together raspberry jam, mustard, and 1 teaspoon orange peel. In another small bowl stir 3 tablespoons of the jam mixture into salsa. Cover; chill jam mixture and salsa mixture. If desired, remove skin from turkey breast. Rinse turkey; pat dry with paper towels. Insert an oven-going meat thermometer into center of turkey breast. The tip should not touch bone.

2. Place turkey breast, bone-side down, on a rack in a shallow roasting pan. Roast, uncovered, for 1¼ to 1½ hours or until juices run clear and turkey is no longer pink (170°F), brushing occasionally with jam mixture during the last 15 minutes of roasting.

3. Remove turkey from oven; cover with foil. Let stand for 15 minutes before slicing. Serve turkey with salsa mixture. If desired, garnish turkey with orange peel strips.

Per serving: 200 cal., 7 g total fat (2 g sat. fat), 66 mg chol., 179 mg sodium, 11 g carbo., 0 g fiber, 23 g pro.
Daily Values: 1% vit. A, 6% vit. C, 2% calcium, 7% iron

Pear-Glazed Roast Turkey

Guests or family will love the rich flavor of the pear glaze that coats this beautiful holiday centerpiece.

Prep: 15 minutes **Roast:** 2¾ hours
Stand: 15 minutes **Oven:** 325°F
Makes: 8 to 10 servings

1 10- to 12-pound turkey
1 tablespoon butter, melted
1 recipe Pear Glaze
1 recipe Pan Gravy (optional)
 Roasted pear quarters* (optional)
 Fresh rosemary sprigs (optional)

1. Preheat oven to 325°F. Rinse inside of the turkey; pat dry with paper towels. If desired, season body cavity with *salt*. Pull neck skin to the back; fasten with a skewer. Tuck drumstick ends under band of skin across tail. If there is no band of skin, tie the drumsticks securely to the tail. If desired, twist wing tips under the back.

2. Place turkey, breast-side up, on a rack in a shallow roasting pan. Brush with the butter. Insert an oven-going meat thermometer into the center of an inside thigh muscle being careful not to touch bone. Cover turkey loosely with foil.

Pear-Glazed Roast Turkey

3. Roast turkey for 2¾ to 3 hours. During the last 45 minutes of roasting, remove foil and cut band of skin or string between drumsticks so thighs cook evenly. During the last 15 minutes of roasting, brush twice with the Pear Glaze. Roast until the thermometer registers 180°F. (The juices should run clear and drumsticks should move easily in sockets.)

4. Remove turkey from oven. If preparing pan gravy, reserve drippings. Cover turkey; let stand for 15 to 20 minutes before carving. If desired, garnish platter with roasted pear quarters and fresh rosemary sprigs. Carve turkey. If desired, serve with pan gravy.

Pear Glaze: In a small saucepan whisk together 1 cup pear nectar, 2 tablespoons packed brown sugar, 1 tablespoon Dijon-style mustard, 1 tablespoon Worcestershire sauce for chicken, ¼ teaspoon salt, ⅛ teaspoon ground nutmeg, and ⅛ teaspoon cayenne pepper. Add 1 tablespoon butter. Bring to boiling; reduce heat. Boil gently, uncovered, for 5 to 8 minutes or until mixture is a glazing consistency.

***Note:** To prepare roasted pear garnish, quarter 4 small pears; add to the roasting pan the last 10 to 20 minutes of roasting.

Per serving: 512 cal., 17 g total fat (5 g sat. fat), 283 mg chol., 315 mg sodium, 9 g carbo., 0 g fiber, 77 g pro.
Daily Values: 2% vit. A, 9% vit. C, 8% calcium, 27% iron

Pan Gravy: While turkey stands after roasting, pour pan drippings into a large measuring cup. Scrape the browned bits from the pan into the cup. Skim and reserve fat from the drippings. Pour ¼ cup of the fat into a medium saucepan (discard any remaining fat). Stir in ¼ cup all-purpose flour. Add enough chicken broth to remaining drippings in the measuring cup to equal 2 cups; add broth mixture all at once to flour mixture in saucepan. Cook and stir over medium heat until thickened and bubbly. Cook and stir for 1 minute more. Season to taste with salt and ground black pepper.

Lemony Herbed Pork Roast

The snazzy marinade for this roast imparts plenty of flavor! Be sure to marinate the roast no more than four hours.

Prep: 20 minutes   **Marinate:** 2 hours
Roast: 1¼ hours   **Stand:** 15 minutes
Oven: 325°F   **Makes:** 6 to 8 servings

- 1 2- to 3-pound boneless pork top loin roast (single loin)
- 2 teaspoons finely shredded lemon peel
- 3 tablespoons lemon juice
- 2 tablespoons olive oil
- 2 cloves garlic, minced
- 1 tablespoon snipped fresh oregano or 1 teaspoon dried oregano, crushed
- ¼ teaspoon salt
- ¼ teaspoon ground black pepper

1. Place meat in a large resealable plastic bag set in a shallow dish. For marinade, combine lemon peel, lemon juice, oil, garlic, oregano, salt, and pepper. Pour marinade over meat; seal bag. Marinate in the refrigerator for 2 to 4 hours, turning bag occasionally.

2. Preheat oven to 325°F. Drain meat, discarding marinade. Place meat on a rack in a shallow roasting pan. Insert an oven-going meat thermometer into center of roast. Roast for 1¼ to 1¾ hours or until thermometer registers 150°F. Cover meat with foil; let stand for 15 minutes before slicing. The meat's temperature should rise 10°F after standing.

Per serving: 243 cal., 11 g total fat (3 g sat. fat), 82 mg chol., 113 mg sodium, 1 g carbo., 0 g fiber, 33 g pro.
Daily Values: 5% vit. C, 3% calcium, 7% iron

Wine Serving Savvy

The temperature at which you serve wine is a personal preference, but extreme temperatures can change the flavor and complexity. White and rosé wines are served chilled (50°F to 55°F); red wines are served slightly below room temperature (62°F to 67°F); and champagne and sparkling wines are served very cold (40°F to 50°F). To chill wine, place in the refrigerator at least 1 to 2 hours before serving. If you need to quick-chill a wine, place the bottle in a bucket filled with water and ice for about 5 minutes. If a wine is too cool, place the bottle in a bucket of warm (70°F) water for about 5 minutes.

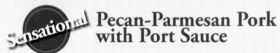
Pecan-Parmesan Pork with Port Sauce

in meat registers 155°F. Cover with foil; let stand 15 minutes. The temperature of the meat should rise 5°F after standing.

3. Meanwhile, for sauce, in a medium saucepan stir together port, figs, and brown sugar. Bring to boiling; reduce heat. Simmer, uncovered, for 10 to 15 minutes or until mixture is reduced to 2¼ cups. Cool slightly.

4. Transfer half of the sauce mixture at a time to a blender or food processor. Cover and blend or process until nearly smooth. Pour mixture through a sieve over a bowl, pressing solids to release juices. Discard solids. Return sauce to saucepan. Cook and stir over low heat just until heated through. Slice tenderloin and serve with warm sauce. If desired, garnish with halved kumquats.

Per serving: 428 cal., 15 g total fat (3 g sat. fat), 78 mg chol., 253 mg sodium, 31 g carbo., 4 g fiber, 29 g pro.
Daily Values: 1% vit. A, 2% vit. C, 15% calcium, 20% iron

Sensational Pecan-Parmesan Pork with Port Sauce

Be sure to use the finest Parmesan cheese—Parmigiano-Reggiano if possible—in this lovely holiday main dish. If desired, serve with Mashed Potatoes and Parsnips (see recipe, page 23).

Prep: 25 minutes **Roast:** 25 minutes
Stand: 15 minutes **Oven:** 425°F
Makes: 8 servings

  1 cup pecan pieces
  ⅔ cup finely shredded Parmesan cheese
  3 tablespoons yellow mustard
  1 tablespoon Worcestershire sauce
  2 1-pound pork tenderloins
  2 cups port or dry Marsala
  1 cup snipped dried Calmyrna or Mission figs
    (5½ to 6 ounces)
  2 tablespoons packed brown sugar
    Kumquats (optional)

1. Preheat oven to 425°F. In a blender or food processor combine pecans, cheese, mustard, and Worcestershire sauce. Cover and blend or process until finely chopped. Press mixture onto all sides of tenderloins to coat with a thin layer.

2. Place pork, side-by-side, on a rack in a shallow roasting pan. Roast, uncovered, for 25 to 35 minutes or until an instant-read thermometer inserted

Simple Raspberry-Pepper Glazed Ham

Chipotle peppers in the raspberry sauce give the ham a definite kick. If a milder flavor is desired, only use two chipotle peppers.

Prep: 15 minutes **Bake:** 1¾ hours
Stand: 15 minutes **Oven:** 325°F
Makes: 16 to 20 servings

  1 9- to 10-pound cooked bone-in ham
    (rump half or shank portion)
  1 recipe Raspberry Sauce
  1 tablespoon peppercorns, coarsely cracked

1. Preheat oven to 325°F. If desired, score ham in a diamond pattern by making shallow diagonal cuts at 1-inch intervals. Place ham, flat-side down, on a rack in a shallow roasting pan. Insert an oven-going meat thermometer into the thickest portion of the meat; tip should not touch bone. Bake for 1½ hours. Meanwhile, prepare Raspberry Sauce.

2. Spoon or brush some of the Raspberry Sauce over the ham. Bake ham for 15 to 30 minutes more or until thermometer registers 140°F, spooning or brushing twice with additional sauce. Remove from oven. Sprinkle with coarsely cracked peppercorns. To serve, carve the ham. Reheat any remaining Raspberry Sauce until bubbly; pass with ham.

Raspberry Sauce: In a small saucepan combine 1½ cups seedless raspberry preserves; 2 tablespoons white vinegar; 2 or 3 canned chipotle peppers in adobo sauce, drained and chopped (see Note, page 11); and 3 cloves garlic, minced. Bring just to boiling; reduce heat. Simmer, uncovered, for 5 minutes, stirring frequently. Makes 1¾ cups sauce.

Per serving: 321 cal., 8 g total fat (3 g sat. fat), 106 mg chol., 116 mg sodium, 21 g carbo., 1 g fiber, 38 g pro.
Daily Values: 1% vit. A, 8% vit. C, 2% calcium, 10% iron

Southern-Style Pork Loin Roast

Here's an outstanding main dish for your holiday table! Round out the meal perfectly with the addition of candied sweet potatoes and pecans.

Prep: 45 minutes **Roast:** 2½ hours
Stand: 20 minutes **Oven:** 325°F/375°F
Makes: 10 to 12 servings

- 1 6- to 7-pound boneless pork top loin roast (double loin, tied)
- ¾ cup peach preserves
- 1 tablespoon packed brown sugar
- 1 tablespoon grated fresh ginger
- 1 teaspoon finely shredded lemon peel
- 1 tablespoon lemon juice
- ¼ teaspoon ground nutmeg
- 1 cup panko (Japanese-style) bread crumbs
- 1 14-ounce can chicken broth
  Butter
- 2 cups half-and-half or light cream
- ¼ cup all-purpose flour
- 2 tablespoons bourbon or chicken broth
- 1 tablespoon snipped fresh Italian (flat-leaf) parsley

1. Preheat oven to 325°F. Place pork roast on a rack in a shallow roasting pan. Sprinkle lightly with *salt* and *ground black pepper.* Insert an oven-going meat thermometer into center of roast. Roast about 2 hours or until meat thermometer registers 140°F.

2. Meanwhile, for glaze, in a small bowl combine peach preserves, brown sugar, ginger, lemon peel, lemon juice, and nutmeg.

3. When the temperature of the roast registers 140°F, increase oven temperature to 375°F. Spoon peach glaze over roast. Sprinkle panko crumbs over the glaze and lightly pat into place to adhere. Pour chicken broth into bottom of the roasting pan. Continue roasting about 30 minutes more or until the meat thermometer registers 150°F. Cover meat with foil; let stand 20 minutes. The temperature of the meat should rise 10°F after standing.

4. Pour pan drippings into a large measuring cup through a fine mesh strainer; discard solids. Skim fat from drippings; reserve ¼ cup of the fat. If there is not enough fat, add butter to equal ¼ cup. Measure 1 cup of the remaining drippings; if necessary, add enough water to equal 1 cup. Add half-and-half to drippings.

5. In a medium saucepan combine reserved fat and flour. Gradually stir the drippings-cream mixture and bourbon into the flour mixture in saucepan. Cook and stir over medium heat until thickened and bubbly. Cook and stir for 1 minute more. Stir in parsley and season to taste with *salt* and *pepper.*

Per serving: 526 cal., 22 g total fat (10 g sat. fat), 150 mg chol., 509 mg sodium, 27 g carbo., 1 g fiber, 50 g pro.
Daily Values: 7% vit. A, 8% vit. C, 11% calcium, 11% iron

Southern-Style Pork Loin Roast

Herbed Dressing

Fresh mushrooms add a twist to this favorite.

Prep: 40 minutes **Bake:** 45 minutes
Oven: 350°F **Makes:** 12 servings

- 4½ cups sliced fresh mushrooms (12 ounces)
- 1 cup sliced celery (2 stalks)
- 1 cup chopped onion (1 large)
- 6 tablespoons butter or margarine
- ⅓ cup snipped fresh basil or 1 tablespoon dried basil, crushed
- ½ teaspoon ground black pepper
- 12 cups dry bread cubes*
- ¾ cup chopped pecans, toasted (see tip, page 63)
- 1 14-ounce can chicken broth

1. Preheat oven to 350°F. In a 12-inch skillet cook mushrooms, celery, and onion in hot butter over medium heat about 5 minutes or just until vegetables are tender, stirring occasionally. Remove from heat; stir in basil and pepper. Transfer mixture to a large bowl. Add bread cubes and pecans; toss to combine. Add chicken broth, tossing gently until mixture is evenly moistened. Spoon bread mixture into a 3-quart rectangular baking dish.

2. Bake, covered, for 30 minutes. Uncover; bake about 15 minutes more or until heated through.

*Note: To dry bread cubes, preheat oven to 300°F. Cut 18 slices fresh bread into ½-inch cubes. Spread cubes in a large shallow baking pan. Bake for 10 to 15 minutes or until dry, stirring twice; cool.

Per side-dish serving: 213 cal., 12 g total fat (4 g sat. fat), 16 mg chol., 438 mg sodium, 23 g carbo., 2 g fiber, 5 g pro.
Daily Values: 6% vit. A, 3% vit. C, 7% calcium, 10% iron

Artisanal Bread Stuffing

This savory stuffing can be spooned into a casserole and baked as a side dish.

Prep: 30 minutes **Bake:** 1 hour
Oven: 350°F **Makes:** 10 to 12 servings

- 12 cups ¾- to 1-inch cubes artisanal bread, such as rosemary or sun-dried tomato (about 1¼-pound loaf)
- ½ cup pine nuts
-    Nonstick cooking spray
- 4½ cups coarsely chopped fennel (reserve leafy green tops for another use)
- 1½ cups chopped onion (3 medium)
- 6 tablespoons unsalted butter or margarine
- 1½ cups sliced, pitted kalamata olives
- 3 tablespoons snipped fresh thyme or 1 tablespoon dried thyme, crushed
- ¾ teaspoon coarsely ground black pepper
- 2¼ cups chicken broth
-    Fresh thyme sprigs (optional)

1. Preheat oven to 350°F. In a large roasting pan toast bread cubes and pine nuts for 15 to 20 minutes or until the cubes are toasted and pine nuts are light brown, tossing once. Set aside.

2. Meanwhile, lightly coat a 3-quart casserole with cooking spray; set aside. In a large skillet cook fennel and onion in hot butter over medium heat about 10 minutes or until tender, stirring occasionally. Remove from heat. Stir in olives, snipped thyme, and pepper. Transfer mixture to an extra-large bowl. Add bread cubes and pine nuts; toss to combine. Add chicken broth; toss until evenly moistened.

3. Spoon bread mixture into prepared casserole. Bake, covered, for 45 minutes. Uncover; bake about 15 minutes more or until heated through.

Make-Ahead Directions: Prepare bread cubes and pine nuts as above in Step 1. Store in an airtight container at room temperature for up to one day. To prepare, continue as directed in Step 2.

Per serving: 319 cal., 16 g total fat (6 g sat. fat), 20 mg chol., 818 mg sodium, 38 g carbo., 5 g fiber, 8 g pro.
Daily Values: 7% vit. A, 12% vit. C, 7% calcium, 14% iron

Artisanal Bread Stuffing

Chilled Spinach Couscous

Quick-cooking couscous is transformed with the additions of spinach, fresh dillweed, and feta cheese.

Prep: 15 minutes **Stand:** 30 minutes
Chill: 2 hours **Makes:** 8 to 10 servings

2¼ cups water
½ teaspoon salt
1 10-ounce package quick-cooking couscous
⅓ cup olive oil
3 tablespoons lemon juice
4 cups torn fresh spinach
¼ cup sliced green onion (2)
3 tablespoons snipped fresh dillweed
⅓ cup crumbled feta cheese

1. In a large saucepan bring water and salt to boiling. Remove from heat. Stir in couscous; cover and let stand for 5 minutes. Fluff couscous with a fork.

2. Meanwhile, combine oil and lemon juice. Add oil mixture to couscous, stirring to coat. Let stand until completely cool, about 25 minutes.

3. Stir in spinach, green onion, and dillweed. Cover and chill for 2 to 12 hours or until thoroughly chilled. Sprinkle with feta cheese before serving.

Per serving: 235 cal., 11 g total fat (2 g sat. fat), 5 mg chol., 231 mg sodium, 29 g carbo., 2 g fiber, 6 g pro.
Daily Values: 29% vit. A, 15% vit. C, 6% calcium, 5% iron

Roasted Vegetable Couscous

Roasting the vegetables in this colorful side dish gives it an elevated level of flavors.

Prep: 20 minutes **Roast:** 30 minutes
Stand: 5 minutes **Oven:** 375°F
Makes: 6 to 8 servings

Nonstick cooking spray
1 Japanese eggplant or 1 small eggplant, cut into bite-size pieces
1 small red onion, cut into thin wedges

Roasted Vegetable Couscous

1 yellow or red sweet pepper,* cut into bite-size pieces
1 or 2 yellow banana peppers, cut into bite-size pieces
1 cup water or chicken broth
¾ cup quick-cooking couscous
1 recipe Balsamic-Mustard Dressing

1. Preheat oven to 375°F. Lightly coat a shallow baking pan with cooking spray. Place eggplant, onion, sweet pepper, and banana pepper in prepared pan. Roast for 30 to 35 minutes or until tender.

2. In a medium saucepan bring the water to boiling. Stir in couscous. Remove from heat. Cover; let stand for 5 minutes. Fluff couscous with a fork.

3. In a large bowl combine vegetables, couscous, and Balsamic-Mustard Dressing. Toss gently to coat. Serve chilled or at room temperature.

Balsamic-Mustard Dressing: In a screw-top jar combine ¼ cup white or regular balsamic vinegar, 1 tablespoon olive oil, 1½ teaspoons Dijon-style mustard, ¼ teaspoon salt, and ¼ teaspoon garlic powder. Cover and shake well.

***Note:** If desired, use half of a yellow sweet pepper and half of a red sweet pepper.

Per serving: 139 cal., 3 g total fat (0 g sat. fat), 0 mg chol., 134 mg sodium, 24 g carbo., 2 g fiber, 4 g pro.
Daily Values: 2% vit. A, 107% vit. C, 2% calcium, 3% iron

Sweet Potato Fries

Prep: 15 minutes **Bake:** 20 minutes
Oven: 425°F **Makes:** 4 servings

- 1 pound medium sweet potatoes
- 1 tablespoon butter or margarine, melted
- ¼ teaspoon seasoned salt
  Dash ground nutmeg

1. Preheat oven to 425°F. Lightly coat a 15×10×1-inch baking pan with *nonstick cooking spray.* Scrub potatoes. Cut lengthwise into quarters. Cut quarters in half. Arrange potatoes in a single layer in pan.

2. Combine butter, seasoned salt, and nutmeg. Brush mixture onto potatoes. Bake for 20 to 30 minutes or until brown and tender, turning once.

Per serving: 113 cal., 3 g total fat (2 g sat. fat), 8 mg chol., 142 mg sodium, 20 g carbo., 2 g fiber, 1 g pro.
Daily Values: 314% vit. A, 23% vit. C, 2% calcium, 3% iron

Sweet Potato Casserole

This casserole is so sweet and lovely that it almost could double as dessert!

Prep: 45 minutes **Bake:** 30 minutes
Oven: 350°F **Makes:** 6 to 8 servings

- 2 pounds sweet potatoes
- ½ cup sugar
- ¼ cup butter or margarine, melted
- ¼ cup milk
- 2 eggs, lightly beaten
- 1 teaspoon vanilla
- ½ cup packed brown sugar
- ½ cup chopped pecans
- ¼ cup all-purpose flour
- 1 tablespoon butter, melted

1. Preheat oven to 350°F. Wash and peel sweet potatoes; cut off woody portions and ends. Cut crosswise

Sweet Potato Casserole

into quarters. In a large saucepan cook potatoes, covered, in enough boiling salted water to cover for 25 to 30 minutes or until tender; drain.

2. Transfer potatoes to a large mixing bowl. Mash lightly. Stir in sugar, ¼ cup melted butter, milk, eggs, and vanilla. Transfer sweet potato mixture to a 2-quart casserole. In a small bowl combine brown sugar, pecans, flour, and 1 tablespoon melted butter. Sprinkle over sweet potato mixture. Bake, uncovered, for 30 to 35 minutes or until hot and bubbly.

Per serving: 462 cal., 19 g total fat (7 g sat. fat), 97 mg chol., 182 mg sodium, 71 g carbo., 6 g fiber, 6 g pro.

Daily Values: 373% vit. A, 5% vit. C, 9% calcium, 11% iron

Cream Cheese Mashed Potatoes

Prep: 10 minutes **Cook:** 5 minutes
Makes: 6 servings

- 2 **cups water**
- ¾ **to 1 cup milk**
- 2 **tablespoons butter or margarine**
- ¼ **teaspoon salt**
- 2 **cups packaged instant mashed potato flakes**
- ½ **of an 8-ounce tub cream cheese spread with chive and onion**
  Butter (optional)

1. In a 1½-quart microwave-safe casserole, combine water, ¾ cup of the milk, 2 tablespoons butter, and salt. Stir in potato flakes. Cook, covered, on 100-percent power (high) for 4 to 5 minutes or until liquid is absorbed.

2. Stir to rehydrate potatoes. Stir in cream cheese. Add the remaining milk, if necessary, to reach desired consistency. Cook, covered, on high about 1 minute more or until heated through. If desired, serve with additional butter.

Per serving: 173 cal., 11 g total fat (7 g sat. fat), 31 mg chol., 238 mg sodium, 16 g carbo., 1 g fiber, 3 g pro.

Daily Values: 8% vit. A, 22% vit. C, 7% calcium, 1% iron

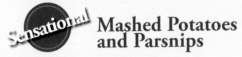

Mashed Potatoes and Parsnips

This decadent garlicky potato/parsnip duo is an ideal accompaniment to Pecan-Parmesan Pork with Port Sauce (see recipe, page 18).

Prep: 15 minutes **Bake:** 25 minutes
Cook: 20 minutes **Oven:** 425°F
Makes: 12 servings

- 3 **pounds potatoes, such as russet potatoes, peeled and quartered**
- 1½ **pounds parsnips, peeled and cut into large pieces**
- 1 **bulb garlic**
- 2 **teaspoons olive oil**
- ¾ **cup milk**
- ½ **cup butter or margarine**
- ¾ **teaspoon salt**
- ⅛ **teaspoon freshly ground black pepper**
  Salt and ground black pepper (optional)

1. In a 4-quart Dutch oven cook potatoes and parsnips, covered, in enough boiling salted water to cover for 20 to 25 minutes or until tender. Drain.

2. Preheat oven to 425°F. Peel away the dry outer layers of skin from bulb of garlic, leaving cloves intact. Cut off the pointed top portion (about ¼ inch), leaving the bulb intact but exposing individual cloves. Place the garlic bulb, cut side up, in a muffin cup or custard cup. Drizzle with olive oil. Cover with foil and bake for 25 to 35 minutes or until the cloves feel soft when pressed. Set aside just until cool enough to handle. Squeeze out the garlic paste from individual cloves. Mash with a fork; set aside.

3. Press the potatoes and parsnips through a potato ricer or food mill (or mash with a potato masher) and return them to the Dutch oven.

4. In a small saucepan bring milk and butter just to boiling. Stir milk mixture, mashed garlic, ¾ teaspoon salt, and ⅛ teaspoon pepper into the potato mixture. Heat through. If desired, season to taste with additional salt and pepper.

Per serving: 187 cal., 9 g total fat (5 g sat. fat), 22 mg chol., 214 mg sodium, 25 g carbo., 2 g fiber, 3 g pro.

Daily Values: 5% vit. A, 31% vit. C, 4% calcium, 5% iron

Orange-Glazed Baby Carrots

Three ingredients provide a host of flavors in this super simple side dish that adds not only taste, but color, to the holiday table.

Start to Finish: 15 minutes **Makes:** 4 servings

- 2 cups packaged peeled fresh baby carrots
- 1 tablespoon butter or margarine
- 2 tablespoons orange marmalade

1. In a medium saucepan cook carrots, covered, in lightly salted boiling water for 5 minutes. Drain; set aside.

2. In the same saucepan melt butter over medium heat. Add the carrots and orange marmalade. Cook and stir for 2 to 3 minutes or until carrots are tender and glazed.

Per serving: 77 cal., 3 g total fat (2 g sat. fat), 8 mg chol., 57 mg sodium, 13 g carbo., 2 g fiber, 1 g pro.
Daily Values: 310% vit. A, 8% vit. C, 2% calcium, 2% iron

Carrots and Parsnips

This stunning toasted side dish features two tasty root vegetables and a host of delicious herbs and spices.

Start to Finish: 50 minutes
Makes: 10 to 12 servings

- 1½ pounds small parsnips, peeled and halved lengthwise
- 1½ pounds small carrots, peeled and halved lengthwise
- 3 tablespoons olive oil
- ¾ teaspoon fennel seeds, crushed
- ½ teaspoon ground coriander (optional)
- ¼ teaspoon ground cinnamon
- 4 cloves garlic, thinly sliced
- 2 tablespoons chopped fresh cilantro
- 1 teaspoon finely shredded lemon peel
- 2 tablespoons lemon juice
- ½ teaspoon salt
- ⅛ teaspoon freshly ground black pepper
- 1 tablespoon olive oil

1. Cut any long carrots and parsnips in half crosswise. In a 12-inch skillet cook parsnips, covered, in a small amount of boiling salted water for 2 minutes. Add carrots; return to boiling. Cook for 4 minutes more. Drain; set aside. Carefully wipe skillet dry.

2. In the same skillet heat the 3 tablespoons oil over medium heat. Add fennel seeds, coriander (if desired), and cinnamon. Cook about 1 minute or until fragrant; stir occasionally. Add parsnips, carrots, and garlic. Cook for 10 to 12 minutes or until vegetables are tender, turning occasionally. Remove from heat. Stir in cilantro, lemon peel and juice, salt, and pepper. Drizzle with the 1 tablespoon olive oil.

Per serving: 130 cal., 6 g total fat (1 g sat. fat), 0 mg chol., 171 mg sodium, 20 g carbo., 6 g fiber, 2 g pro.
Daily Values: 149% vit. A, 25% vit. C, 5% calcium, 4% iron

Broccoli with Lemon

A splash of lemon and a bit of dillweed pair up perfectly with healthful broccoli.

Start to Finish: 25 minutes **Makes:** 6 to 8 servings

- ½ cup chopped onion (1 medium)
- 1 clove garlic, minced
- 1 tablespoon olive oil

Carrots and Parsnips

½ cup reduced-sodium chicken broth

1½ pounds broccoli, cut into spears

1 tablespoon lemon juice

1 teaspoon all-purpose flour

2 tablespoons snipped fresh dillweed or
  1 teaspoon dried dillweed
  Lemon slices (optional)

1. In a large saucepan cook and stir onion and garlic in hot oil over medium heat about 3 minutes or until tender. Add broth; bring to boiling. Add broccoli and return to boiling. Reduce heat; cook, covered, for 8 to 10 minutes or until broccoli is tender. Transfer vegetables to a serving bowl, reserving broth in pan. (Add additional broth, if necessary, to measure ½ cup.)

2. Combine lemon juice and flour; add to broth in saucepan. Cook and stir until thickened and bubbly; cook and stir for 1 minute more. Add dillweed and season to taste with *salt* and *ground black pepper*. Spoon sauce over vegetables; toss to coat. If desired, garnish with lemon slices.

Per serving: 49 cal., 3 g total fat (0 g sat. fat), 0 mg chol., 119 mg sodium, 6 g carbo., 2 g fiber, 3 g pro.

Daily Values: 20% vit. A, 95% vit. C, 4% calcium, 4% iron

Broccoli with Orange Hollandaise

Another time, try this sauce in place of the original hollandaise on Eggs Benedict.

Prep: 50 minutes **Cook:** 10 minutes
Stand: 45 minutes **Makes:** 8 to 10 servings

½ cup butter

6 cups broccoli florets

3 egg yolks, lightly beaten

1 teaspoon finely shredded orange peel
  (set aside)

1 tablespoon orange juice

1 tablespoon water
  Salt and ground white pepper

⅓ cup sliced almonds, toasted (see tip, page 63)

1. Cut the butter into thirds and bring it to room temperature (allow about 45 minutes).

Broccoli with Orange Hollandaise

2. In a large saucepan cook broccoli, covered, in a small amount of boiling salted water for 8 to 10 minutes or until crisp-tender. Drain and place on a serving platter. Cover to keep warm.

3. For hollandaise sauce, in the top of a double boiler combine egg yolks, orange juice, and water. Add a piece of the butter. Place over gently boiling water (upper pan should not touch water). Cook, stirring rapidly with a whisk, until butter melts and the sauce begins to thicken. (Sauce may appear to curdle at this point but will smooth out when remaining butter is added.) Add the remaining butter, 1 piece at a time, stirring constantly until melted. Continue to cook and stir for 2 to 2½ minutes more or until sauce thickens. Immediately remove from heat. If sauce is too thick or curdles, immediately whisk in 1 to 2 tablespoons hot water. Stir in orange peel and season to taste with salt and pepper.

4. Spoon hollandaise sauce over broccoli and sprinkle with toasted almonds.

Per serving: 154 cal., 14 g total fat (8 g sat. fat), 109 mg chol., 180 mg sodium, 5 g carbo., 2 g fiber, 3 g pro.

Daily Values: 18% vit. A, 104% vit. C, 5% calcium, 4% iron

Easy Mushroom Gravy

For an even easier sauce, use two 4-ounce cans sliced mushrooms, drained, instead of the fresh mushrooms—and skip the first cooking step.

Prep: 15 minutes **Cook:** 5 minutes
Makes: 2 cups gravy (eight ¼-cup servings)

3   cups wild mushrooms or button
       mushrooms, sliced
1   tablespoon olive oil or cooking oil
1   12-ounce jar turkey gravy
½   cup dairy sour cream or
       light dairy sour cream
½   teaspoon dried sage or thyme, crushed

1. In a large skillet cook mushrooms in hot oil over medium heat until tender. In a medium bowl whisk together gravy, sour cream, and sage; add to mushrooms in skillet. Cook and stir until heated through. Serve over roasted meat, poultry, or potatoes.

Per serving: 67 cal., 5 g total fat (2 g sat. fat), 5 mg chol., 284 mg sodium, 4 g carbo., 0 g fiber, 2 g pro.
Daily Values: 2% vit. A, 1% vit. C, 2% calcium, 1% iron

Molasses-Spice Gravy

Be sure to use full-flavor molasses for the maximum flavor punch from this hearty—but healthful—gravy.

Prep: 20 minutes **Cook:** 30 minutes
Makes: about 3 cups gravy (twelve ¼-cup servings)

2   14-ounces cans chicken broth
½   of a large sweet potato, peeled and
       coarsely chopped (8 ounces)
⅔   cup peeled, sliced fresh carrot
       (about 1 large)
½   cup chopped onion (1 medium)
1   to 2 tablespoons full-flavor molasses
½   teaspoon ground allspice
¼   teaspoon salt
⅛   teaspoon freshly ground black pepper

1. In a medium saucepan combine chicken broth, sweet potato, carrot, and onion. Bring to boiling; reduce heat. Simmer, covered, about 20 minutes or until vegetables are tender. Remove from heat; cool slightly.

2. Pour half the vegetable mixture into a deep bowl or blender container. Blend with an immersion blender or in a blender until smooth. Repeat with remaining mixture. Return all to saucepan. Bring to boiling; reduce heat. Simmer, uncovered, for 10 minutes, stirring occasionally. Remove from heat. Stir in molasses, allspice, salt, and pepper.

Per serving: 25 cal., 0 g total fat (0 g sat. fat), 1 mg chol., 280 mg sodium, 5 g carbo., 1 g fiber, 1 g pro.
Daily Values: 53% vit. A, 6% vit. C, 1% calcium, 1% iron

Keep Spices Fresh!

Dried herbs and spices can be quite sensitive to their environment, so take care when storing them. Keep bottles tightly capped in a cool dry place away from direct sunlight, moisture, and heat. Don't store them above the stove, and quickly replace bottle lids after using. Most dried herbs and spices last from 1 to 3 years if stored properly. To check the freshness of dried spices and herbs, rub them in your hand to make sure the aroma is still intense. If not, you'll probably want to purchase some new herbs and spices for Christmas dinner!

Molasses-Spice Gravy

Simple

Cranberry Relish

This simple sauce goes together in minutes and is the perfect accompaniment to ham, pork, beef, or roasted poultry.

Prep: 25 minutes **Chill:** 2 hours **Makes:** about 2 cups (sixteen 2-tablespoon servings)

- 1 **12-ounce package (3 cups) fresh cranberries**
- ¾ **cup cranberry-apple drink**
- 3 **tablespoons sugar**
- ½ **teaspoon ground cinnamon**
- ¼ **teaspoon ground nutmeg**
  Dash ground cloves
- ½ **cup coarsely chopped pecans, toasted (see tip, page 63)**

1. In a medium saucepan combine cranberries, cranberry-apple drink, sugar, cinnamon, nutmeg, and cloves. Cook and stir over medium-high heat until boiling and cranberries pop; reduce heat.

2. Simmer, uncovered, for 6 to 8 minutes or until mixture thickens, stirring frequently. Transfer to a small bowl. Cover and chill for 2 to 48 hours. Just before serving, stir in pecans.

Per serving: 37 cal., 2 g total fat (0 g sat. fat), 0 mg chol., 2 mg sodium, 4 g carbo., 1 g fiber, 0 g pro.
Daily Values: 1% vit. A, 11% vit. C, 1% calcium, 2% iron

Sensational

Holiday Cranberry Salsa

Jalapeño chile peppers, onion, oranges, and fresh cilantro add unexpected flavor to this extraordinary salsa. Serve it with poultry, pork, or ham.

Prep: 25 minutes **Chill:** 4 hours **Makes:** about 4 cups (thirty-two 2-tablespoon servings)

- 2 **cups fresh cranberries, coarsely chopped**
- 1 **or 2 fresh jalapeño chile peppers, seeded and finely chopped***
- 1 **teaspoon finely shredded orange peel**
- 1 **large orange, peeled, sectioned, and cut up (½ cup)**
- ½ **cup chopped cucumber**

Holiday Cranberry Salsa

- ¼ **cup chopped yellow sweet pepper**
- ¼ **cup sliced celery**
- ¼ **cup chopped red onion**
- 1 **tablespoon snipped fresh cilantro**
- 3 **tablespoons honey**
- 2 **tablespoons lime juice**
- 2 **teaspoons olive oil**
- ¼ **teaspoon salt**

1. In a large bowl combine cranberries, jalapeño pepper, orange peel, orange sections, cucumber, sweet pepper, celery, onion, and cilantro.

2. In a small bowl combine honey, lime juice, olive oil, and salt. Add to cranberry mixture, tossing gently to coat. Cover and chill for 4 to 24 hours before serving.

***Note:** Because hot chile peppers, such as jalapeños, contain oils that can burn skin and eyes, avoid direct contact with chiles as much as possible. When working with chile peppers, wear plastic or rubber gloves. If your bare hands do touch the chile peppers, wash them well with soap and water.

Per serving: 15 cal., 0 g total fat (0 g sat. fat), 0 mg chol., 19 mg sodium, 3 g carbo., 0 g fiber, 0 g pro.
Daily Values: 1% vit. A, 11% vit. C

Appetizer Spread

What better way to gather during the busy holiday season than with an appetizer party? All you need to do is set out a brimming buffet of bite-size nibbles, quick dips, and dazzling beverages. Keep it simple with all-time favorites like Artichoke Dip (four ingredients plus dippers) or munchable Honey Spiced Nuts (goes together in less than 30 minutes). Or sample some dishes that are a step above, such as Shoyster Cocktail (a delectable duo of oysters and shrimp in a piquant sauce) or Baked Brie with Caramelized Onions and Hazelnuts (which calls upon America's culinary darling—caramelized onions—for its memorable flavor). Serve some first-rate cocktails such as Poinsettia Mimosas or Raspberry Wine Punch—both of which are delightfully colorful and delicious. Provide a selection of wine, bottled water, and soft drinks, and let the holidays begin!

2. In a pitcher combine raspberry puree, wine, and raspberry liqueur. If desired, serve over ice.

Per serving: 146 cal., 0 g total fat (0 g sat. fat), 0 mg chol., 14 mg sodium, 19 g carbo., 1 g fiber, 0 g pro.
Daily Values: 1% vit. A, 1% vit. C, 2% calcium, 5% iron

Poinsettia Mimosas

The up-and-down motion in preparing this cocktail mixes the drink without destroying the carbonation of the champagne. For the kids, substitute orange juice and sparkling apple or pear juice.

Start to Finish: 10 minutes
Makes: 12 to 14 (4-ounce) servings

    3 or 4 tangerines (optional)
       Maraschino cherries (optional)
    3 cups cranberry juice cocktail, chilled
    ¼ cup Triple Sec, orange liqueur,
          or orange juice
    2 tablespoons maraschino cherry juice
          or grenadine syrup
    1 750-ml bottle champagne or
          sparkling apple juice or one 32-ounce
          bottle carbonated water or lemon-lime
          carbonated beverage, chilled
       Small carambola (star fruit) slices,
          seeded (optional)

1. If desired, use a lemon zester, vegetable peeler, or a thin sharp knife to thinly peel the tangerines into about 6-inch spirals of peel. Place a tangerine spiral into each chilled champagne flute. If desired, add 1 or 2 maraschino cherries. In a glass pitcher combine cranberry juice, Triple Sec, and maraschino cherry juice.

2. For each serving, half fill the chilled champagne flute with cranberry juice mixture (about 2 ounces). Pour in the champagne and fill almost to the top (about 2 ounces). Gently stir with an up-and-down motion. If desired, garnish the rim of the flute with a star fruit slice.

Per serving: 103 cal., 0 g total fat (0 g sat. fat), 0 mg chol., 3 mg sodium, 15 g carbo., 0 g fiber, 0 g pro.
Daily Values: 37% vit. C, 1% iron

Poinsettia Mimosas

Raspberry Wine Punch

Make this gorgeous cocktail up to 24 hours in advance and refrigerate until ready to serve. For a pretty presentation, moisten the rims of glasses and dip them in sugar before serving.

Start to Finish: 15 minutes
Makes: 8 (about 4-ounce) servings

    1 10-ounce package frozen red raspberries
          in syrup, thawed
    1 750-ml bottle sweet white wine, such as
          white Zinfandel, chilled
    ¼ cup raspberry liqueur
       Crushed ice or ice cubes (optional)

1. Place raspberries and syrup in a blender or food processor. Cover and blend or process until berries are smooth. Press berries through a fine-mesh sieve; discard seeds. You should have about ¾ cup sieved puree.

Honey Spiced Nuts

Sweet and hot, these nuts will be a hit at any party. Use cashews, whole almonds, or macadamia nuts here—or go all out and use a mixture of premium whole nuts.

Prep: 10 minutes **Bake:** 15 minutes **Oven:** 325°F
Makes: about 2½ cups (ten ¼-cup servings)

- 2 tablespoons butter
- 2 tablespoons honey
- 2 teaspoons ground cumin
- 1 teaspoon salt
- ¼ teaspoon cayenne pepper
- 2½ cups broken pecans or walnuts

1. Preheat oven to 325°F. In a large saucepan melt butter over medium heat. Stir in honey, cumin, salt, and cayenne pepper. Remove from heat. Add nuts. Stir until nuts are coated. Spread nuts in a 13×9×2-inch baking pan.

2. Bake, uncovered, for 15 to 18 minutes or until nuts are toasted, stirring once or twice. Spread on a piece of foil; let cool.

Make-Ahead Directions: Prepare as directed. Store in an airtight container at room temperature for up to 2 weeks or in the freezer for up to 3 months.

Per serving: 223 cal., 22 g total fat (3 g sat. fat), 6 mg chol., 251 mg sodium, 7 g carbo., 3 g fiber, 3 g pro.
Daily Values: 2% vit. A, 1% vit. C, 2% calcium, 5% iron

 Sweet Curried Party Nuts

This snack features a trio of nuts, pumpkin seeds, and pretzels. Watch out! Once the munching starts, it is difficult to stop.

Prep: 15 minutes **Bake:** 40 minutes **Oven:** 300°F
Makes: about 12 cups (twenty-four ½-cup servings)

- 3½ cups bite-size pretzel twists
- 2¼ cups lightly salted cocktail peanuts
     (one 12-ounce container)
- 1½ cups blanched whole almonds
- 1 cup unsalted pistachio nuts
- 1 cup shelled pumpkin seeds (pepitas)
- ½ cup light-colored corn syrup
- 6 tablespoons butter
- ⅓ cup packed brown sugar
- 2 tablespoons curry powder
- ½ teaspoon salt
- ¼ teaspoon cayenne pepper

1. Preheat oven to 300°F. Line 1 to 2 very large baking sheets with foil; set aside.

2. In a large roasting pan combine pretzel twists, peanuts, almonds, pistachio nuts, and pumpkin seeds; set aside.

3. In a small saucepan combine corn syrup, butter, brown sugar, curry powder, salt, and cayenne pepper. Cook and stir over medium heat until butter is melted and sugar is dissolved. Pour syrup mixture over nut mixture; toss to coat.

4. Bake, uncovered, for 40 to 45 minutes or until mixture is golden, stirring once or twice. Spread nut mixture on prepared baking sheet(s); let cool.

Make-Ahead Directions: Prepare as directed. Store in an airtight container at room temperature for up to 2 weeks or in the freezer for up to 3 months.

Per serving: 273 cal., 20 g total fat (4 g sat. fat), 8 mg chol., 227 mg sodium, 18 g carbo., 3 g fiber, 9 g pro.
Daily Values: 3% vit. A, 1% vit. C, 4% calcium, 11% iron

Appetizer Math

When hosting a party it is important to keep portion size and number of tidbits per person in mind. For an appetizer-only party, plan on 10 to 12 bites/snacks per person. If dinner is to follow, plan to serve 4 to 6 bites per person.

Sweet, Hot, and Sour Meatballs

Frozen meatballs make this appetizer a snap to put together. To serve at a party or open house, transfer the meatballs to a slow cooker. Turn to the warm or low setting and let stand up to two hours. Stir occasionally.

Prep: 5 minutes **Bake:** 20 minutes **Oven:** 350°F
Makes: 32 meatballs (ten 3-meatball servings)

- 1 **16-ounce package frozen cooked meatballs (32)**
- ⅓ **cup apple jelly**
- 3 **tablespoons spicy brown mustard**
- 3 **tablespoons whiskey or apple juice**
- ½ **teaspoon Worcestershire sauce**
   Few dashes bottled hot pepper sauce

1. Preheat oven to 350°F. Place meatballs in a single layer in a shallow baking pan. Bake, uncovered, about 20 minutes or until heated through (160°F).

2. Meanwhile, in a large saucepan stir together apple jelly, mustard, whiskey, Worcestershire sauce, and hot pepper sauce. Cook and stir over medium heat until jelly is melted and mixture bubbles. Using a slotted spoon, transfer meatballs from baking pan to saucepan with jelly mixture; stir gently to coat. Return to boiling; reduce heat. Simmer, uncovered, for 3 to 5 minutes or until sauce thickens, stirring occasionally.

Per serving: 183 cal., 12 g total fat (5 g sat. fat), 16 mg chol., 425 mg sodium, 11 g carbo., 1 g fiber, 6 g pro.
Daily Values: 3% calcium, 3% iron

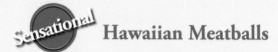 ## Hawaiian Meatballs

Beware! These lovely looking meatballs pack quite a spicy punch from the double dose of chipotles in adobo.

Prep: 30 minutes **Bake:** 10 minutes
Cook: 10 minutes **Oven:** 350°F
Makes: 48 meatballs (twelve 4-meatball servings)

   Nonstick cooking spray
- 1 **egg, lightly beaten**
- ¼ **cup fine dry bread crumbs**
- ¼ **cup finely chopped onion**

Sweet, Hot, and Sour Meatballs

2 to 3 tablespoons finely chopped canned
  chipotle peppers in adobo
2 cloves garlic, minced
¼ teaspoon salt
1 pound lean ground turkey or chicken
½ of a 16-ounce can or one 8-ounce can
  jellied cranberry sauce
1 cup bottled chili sauce
  Canned pineapple rings (optional)

1. Preheat oven to 350°F. Lightly coat a 15×10×1-inch baking pan with cooking spray; set aside. For meatballs, in a large bowl combine egg, bread crumbs, onion, 1 tablespoon of the chipotle in adobo, garlic, and salt. Add ground turkey; mix well. Shape into 48 meatballs (about ¾-inch diameter).

2. Arrange meatballs in a single layer in prepared pan. Bake, uncovered, for 10 to 15 minutes or until no pink remains. Drain well.

3. Meanwhile, for sauce, in a large skillet stir together cranberry sauce, chili sauce, and remaining 1 to 2 tablespoons chipotle in adobo. Cook over medium heat until cranberry sauce is melted, stirring occasionally. Transfer meatballs from baking pan to skillet with sauce. Simmer, uncovered, for 10 minutes, stirring occasionally. If desired, serve on pineapple rings.

Per serving: 122 cal., 5 g total fat (2 g sat. fat), 38 mg chol., 344 mg sodium, 12 g carbo., 1 g fiber, 7 g pro.
Daily Values: 3% vit. C, 1% calcium, 4% iron

Jam-Topped Cheese Tartlets

Try any variety of sweet and savory preserves—almost anything will pair well with the cheese combo in these morsels.

Prep: 30 minutes **Bake:** 12 minutes
Oven: 450°F/375°F **Makes:** 24 appetizers

½ of a 15-ounce package rolled refrigerated
  unbaked piecrust (1 crust)
1 5.3-ounce package soft goat cheese
  (chèvre)
1 3-ounce package cream cheese, softened
1 egg

Jam-Topped Cheese Tartlets

1 teaspoon all-purpose flour
¼ cup desired fruit preserves, jam, or jelly,
  such as apricot, tomato, orange, peach,
  jalapeño, or apple
  Fresh thyme, basil, oregano, sage,
  or parsley leaves

1. Preheat oven to 450°F. For pastry shells, on a lightly floured surface, roll pastry to a 13-inch circle. Using a 2¼-inch scalloped or round cookie cutter, cut 24 rounds, rerolling scraps, if needed. Press rounds into 1¾-inch muffin cups. Prick bottoms of pastry with a fork and bake for 4 to 5 minutes or until set and lightly browned. Let cool on a wire rack. Reduce oven temperature to 375°F.

2. For filling, in a medium bowl whisk together goat cheese, cream cheese, egg, and flour until nearly smooth. Spoon about 1 tablespoon of the mixture into each pastry shell.

3. Bake for 8 to 10 minutes or until filling is set. Remove from pans to a wire rack.

4. Meanwhile, in a small saucepan stir preserves over low heat until melted. Spoon ½ teaspoon warm preserves over each tartlet. Garnish each with a fresh herb leaf. Serve warm.

Per appetizer: 81 cal., 5 g total fat (3 g sat. fat), 17 mg chol., 70 mg sodium, 7 g carbo., 0 g fiber, 2 g pro.
Daily Values: 1% vit. A, 1% calcium, 1% iron

 ## Caramelized Onion Tartlets

Choose a creamy "young" Gorgonzola cheese for this recipe. It will be milder in flavor and easier to spread than a more aged Gorgonzola. Because of the strong flavor of the cheese, you might want to try a dessert wine with this sumptuous appetizer. Sample port, a French Sauternes, or Vin Santo for an interesting match. Or rely on a robust red.

Prep: 30 minutes **Bake:** 13 minutes
Cook: 16 minutes **Oven:** 450°F
Makes: 4 appetizer servings

- 1 **recipe Caraway Seed Pastry**
- 1 **cup chopped sweet onion, such as Vidalia or Walla Walla (1 large)**
- 1 **tablespoon olive oil**
- 1 **tablespoon sugar**
- ¼ **teaspoon salt**
- ⅛ **teaspoon freshly ground black pepper**
   Dash ground nutmeg
- 1 **ounce creamy Gorgonzola cheese, crumbled (¼ cup)**
- 1 **tablespoon milk**
- 1 **tablespoon snipped fresh parsley**
- 4 **cups mixed baby salad greens**
- ¼ **cup bottled balsamic vinaigrette salad dressing**

1. Preheat oven to 450°F. Prepare Caraway Seed Pastry; divide into four portions. On a lightly floured surface, slightly flatten one portion of the dough. Roll dough from center to edge into a 5-inch circle. Line a 4-inch tart pan with a removable bottom with the pastry. Press pastry into fluted side of tart pan; trim edge. Prick bottom and side of pastry. Repeat with remaining three portions of dough. Line pastry shells with a double thickness of foil. Bake pastry shells for 8 minutes. Remove foil. Bake for 5 to 6 minutes more or until pastry shells are golden. Cool pastry shells on a wire rack.

2. In a medium skillet cook onion in hot olive oil, covered, over medium-low heat for 13 to 15 minutes or until onion is tender, stirring occasionally. Uncover. Stir in sugar. Cook and stir over medium-high heat for 3 to 5 minutes more or until onion is golden. Stir in salt, pepper, and nutmeg. Cool slightly.

3. In a small bowl stir together Gorgonzola cheese and milk until mixture is smooth. Spread evenly in cooled pastry shells. Spoon the caramelized onion mixture into pastry shells over the Gorgonzola mixture. Sprinkle with parsley.

4. To serve, carefully remove pastry shells from tart pans. Divide salad greens among four serving plates; drizzle with salad dressing. Place tarts on plates with greens.

Caraway Seed Pastry: In a bowl stir together ¾ cup all-purpose flour and ¼ teaspoon salt. Using a pastry blender, cut in ¼ cup cold unsalted butter until pieces are the size of small peas. Stir in ¾ teaspoon caraway seeds. Add 3 to 4 tablespoons cold water, 1 tablespoon at a time, gently tossing until all of the flour mixture is moistened. Form into a ball.

Make-Ahead Directions: Prepare pastry shells as directed in Step 1. Cool completely. Place in an airtight container; cover. Store at room temperature for up to three days or freeze for up to three months. When ready to serve, prepare onion and cheese mixture as directed in Steps 2 and 3; serve as directed.

Per serving: 326 cal., 23 g total fat (10 g sat. fat), 39 mg chol., 573 mg sodium, 27 g carbo., 2 g fiber, 5 g pro.
Daily Values: 21% vit. A, 12% vit. C, 8% calcium, 8% iron

 ## Blue Cheese Walnut Mousse

Use a favorite variety of domestic or imported blue cheese in this simple-to-fix, delicious appetizer. Maytag Blue cheese from Iowa is a good, relatively mild choice.

Start to Finish: 10 minutes
Makes: 1 cup (eight 2-tablespoon servings)

- 1 **3-ounce package cream cheese, softened**
- 2 **ounces blue cheese, crumbled (½ cup)**
- ¼ **cup dairy sour cream**
- ½ **teaspoon Worcestershire sauce**
- ¼ **cup chopped walnuts, toasted (see tip, page 63)**
- 1 **tablespoon snipped fresh chives**
   Assorted crackers, apple slices, and/or pear slices

1. In a small bowl stir together cream cheese, blue cheese, sour cream, and Worcestershire sauce. Stir in walnuts and chives. Serve with crackers and/or fruit.

Per serving mousse: 99 cal., 9 g total fat (5 g sat. fat), 20 mg chol., 138 mg sodium, 1 g carbo., 0 g fiber, 3 g pro.
Daily Values: 5% vit. A, 1% vit. C, 6% calcium, 2% iron

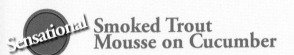

Sensational Smoked Trout Mousse on Cucumber

For a twist, substitute smoked salmon for smoked trout. Or, use half trout and half salmon for another flavor option.

Start to Finish: 25 minutes
Makes: about 36 appetizers

- 3 large cucumbers (each 8 inches long)
- 1 8-ounce package cream cheese, softened
- 4 ounces soft goat cheese (chèvre)
- ¼ cup chopped green onion
- 2 tablespoons snipped fresh Italian (flat-leaf) parsley
- 3 tablespoons snipped fresh dillweed
- 8 ounces smoked trout fillets, skin and bones removed and flaked
  Fresh dillweed sprigs (optional)

1. Wash cucumbers; cut into ½-inch slices. Pat slices dry with paper towels.

2. In a medium mixing bowl beat cream cheese and goat cheese with an electric mixer on medium speed until smooth. Stir in green onion, parsley, and snipped dillweed. Stir in trout.

3. Spoon trout mixture onto cucumber slices. If desired, garnish with dill sprigs.

Make-Ahead Directions: Prepare as directed through Step 2. Cover and chill cucumber slices and trout mixture for up to 4 hours. Continue as directed in Step 3.

Per appetizer: 48 cal., 3 g total fat (2 g sat. fat), 16 mg chol., 54 mg sodium, 2 g carbo., 0 g fiber, 2 g pro.
Daily Values: 3% vit. A, 2% vit. C, 2% calcium, 1% iron

Simple Sweet Pepper Bruschetta

White cheese, red sweet peppers, and green oregano make this appetizer holiday-perfect and super delicious.

Start to Finish: 20 minutes **Makes:** 16 appetizers

- 16 bias-cut slices (about ¾-inch) Italian country bread or crusty sourdough bread
- 1 cup soft goat cheese (chèvre) or other spreadable soft white cheese (about 10 ounces)
- ½ cup purchased basil pesto
- ⅔ cup roasted red sweet peppers, drained and cut into ½-inch strips
  Snipped fresh oregano (optional)

1. Preheat broiler. Place bread slices on a baking sheet. Broil about 4 inches from the heat for 1 to 2 minutes or until bread is toasted, turning once.

2. Spread toasted bread with goat cheese. Spread pesto on cheese; top with roasted red pepper strips. If desired, garnish with fresh oregano.

Per appetizer: 202 cal., 11 g total fat (4 g sat. fat), 15 mg chol., 325 mg sodium, 17 g carbo., 1 g fiber, 7 g pro.
Daily Values: 5% vit. A, 28% vit. C, 8% calcium, 7% iron

Sweet Pepper Bruschetta

Gorgonzola and Artichoke Bruschetta

When buying watercress, look for crisp, bright green leaves and healthy stems. Rinse the watercress just before assembling the bruschetta. Be sure to dry the leaves thoroughly by patting with paper towels.

Prep: 40 minutes **Chill:** 1 hour **Bake:** 1 minute
Oven: 400°F **Makes:** 24 appetizers

- 1 6-ounce jar marinated artichoke hearts
- 12 ounces Gorgonzola cheese or goat cheese (chèvre)
- ½ cup seasoned fine dry bread crumbs
- 1 8-ounce loaf baguette-style French bread, cut into 24 slices and toasted
- 2 tablespoons Dijon-style mustard or tarragon mustard
- 1½ cups watercress trimmed and chopped, or baby spinach

1. Drain the artichoke hearts, reserving the marinade. Cut the artichoke hearts into 24 thin wedges; set aside. Cut cheese into twenty-four ¼-inch wedges or slices. Brush the wedges with some of the reserved marinade; let stand for 5 minutes. Place the bread crumbs in a shallow dish. Coat the cheese wedges with the bread crumbs. Place on a baking sheet. Cover and chill for 1 hour.

2. Preheat oven to 400°F. Brush toasted bread slices very lightly with mustard. Place the watercress on top of the baguette slices; set aside.

3. Bake breaded cheese for 1 to 2 minutes or just until cheese begins to bubble around the edges and begins to soften (do not overbake). Place warm cheese on baguette slices. Top with artichoke wedges. Serve immediately.

Per appetizer: 98 cal., 6 g total fat (3 g sat. fat), 13 mg chol., 322 mg sodium, 7 g carbo., 1 g fiber, 4 g pro.
Daily Values: 5% vit. A, 3% vit. C, 9% calcium, 2% iron

Gouda and Red Onion Pizza

This easy-on-the-cook pizza takes hardly any time to prepare with the use of purchased pizza dough, but packs a powerful—and impressive—flavor punch with the additions of onion, plenty of Gouda cheese, and snipped thyme.

Prep: 25 minutes **Bake:** 12 minutes
Oven: 400° F **Makes:** 12 appetizers

- 1 large red onion, halved lengthwise and thinly sliced (about 2 cups)
- 2 tablespoons olive oil
- 1 tablespoon snipped fresh thyme or 1 teaspoon dried thyme, crushed
- ¼ teaspoon salt
- ¼ teaspoon freshly ground black pepper
- 1 tablespoon cornmeal
- 1 13.8-ounce package refrigerated pizza dough
- 8 ounces Gouda cheese or Edam cheese, shredded (2 cups)

1. Preheat oven to 400°F. In a large skillet cook onion in 1 tablespoon of the hot oil over medium heat for 5 to 7 minutes until onion is tender but not brown, stirring often. Remove from heat. Stir in thyme, salt, and pepper; set aside.

Gorgonzola and Artichoke Bruschetta

2. Grease a baking sheet and sprinkle with the cornmeal. Pat pizza dough into a 12×8-inch rectangle on the baking sheet. Brush pizza dough with remaining 1 tablespoon oil. Sprinkle pizza dough with cheese to within ½ inch of edges. Spoon onion mixture over the cheese.

3. Bake for 12 to 15 minutes or until crust is golden. Cut into 12 pieces.

Per appetizer: 166 cal., 9 g total fat (4 g sat. fat), 22 mg chol., 308 mg sodium, 15 g carbo., 1 g fiber, 7 g pro.
Daily Values: 2% vit. A, 2% vit. C, 14% calcium, 5% iron

 **Blue Cheese-Apple Pizza**

Using a tart apple, such as McIntosh, Jonathan, or Granny Smith, is key for this flavor combination!

Prep: 30 minutes **Rise:** 45 minutes
Bake: 20 minutes **Oven:** 450°F
Makes: 12 appetizers

- 1 teaspoon active dry yeast
- ¾ cup warm water (105°F to 115°F)
- 1 cup all-purpose flour
- ¾ cup whole wheat flour
- 1 teaspoon sugar
- 1 teaspoon salt
- 1 tablespoon cooking oil
- 3 ounces blue cheese, crumbled (¾ cup)
- 1 large tart red or green apple, such as McIntosh, Jonathan, or Granny Smith, cored and thinly sliced (about 1⅓ cups)
- 2 ounces Monterey Jack cheese, shredded (½ cup)
- ½ cup coarsely chopped walnuts
- 1½ teaspoons snipped fresh rosemary

1. In a small bowl dissolve yeast in warm water; let stand 5 minutes. In a large bowl stir together all-purpose flour, whole wheat flour, sugar, and salt. Make a well in the center of the dry ingredients. Add yeast mixture and oil; stir until combined. Turn out onto a well-floured surface. Knead gently about 20 times or until a soft dough forms. Place dough in a greased bowl. Turn dough once to grease dough surface. Cover; let rise in a warm place until double in size (45 to 60 minutes).

Blue Cheese-Apple Pizza

2. Preheat oven to 450°F. Grease a 12-inch pizza pan. Turn dough out onto a well-floured surface. Roll dough into a 13-inch circle. Transfer to prepared pizza pan. Build up edges slightly. Bake crust about 10 minutes or until just beginning to brown. Remove from oven.

3. Sprinkle with blue cheese. Top with apple slices. Sprinkle with Monterey Jack cheese, walnuts, and rosemary. Bake for 10 to 12 minutes more or until the edge of crust is browned. Cut into 12 wedges.

Per appetizer: 154 cal., 8 g total fat (3 g sat. fat), 10 mg chol., 319 mg sodium, 16 g carbo., 2 g fiber, 6 g pro.
Daily Values: 2% vit. A, 1% vit. C, 8% calcium, 6% iron

Buffalo Chicken Wings

Look for chicken wing seasoning mix in the spice aisle of the supermarket. If desired, serve these appetizers with purchased blue cheese dressing instead of the sour cream mixture.

Prep: 15 minutes **Bake:** 1 hour
Oven: 350°F **Makes:** 10 servings

   2 to 2½ pounds frozen chicken wing pieces
   1 1.75-ounce package Buffalo chicken wing
      seasoning mix with cooking bag
   1 8-ounce container dairy sour cream
      ranch-flavor dip
   2 ounces blue cheese, crumbled (½ cup)
   2 tablespoons milk
      Celery sticks

1. Preheat oven to 350°F. Place frozen wing pieces in the cooking bag. Add seasoning and shake to coat. Close bag with nylon tie. Place bag in a shallow baking pan and arrange pieces in a single layer. Cut two slits in the top of the bag to allow steam to escape. Bake about 1 hour or until chicken pieces are tender and no longer pink, carefully cutting bag open to check doneness.

2. Meanwhile, in a small bowl combine the ranch dip, blue cheese, and milk. Cover and chill until serving time.

3. Place wings in a serving dish, spooning some of the cooking liquid over wings to moisten (discard remaining cooking liquid). Serve wings with blue cheese mixture and celery sticks.

Per serving: 269 cal., 20 g total fat (7 g sat. fat), 114 mg chol., 735 mg sodium, 4 g carbo., 1 g fiber, 18 g pro.
Daily Values: 10% vit. A, 7% calcium, 1% iron

Persimmon-Glazed Chicken Wings

 Persimmon-Glazed
Chicken Wings

Persimmons are widely available in the winter months. Look for ripe fruit that has an orange-red skin and very soft flesh. If eaten when underripe, persimmons have a somewhat bitter flavor.

Prep: 20 minutes **Chill:** 1 hour **Bake:** 50 minutes
Oven: 375°F **Makes:** about 10 servings

  2 pounds chicken wings
  1 large ripe persimmon (preferably Hachiya)
  ¼ cup maple syrup or maple-flavored syrup
  ¼ cup Dijon-style mustard
  3 tablespoons cider vinegar
  2 tablespoons Asian chili sauce
  2 tablespoons dark rum (optional)
  1 tablespoon chopped fresh chives or
     finely chopped green onion
  2 teaspoons soy sauce
     Salt
     Ground black pepper

1. If desired, remove and discard wing tips from chicken wings; separate each wing into two pieces at the joint.

2. Coarsely chop persimmon and place in a blender or food processor. Cover and blend or process until almost smooth. In a large nonmetal bowl stir together persimmon, maple syrup, mustard, vinegar, chili sauce, rum (if desired), chives, and soy sauce. Add chicken and toss to coat. Cover and chill for 1 to 4 hours.

3. Preheat oven to 375°F. Line a shallow roasting pan with foil. Drain wings, reserving marinade. Place wings in pan; season with salt and pepper. Bake for 30 minutes, brushing with marinade after 15 minutes. Brush wings again; turn wings over and brush with additional marinade. Bake 20 minutes more, brushing with marinade after 10 minutes. Discard any remaining marinade. Serve chicken wings warm.

Per serving: 90 cal., 2 g total fat (0 g sat. fat), 26 mg chol., 322 mg sodium, 7 g carbo., 0 g fiber, 10 g pro.
Daily Values: 2% vit. A, 4% vit. C, 1% calcium, 3% iron

Quick Bites

Here are some suggestions for quick-to-fix or last-minute snacks and appetizers for your next party or impromptu gathering:

• Spread purchased olive tapenade on crostini.
• Scoop finely chopped chicken, turkey, or tuna salad into endive leaves.
• Spread egg salad on cucumber slices and garnish with fresh dillweed.
• Spread purchased pâté on apple or pear slices.
• Remove the string from snow peas or sugar snap peas, separate along one side, and pipe boursin or chèvre cheese into them.
• Offer a bowl of cleaned radishes with a ramekin of softened butter and a dish of kosher salt for dipping.

 Crab Cakes with
Cranberry-Mustard
Sauce

To make these crab cakes extra-special, serve them on a bed of salad greens. Another option is to use mini crab cakes—look for them at a warehouse market.

Start to Finish: 30 minutes
Makes: 8 appetizer servings

  4 6-ounce packages frozen crab cakes
     (8 crab cakes total)
  1 9-ounce jar (1¼ cups) cranberry chutney
  2 tablespoons honey
  1 tablespoon horseradish mustard
     Mesclun mix or micro salad greens

1. Heat crab cakes according to package directions.

2. Meanwhile, for sauce, in a small saucepan heat and stir chutney, honey, and mustard over medium heat until bubbly. Remove from heat. To serve, arrange greens on a serving platter. Top with crab cakes. Transfer sauce to a serving bowl. Serve immediately.

Per serving: 221 cal., 7 g total fat (1 g sat. fat), 128 mg chol., 299 mg sodium, 23 g carbo., 0 g fiber, 17 g pro.
Daily Values: 6% vit. A, 5% vit. C, 9% calcium, 5% iron

Cilantro Crab Cakes with Serrano Aïoli

Cilantro Crab Cakes with Serrano Aïoli

Water chestnuts add an unexpected crunch to these flavor-packed crab cakes. If possible, use panko (Japanese-style bread crumbs) in this recipe for maximum crispness.

Prep: 25 minutes **Cook:** 6 minutes per batch
Makes: about 30 crab cakes
(fifteen 2-cake servings)

  2 **eggs**
  1 **medium red sweet pepper, finely chopped**
  ½ **of an 8-ounce can water chestnuts, drained and finely chopped (½ cup)**
  ½ **cup panko (Japanese-style bread crumbs) or fine dry bread crumbs**
  2 **tablespoons snipped fresh cilantro**
  ½ **teaspoon salt**

  ¼ **teaspoon ground white pepper or ground black pepper**
  1 **16-ounce can crabmeat, drained, flaked, and cartilage removed**
  ⅔ **cup panko (Japanese-style) bread crumbs or fine dry bread crumbs**
  ¼ **cup cooking oil**
  1 **recipe Serrano Aïoli**
     Fresh cilantro sprigs (optional)
     Lime wedges (optional)

1. In a large bowl beat eggs lightly with a fork. Stir in sweet pepper, water chestnuts, ½ cup bread crumbs, snipped cilantro, salt, and pepper. Add crabmeat; mix well. Form mixture into about thirty 1½-inch patties.

2. Place ⅔ cup bread crumbs in a shallow dish; dip patties into bread crumbs, turning to coat. In a large skillet heat 2 tablespoons of the oil over medium heat. Add half of the crab cakes; cook for 6 to 8 minutes or until golden, turning once. Drain on paper towels; keep warm. Repeat cooking with remaining 2 tablespoons oil and remaining crab cakes.

3. Serve crab cakes warm with Serrano Aïoli. If desired, garnish with cilantro sprigs and serve with lime wedges.

Serrano Aïoli: In a small bowl combine ⅔ cup mayonnaise or salad dressing; 1 tablespoon lime juice; 1 to 2 fresh serrano chile peppers, seeded and finely chopped;* ½ teaspoon salt; and ¼ teaspoon ground white pepper or ground black pepper. Cover and chill for up to 24 hours. Makes ¾ cup.

Make-Ahead Directions: Prepare and form crab cakes as directed in Step 1. Cover and chill for up to 24 hours. To serve, continue as directed in Steps 2 and 3.

*Note: Because chile peppers contain oils that can burn skin and eyes, avoid direct contact with them as much as possible. When working with chile peppers, wear plastic or rubber gloves. If your bare hands do touch the peppers, wash them well with soap and warm water.

Per serving: 165 cal., 13 g total fat (2 g sat. fat), 59 mg chol., 333 mg sodium, 4 g carbo., 0 g fiber, 8 g pro.
Daily Values: 6% vit. A, 24% vit. C, 4% calcium, 2% iron

 ## Orange Martini Shrimp Cocktail

Serve these vodka-infused shrimp in martini or wine glasses or simply arranged on a pretty glass platter.

Prep: 15 minutes **Chill:** 2 hours
Makes: 6 servings

18 fresh or frozen extra jumbo shrimp in shells
   (about 1 pound)
⅓ cup orange-flavored vodka
1 tablespoon cooking oil
1 tablespoon snipped fresh mint
1 teaspoon finely shredded orange peel
   Crushed ice
   Orange peel twists
   Dry vermouth (optional)

1. Thaw shrimp, if frozen. Peel and devein shrimp, leaving tails intact. Cook shrimp in lightly salted boiling water for 2 to 3 minutes or until shrimp turn opaque, stirring occasionally; drain. Rinse in a colander under cold running water; drain. Place shrimp in a plastic bag set in a medium bowl; set aside.

2. In a small bowl combine vodka, oil, mint, and orange peel. Pour mixture over shrimp; seal bag. Marinate in the refrigerator for 2 to 4 hours, turning bag occasionally.

3. To serve, place about ⅓ cup crushed ice in each of six chilled martini glasses or small serving bowls. Drain shrimp; discard marinade. Arrange shrimp in each glass on top of ice. Garnish with orange peel twists. If desired, drizzle each with 1 to 2 teaspoons vermouth.

***Note:** If you can't find orange-flavored vodka in local stores, use ¼ cup plain vodka and 2 tablespoons orange juice.

Per serving: 130 cal., 4 g total fat (0 g sat. fat), 115 mg chol.,
112 mg sodium, 1 g carbo., 0 g fiber, 15 g pro.
Daily Values: 3% vit. A, 6% vit. C, 4% calcium, 11% iron

Shrimp Math

When choosing shrimp, follow the guidelines below. Be sure to buy pink shrimp with no fishy odor. Twelve ounces shrimp in shell equals eight ounces peeled and deveined.

Extra small: 61 to 70 per pound
Small: 50 to 60 per pound
Medium: 41 to 50 per pound
Medium large: 36 to 40 per pound
Large: 31 to 40 per pound
Extra large: 26 to 30 per pound
Jumbo: 20 to 25 per pound
Extra jumbo: 16 to 20 per pound
Colossal: Fewer than 15 per pound

Orange Martini Shrimp Cocktails

 ## Shoyster Cocktail

This snack is based on oysters and shrimp packed with just the right amount of heat and tang for a holiday open house. People will gobble it up!

Prep: 25 minutes **Chill:** 2 hours
Makes: 8 servings

- 12 fresh or frozen medium shrimp in shells
- 12 fresh shucked oysters
- ½ cup chopped tomato
- ½ cup cocktail sauce
- ⅓ cup finely chopped onion
- 1 medium fresh Anaheim or banana chile pepper, seeded and finely chopped*
- 2 tablespoons snipped fresh parsley
- 1 tablespoon lime juice
- ¼ teaspoon bottled hot pepper sauce
- 1 clove garlic, minced
- 1 medium avocado, halved, pitted, peeled, and chopped
    Leaf lettuce (optional)
    Toasted baguette slices (optional)
    Lemon wedges (optional)

1. Thaw shrimp, if frozen. Peel and devein shrimp. In a medium saucepan cook shrimp and oysters in lightly salted boiling water for 2 minutes or until edges of oysters curl and shrimp turn opaque. Drain well. Cut shrimp in half lengthwise.

2. In a medium bowl combine oysters, shrimp, tomato, cocktail sauce, onion, chile pepper, parsley, lime juice, hot pepper sauce, and garlic. Cover and chill for 2 to 6 hours. Stir in avocado just before serving. If desired, serve in individual lettuce-lined dishes with baguette slices and lemon wedges.

*Note: Because chile peppers contain oils that can burn skin and eyes, avoid direct contact with them as much as possible. When working with chile peppers, wear plastic or rubber gloves. If your bare hands do touch the peppers, wash them well with soap and warm water.

Per serving: 93 cal., 4 g total fat (1 g sat. fat), 21 mg chol., 285 mg sodium, 11 g carbo., 2 g fiber, 4 g pro.
Daily Values: 11% vit. A, 35% vit. C, 2% calcium, 10% iron

 ## Savory Party Dip

This dip can be assembled so quickly that it is perfect for last-minute guests. Be sure to chill at least an hour before serving. The bonus? All of the ingredients are usually on hand.

Prep: 10 minutes **Chill:** 1 hour
Makes: 1⅝ cups (thirteen 2-tablespoon servings)

- 1 cup mayonnaise or salad dressing
- 1 cup dairy sour cream
- 6 green onion tops, cut up (about ¾ cup)
- ¼ teaspoon garlic powder
    Bias-sliced green onion (optional)
    Assorted crackers, pepperoncini, and/or olives

1. In a food processor or blender, combine mayonnaise, sour cream, green onion tops, and garlic powder. Cover and process or blend until smooth. Cover and chill for 1 to 24 hours. If desired, top with additional sliced green onion. Serve with crackers, pepperoncini, and/or olives.

Per serving dip: 157 cal., 17 g total fat (4 g sat. fat), 13 mg chol., 101 mg sodium, 1 g carbo., 0 g fiber, 1 g pro.
Daily Values: 3% vit. A, 2% vit. C, 2% calcium, 1% iron

Savory Party Dip

Layered Fiesta Shrimp Dip

 **Layered Fiesta Shrimp Dip**

Family and holiday guests will love the sweet-spicy flavors in this jazzy version of a Mexican layer dip.

Start to Finish: 20 minutes
Makes: about 4 cups dip (16 to 20 servings)

   2 8-ounce packages cream cheese, softened
   2 tablespoons mayonnaise or salad dressing
   1 fresh jalapeño chile pepper, seeded and finely chopped (see Note, page 11)
   2 cloves garlic, minced
   1 cup bottled lime and garlic salsa or habañero lime salsa
  12 ounces fresh or frozen peeled, cooked shrimp, halved lengthwise, if desired
   1 cup chopped mango
   1 cup chopped, seeded roma tomatoes
   ¼ cup sliced green onion
   2 tablespoons snipped fresh cilantro
      Cilantro sprigs (optional)
      Tortilla chips or crostini*

1. In a medium mixing bowl beat cream cheese, mayonnaise, jalapeño pepper, and garlic with an electric mixer on medium to high speed until creamy. Spread mixture on a 12-inch diameter serving platter. Spread salsa over cream cheese layer to cover. Top with shrimp.

2. In a medium bowl combine mango, tomato, green onion, and cilantro. Sprinkle mango mixture evenly over shrimp. If desired, garnish with cilantro sprigs. Serve immediately or cover and refrigerate for up to 4 hours. Serve with tortilla chips or crostini.

*Tip: To make crostini, preheat oven to 400°F. Bias-slice an 8-ounce loaf of baguette-style French bread into forty ¼-inch slices. Arrange bread on baking sheets. Using 2 tablespoons olive oil, lightly brush one side of each slice with some of the oil. Bake for 4 minutes. Turn slices and bake about 4 minutes or until golden.

Per serving dip with chips: 221 cal., 15 g total fat (7 g sat. fat), 64 mg chol., 301 mg sodium, 14 g carbo., 1 g fiber, 8 g pro.
Daily Values: 14% vit. A, 11% vit. C, 6% calcium, 7% iron

 ## Orange-Pecan Topped Brie

This appetizer has only four ingredients plus bread.

Prep: 10 minutes **Bake:** 15 minutes **Oven:** 350°F
Makes: 8 to 10 servings

- 1 15-ounce round Brie cheese
- ½ cup orange marmalade
- 2 tablespoons packed brown sugar
- ⅓ cup coarsely chopped pecans, toasted (see tip, page 63)
  Toasted baguette slices, assorted crackers, and/or sliced apples

1. Preheat oven to 350°F. Place the round of cheese on an ovenproof plate or pie plate. In a small bowl stir together orange marmalade and brown sugar. Spread on top of cheese. Sprinkle with toasted pecans.

2. Bake for 15 to 20 minutes or until cheese is slightly softened and topping is bubbly. Serve with baguette slices, crackers, and/or sliced apples.

Per serving with baguette slices: 359 cal., 19 g total fat (10 g sat. fat), 53 mg chol., 542 mg sodium, 34 g carbo., 2 g fiber, 14 g pro.
Daily Values: 7% vit. A, 2% vit. C, 14% calcium, 7% iron

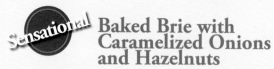 ## Baked Brie with Caramelized Onions and Hazelnuts

Almost everyone is amazed at how sweet onions become when they are caramelized. Here, the onions elevate baked Brie to showcase appetizer status.

Prep: 25 minutes **Bake:** 15 minutes
Oven: 350°F **Makes:** 8 to 10 servings

Orange-Pecan Topped Brie

- ½ cup chopped yellow onion (1 medium)
- 2 tablespoons butter
- 1 15-ounce round Brie cheese
- 3 tablespoons apricot preserves
- ¼ cup chopped hazelnuts (filberts) or pecans
  French bread slices and/or sliced apples
  or pears

1. Preheat oven to 350°F. For caramelized onions, in a small saucepan cook onion in hot butter, covered, over low heat for 10 to 15 minutes or until tender and golden, stirring occasionally.

2. Place the round of cheese on an ovenproof plate or baking sheet. Spread the apricot preserves on top of the cheese. Top with the caramelized onion and sprinkle with nuts.

3. Bake for 15 to 20 minutes or until cheese is slightly softened. If baked on a baking sheet, carefully transfer warm Brie to a serving platter. Serve with French bread slices and/or sliced fruit.

Per serving cheese and topping: 254 cal., 20 g total fat (11 g sat. fat), 61 mg chol., 355 mg sodium, 7 g carbo., 1 g fiber, 12 g pro.
Daily Values: 8% vit. A, 2% vit. C, 11% calcium, 3% iron

Artichoke Dip

Another time, serve this savory dip with toasted pita bread triangles.

Prep: 10 minutes **Chill:** 2 hours
Makes: about 1¼ cups (ten 2-tablespoon servings)

- 1 14-ounce can artichoke hearts
- ½ cup mayonnaise or salad dressing
- ¼ cup grated Parmesan cheese
- 1 clove garlic, minced
  Assorted vegetables

1. Drain artichokes thoroughly, pressing to remove excess liquid. In a medium bowl mash artichokes; stir in mayonnaise, Parmesan cheese, and garlic. Cover and chill for several hours. Serve with vegetable dippers.

Per serving dip: 103 cal., 9 g total fat (2 g sat. fat), 6 mg chol., 210 mg sodium, 4 g carbo., 0 g fiber, 2 g pro.
Daily Values: 1% vit. A, 3% vit. C, 2% calcium, 3% iron

Hot Artichoke and Roasted Pepper Dip

Thinly sliced leek and roasted red pepper take the always popular artichoke dip to new heights.

Prep: 20 minutes **Bake:** 20 minutes **Oven:** 350°F
Makes: 3 cups (twenty-four 2-tablespoon servings)

- 1 medium leek, quartered lengthwise and thinly sliced, or ⅛ cup sliced green onion
- 2 teaspoons butter or margarine
- 1 14-ounce can artichoke hearts, drained and coarsely chopped
- 1 cup bottled roasted red sweet peppers, drained and coarsely chopped
- 1 cup grated Parmesan cheese
- ½ cup mayonnaise
- ½ cup dairy sour cream
- ⅛ teaspoon ground black pepper
- 2 tablespoons grated Parmesan cheese
- 1 tablespoon snipped fresh parsley
  Assorted sweet pepper wedges, flat breads, and/or bagel crisps

1. Preheat oven to 350°F. In a medium skillet cook leek in hot butter over medium heat until tender. Remove from heat. Stir in artichoke hearts, roasted red peppers, 1 cup Parmesan cheese, mayonnaise, sour cream, and black pepper.

2. Spread mixture evenly in an 8-inch quiche dish or 9-inch pie plate. Sprinkle with 2 tablespoons Parmesan cheese and parsley.

3. Bake, uncovered, for 20 minutes or until heated through. Serve with sweet pepper wedges, flat breads, and/or bagel crisps.

Make-Ahead Directions: Prepare as directed through Step 2. Cover and chill for up to 24 hours. Bake as directed in Step 3.

Per serving dip: 69 cal., 6 g total fat (2 g sat. fat), 8 mg chol., 144 mg sodium, 2 g carbo., 1 g fiber, 2 g pro.
Daily Values: 3% vit. A, 30% vit. C, 5% calcium, 3% iron

Favorite Breakfasts & Brunches

Breakfasts and brunches are fun, relaxing ways to celebrate the holidays. Invite some friends for an impromptu morning gathering—perhaps once all the formal celebrations are over. Brew coffee, fill the glasses with OJ, and serve a few of these inspired recipes. Decide to prepare supersimple entreés such as four-ingredient French Toast (so easy children can assist you) and ready-in-less-than-20-minutes Broccoli Omelet. Or try indulgent Lox-Style Strata and raspberry-adorned Lemon Soufflé Pancakes. For an added boost, offer guests a bloody mary or mimosa (part OJ and part sparkling wine or champagne). Whatever you serve, keep your event fun and relaxed. After all, this is a busy time of year. You've earned the chance to take it easy!

Lemon Soufflé Pancakes, page 50

French Toast

Topped with plenty of fresh fruit and warmed citrus curd, this French toast is a perfect heartwarming breakfast for Christmas morning (or anytime!). If desired, skip the citrus curd and pour on maple syrup.

Prep: 10 minutes **Cook:** 4 minutes per batch
Makes: 4 servings

- 4   eggs, beaten
- 1   cup milk
- 2   tablespoons sugar
- 2   teaspoons vanilla
- ½   teaspoon ground cinnamon (optional)
- 8   slices dry white bread
- 2   tablespoons butter
     Orange or lemon curd, warmed (optional)

Sliced strawberries, orange sections, and/or blueberries (optional)

1. In a shallow dish whisk together eggs, milk, sugar, vanilla, and if desired, cinnamon until well combined. Dip bread slices into egg mixture, turning to coat both sides.

2. In a skillet or on a griddle, melt 1 tablespoon of the butter over medium heat; add half of the bread slices and cook for 2 to 3 minutes on each side or until golden brown. Repeat with remaining butter and bread slices. Serve warm. If desired, serve with orange curd and fruit.

Per serving: 553 cal., 19 g total fat (8 g sat. fat), 302 mg chol., 560 mg sodium, 81 g carbo., 7 g fiber, 16 g pro.
Daily Values: 14% vit. A, 35% vit. C, 18% calcium, 20% iron

French Toast

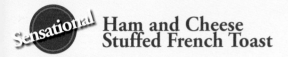

Ham and Cheese Stuffed French Toast

Sweet and savory at the same time, this recipe takes French toast from ordinary to outstanding. Serve with fresh fruit.

Prep: 20 minutes **Cook:** 6 minutes per batch
Makes: 6 servings

- 2 eggs
- 1 cup half-and-half, light cream, or milk
- 1 teaspoon vanilla
- ½ teaspoon ground cinnamon
- 6 ounces Gruyère or Swiss cheese, sliced
- 12 slices firm-texture white, wheat, or rye bread
- 8 ounces cooked, very thinly sliced smoked ham
  Butter
- 1 medium star fruit, sliced (optional)
- 1 kiwifruit, peeled and sliced (optional)

1. In a shallow dish whisk together eggs, half-and-half, vanilla, and cinnamon until well combined; set aside.

2. Divide cheese among 6 of the bread slices. Top each with ham and then a second slice of bread. Dip one at a time in egg mixture, turning to coat both sides of sandwiches (allowing excess egg mixture to drip off).

3. Cook sandwiches, half at a time if necessary, on a hot buttered griddle or in a nonstick skillet over medium heat for 3 to 4 minutes per side or until golden brown. Serve warm. Cut each sandwich in half diagonally. Place two halves on each plate. If desired, garnish with slices of star fruit and kiwi.

Per serving: 449 cal., 28 g total fat (14 g sat. fat), 153 mg chol., 968 mg sodium, 29 g carbo., 0 g fiber, 23 g pro.
Daily Values: 13% vit. A, 1% vit. C, 39% calcium, 15% iron

Lemon Poppy Seed Pancakes with Raspberry Syrup

If desired, substitute banana nut, apple cinnamon, or blueberry muffin mix for the lemon poppy seed and vary the type of frozen fruit—blueberries or strawberries make excellent choices.

Start to Finish: 20 minutes
Makes: 8 pancakes (4 servings)

- 2 eggs
- ⅔ cup milk
- 1 7.6-ounce package lemon poppy seed muffin mix
- 1 10-ounce package frozen red raspberries in syrup, thawed
- 2 teaspoons cornstarch

1. To make pancakes, in a medium bowl beat together eggs and milk. Add the muffin mix all at once. Stir just until moistened (batter should be nearly smooth).

2. For standard-size pancakes, pour or spread about ¼ cup of the batter into a 4-inch circle onto a hot, lightly greased griddle or heavy skillet. Cook over medium heat for 1½ to 2 minutes on each side or until pancakes are brown, turning to second sides when pancakes have bubbly surfaces and edges are slightly dry. Repeat with remaining batter.

3. For syrup, in a small saucepan combine raspberries and cornstarch. Cook and stir until thickened and bubbly. Serve over the pancakes.

Per serving: 405 cal., 10 g total fat (3 g sat. fat), 114 mg chol., 384 mg sodium, 70 g carbo., 3 g fiber, 8 g pro.
Daily Values: 5% vit. A, 2% vit. C, 17% calcium, 25% iron

Lemon Soufflé Pancakes

 **Lemon Soufflé Pancakes**

When folding egg whites, use a rubber spatula. Cut down through the middle of the mixture and sweep upward, giving the bowl a quarter turn before repeating. Continue until mixed.

Prep: 20 minutes **Cook:** 4 minutes per batch
Makes: eight 4-inch or twenty 2-inch pancakes
(4 servings)

    2 cups frozen lightly sweetened
       red raspberries
    1 cup maple syrup
    1 cup all-purpose flour
    2 teaspoons baking powder
    2 teaspoons finely shredded lemon peel
    ¼ teaspoon salt
    1 egg yolk
    ¾ cup milk
    ¼ cup butter, melted
    3 egg whites
       Butter (optional)
       Fresh raspberries (optional)

1. For syrup, thaw 2 cups berries but do not drain. Place berries in a blender or food processor. Cover and blend or process until berries are smooth. Press berries through a fine-mesh sieve into a small saucepan. Discard seeds. Cook and stir over medium heat until just heated through. Stir in syrup; set aside.

2. To make pancakes, in a medium bowl stir together flour, baking powder, lemon peel, and salt. Make a well in the center of flour mixture; set aside. In a small bowl slightly beat egg yolk. Stir in milk and melted butter. Add egg yolk mixture all at once to the flour mixture. Stir just until moistened (batter should be lumpy).

3. In a medium mixing bowl beat egg whites with an electric mixer on medium speed until stiff peaks form (tips stand straight). Gently fold egg whites into batter, leaving a few fluffs of egg white. Do not overmix.

4. For standard-size pancakes, pour ¼ cup of the batter onto a hot, lightly greased griddle or heavy skillet. (Or for dollar-size pancakes, pour about 1 tablespoon batter onto hot lightly greased griddle or heavy skillet.) Cook over medium heat 2 minutes on each side or until pancakes are golden brown, turning when pancakes have bubbly surfaces and edges are slightly dry. Repeat with remaining batter. Serve with raspberry syrup, and if desired, butter and fresh raspberries.

Per serving: 603 cal., 14 g total fat (8 g sat. fat), 87 mg chol., 418 mg sodium, 113 g carbo., 6 g fiber, 9 g pro.
Daily Values: 12% vit. A, 37% vit. C, 18% calcium, 19% iron

Broccoli Omelet

This omelet is so easy to make. It is baked in a rectangular baking pan, so the oven does all the work!

Start to Finish: 20 minutes **Oven:** 400°F
Makes: 6 servings

     Nonstick cooking spray
12   eggs
¼   cup water
½   teaspoon garlic salt
⅛   teaspoon ground black pepper
3   cups packaged shredded broccoli
       (broccoli slaw mix)
1½   cups purchased tomato and basil pasta
       sauce or any favorite tomato pasta
       sauce, heated

1. Preheat oven to 400°F. Coat a 15×10×1-inch baking pan with cooking spray; set aside. For omelet, in a large bowl beat together eggs, water, garlic salt, and pepper. Pour egg mixture into prepared pan. Bake about 10 minutes or until egg mixture is set, but still glossy and moist.

2. Meanwhile, place shredded broccoli in a steamer basket over boiling water. Cover and steam for 3 to 4 minutes or until crisp-tender.

3. To serve, cut omelet into six 5-inch squares. Invert each omelet square onto a serving plate. Spoon some of the broccoli slaw on half of each omelet square; fold other half of omelet over filling. Spoon the warm pasta sauce over omelets. Serve immediately.

Per serving: 185 cal., 10 g total fat (3 g sat. fat), 423 mg chol., 428 mg sodium, 8 g carbo., 2 g fiber, 15 g pro.
Daily Values: 39% vit. A, 65% vit. C, 11% calcium, 14% iron

Omelet with Wilted Greens

Start to Finish: 25 minutes **Makes:** 1 serving

2   slices bacon, chopped
1   teaspoon white wine vinegar
½   teaspoon sugar
½   cup torn sorrel leaves or baby sorrel leaves
½   cup torn red kale leaves (stems removed)
¼   cup torn beet leaves (stems removed)
1   teaspoon snipped fresh oregano
2   eggs
2   tablespoons water
⅛   teaspoon salt
     Dash ground black pepper
1   tablespoon butter or margarine
¼   cup quartered cherry tomatoes
1   tablespoon crumbled feta cheese
     Oregano sprig (optional)

1. For filling, in an 8-inch nonstick skillet or omelet pan, cook the bacon until crisp. Remove bacon from skillet, reserving 1 tablespoon of the drippings in the skillet. Drain bacon on paper towels; set aside. Carefully stir vinegar and sugar into drippings in skillet. Add sorrel, kale, beet leaves, and 1 teaspoon oregano. Using tongs, toss until greens are wilted, 1 to 2 minutes. Remove greens and liquid from skillet; set aside.

2. For omelet, in a small bowl combine eggs, water, salt, and pepper. Beat with a fork until combined but not frothy. Heat the same skillet over medium-high heat until hot. Add butter to skillet. When butter melts, add egg mixture to skillet. Lower heat to medium. Immediately begin stirring egg mixture gently but continuously with a wooden or plastic spatula until mixture resembles small pieces of cooked egg surrounded by liquid egg. Stop stirring. Cook 30 to 60 seconds more or until egg mixture is set but shiny.

3. Spoon filling onto one side of the omelet. Top with bacon. Fold the omelet over filling. Transfer to a warm plate. Top with tomatoes and feta cheese. If desired, garnish with an oregano sprig.

Per serving: 681 cal., 59 g total fat (23 g sat. fat), 514 mg chol., 1,278 mg sodium, 13 g carbo., 2 g fiber, 26 g pro.
Daily Values: 181% vit. A, 111% vit. C, 19% calcium, 18% iron

Spinach Cheese Puff

This puff is light and airy like a soufflé but much less temperamental!

Prep: 30 minutes **Bake:** 40 minutes
Oven: 375°F **Makes:** 6 to 8 servings

- 6 **egg yolks**
- 6 **egg whites**
- 2 **tablespoons grated Parmesan cheese**
- ¼ **cup finely chopped shallots**
- 2 **cloves garlic, minced**
- 3 **tablespoons butter or margarine**
- ¼ **cup finely snipped dried tomatoes (not oil-packed)**
- ¼ **cup all-purpose flour**
- ¼ **teaspoon salt**
- ⅛ **teaspoon cayenne pepper**
- 1 **cup milk**
- 1 **cup shredded Swiss or Gruyère cheese (4 ounces)**
- 8 **ounces fresh spinach, cooked, well-drained, and finely chopped (¾ cup),* or one 10-ounce package frozen chopped spinach, thawed and well drained**
- ¼ **cup finely chopped prosciutto**
- 5 **or 6 dried tomato slices**

1. Allow egg yolks and egg whites to stand at room temperature for 30 minutes. Preheat oven to 375°F. Grease the bottom and sides of a 1½-quart soufflé dish. Sprinkle the inside of the dish with 1 tablespoon of the Parmesan cheese; set aside.

2. In a medium saucepan cook shallots and garlic in butter over medium heat for 1 minute. Stir in dried tomatoes, flour, salt, and cayenne pepper. Cook and stir for 1 minute. Add milk all at once. Cook and stir until thickened and bubbly. Remove from heat. Add Swiss cheese and the remaining 1 tablespoon Parmesan, a little at a time, stirring until melted.

3. In a small bowl beat egg yolks with a fork until combined. Slowly add about half of the cheese sauce to yolks, stirring constantly. Return yolk mixture to the saucepan. Stir in spinach and prosciutto; set aside.

4. In a large mixing bowl beat egg whites with an electric mixer on medium to high speed until stiff peaks form (tips stand straight). Gently fold about one-third of the whites into the spinach sauce to lighten; fold spinach mixture into remaining egg whites. Pour into prepared dish.

5. Bake for 40 to 45 minutes or until puffed and a knife inserted near the center comes out clean. Soak dried tomato slices in hot water about 5 minutes before puff is done. Drain well. Arrange tomato slices on top of puff and serve immediately.

*Note: To cook fresh spinach, place the spinach leaves in a steamer basket over boiling water. Cover and steam for 2 minutes or until wilted. Drain in colander, pressing with a spoon to squeeze out excess liquid. Finely chop spinach.

Per serving: 272 cal., 18 g total fat (10 g sat. fat), 252 mg chol., 477 mg sodium, 12 g carbo., 2 g fiber, 17 g pro.
Daily Values: 67% vit. A, 19% vit. C, 32% calcium, 14% iron

 ## Camembert Soufflé

When choosing Camembert, look for cheese that is soft when touched and doesn't appear to have any hard edges. In a pinch, Brie always makes a fine substitution.

Prep: 20 minutes **Stand:** 30 minutes
Bake: 50 minutes **Oven:** 350°F
Makes: 6 servings

- 5 **egg yolks**
- 7 **egg whites**
- ¼ **cup chopped celery**
- 2 **tablespoons thinly sliced green onion**
- 1 **clove garlic, minced**
- 3 **tablespoons butter or margarine**
- 3 **tablespoons all-purpose flour**
- 1 **teaspoon dry mustard**
- ¼ **teaspoon salt**
  Dash ground black pepper
- 1 **cup milk**
- 5 **ounces Camembert cheese, rind removed, and cheese cut up (½ cup)**
- ½ **cup grated Parmesan cheese or Romano cheese (2 ounces)**

1. Allow egg yolks and egg whites to stand at room temperature for 30 minutes.

2. In a medium saucepan cook celery, green onion, and garlic in hot butter over medium heat about 5 minutes or until tender. Stir in flour, mustard, salt, and pepper. Add milk all at once. Cook and stir until thickened and bubbly. Reduce heat; add Camembert and Parmesan cheeses, a little at a time, stirring until melted. Remove from heat; set aside.

3. Preheat oven to 350°F. In a medium mixing bowl beat egg yolks with an electric mixer on high speed about 5 minutes or until thick and lemon colored. Gradually beat in cheese mixture. Wash beaters with warm, soapy water; dry beaters.

4. In a large mixing bowl beat egg whites with the clean, dry beaters of electric mixer until stiff peaks form (tips stand straight). Gently fold 1 cup of the whites into egg yolk-cheese mixture. Gradually pour over remaining egg whites, folding to combine. Pour into an ungreased 2½-quart soufflé dish.

5. Bake about 50 minutes or until a knife inserted near center comes out clean. Serve immediately.

Per serving: 254 cal., 18 g total fat (10 g sat. fat), 212 mg chol., 531 mg sodium, 7 g carbo., 0 g fiber, 16 g pro.
Daily Values: 14% vit. A, 1% vit. C, 24% calcium, 5% iron

Camembert Soufflé

 Holiday Frittata

In this vegetarian version of a brunch staple, green broccoli and red sweet pepper bring both flavor and a touch of festive color to the table.

Start to Finish: 30 minutes **Makes:** 6 servings

- 1 tablespoon cooking oil
- 1 cup fresh or frozen broccoli florets, thawed
- ¾ cup thinly sliced red sweet pepper (½ of a large)
- ¼ cup chopped onion
- ½ teaspoon dried Italian seasoning, crushed
- ¼ teaspoon salt
- ⅛ teaspoon ground black pepper
- 10 eggs, beaten, or 2½ cups refrigerated or frozen egg product, thawed
- 2 tablespoons milk
- 2 tablespoons finely shredded Parmesan cheese

1. In a large skillet heat oil over medium heat. Add broccoli, sweet pepper, onion, Italian seasoning, salt, and pepper. Cook and stir for 4 to 5 minutes or until vegetables are crisp-tender.

2. In a bowl combine eggs and milk. Pour egg mixture over vegetable mixture in skillet. As eggs begin to set, run a spatula around edge of skillet, lifting egg mixture to allow uncooked portions to flow underneath. Continue cooking and lifting edges until eggs are nearly set (surface will be moist).

3. Remove skillet from heat; sprinkle eggs with cheese. Cover and let stand for 3 to 4 minutes or until set. Cut into six wedges.

Per serving: 166 cal., 11 g total fat (3 g sat. fat), 355 mg chol., 246 mg sodium, 3 g carbo., 1 g fiber, 12 g pro.
Daily Values: 18% vit. A, 53% vit. C, 8% calcium, 10% iron

 Sweet Potato Frittata with Cranberry Salsa

Chutney is the traditional Indian relish responsible for adding pizzazz to this slightly sweet salsa. It contains fruit (usually mangoes or limes), vinegar, sugar, and spices combined in proportions that play up contrasting flavors: sweet, sour, spicy, and piquant.

Prep: 20 minutes **Bake:** 15 minutes
Oven: 350°F **Makes:** 6 servings

- 1 cup fresh cranberries, coarsely chopped
- ¼ cup sugar
- 1 tablespoon water
- ⅓ cup mango chutney
- ¼ cup chopped red onion
- 1 tablespoon butter or margarine
- 1½ cups sliced, halved, peeled sweet potato
- 2 ounces Canadian-style bacon, chopped (about ⅓ cup)
- ¼ cup thinly sliced green onion (2)
  Dash salt
  Dash ground white pepper
- 8 eggs, beaten

1. For cranberry salsa, in a small saucepan combine cranberries, sugar, and water. Bring to boiling, stirring occasionally. Remove from heat. Snip any large pieces of chutney. Stir chutney and red onion into cranberry mixture. Set aside.

Sweet Potato Frittata with Cranberry Salsa

2. Preheat oven to 350°F. In a large ovenproof skillet melt butter over medium heat. Add sweet potato. Cook, covered, for 5 to 7 minutes or until sweet potato is almost tender, turning once. Sprinkle with Canadian bacon, green onion, salt, and pepper.

3. Pour eggs over potato mixture in skillet. Bake, uncovered, for 15 to 18 minutes or until egg mixture is set. Cut into wedges. Serve with warm cranberry salsa.

Per serving: 258 cal., 10 g total fat (4 g sat. fat), 294 mg chol., 283 mg sodium, 32 g carbo., 2 g fiber, 11 g pro.
Daily Values: 156% vit. A, 30% vit. C, 5% calcium, 8% iron

 Two-Cheese Vegetable Quiche

This lovely, colorful quiche is a perfect brunch or luncheon entrée. If serving this to vegetarians, be sure to choose a piecrust that is made without lard.

Prep: 25 minutes **Bake:** 50 minutes
Stand: 10 minutes **Oven:** 450°F/325°F
Makes: 6 servings

- ½ of a 15-ounce package rolled refrigerated unbaked piecrust (1 crust)
- ½ cup shredded Swiss cheese (2 ounces)
- ½ cup shredded cheddar cheese (2 ounces)
- ½ cup purchased shredded carrot
- ⅓ cup sliced green onion
- 1 tablespoon all-purpose flour
- 4 eggs
- 1 10.75-ounce can condensed cream of broccoli soup
- ½ cup milk
- ⅛ teaspoon garlic powder
- ⅛ teaspoon ground black pepper

1. Let piecrust stand according to package directions. Preheat oven to 450°F. Roll out piecrust according to package directions. Ease pastry into a 9-inch pie plate. Trim pastry to ½ inch beyond edge of plate. Fold under extra dough. Crimp edges. Line the unpricked pastry with a double thickness of foil. Bake for 8 minutes. Remove foil. Bake for 5 to 6 minutes more or until pastry is set and dry. Remove from oven. Reduce oven temperature to 325°F.

2. Meanwhile, for filling, in a medium bowl toss together Swiss cheese, cheddar cheese, carrot, green onion, and flour; set aside. In a large bowl beat eggs with a fork. Stir in soup, milk, garlic powder, and pepper. Stir in cheese mixture.

3. Pour filling into hot, baked pastry shell. Bake in the 325°F oven for 50 to 55 minutes or until a knife inserted near the center comes out clean. If necessary, cover edge of crust with foil to prevent over-browning. Let stand for 10 minutes before serving.

Per serving: 338 cal., 20 g total fat (9 g sat. fat), 170 mg chol., 591 mg sodium, 26 g carbo., 1 g fiber, 12 g pro.
Daily Values: 45% vit. A, 4% vit. C, 20% calcium, 5% iron

Spinach and Sausage Quiche

Make this quiche even more upscale by substituting French Gruyère (Compté) for the Swiss cheese and provolone for the mozzarella. If necessary, during baking, cover edge of crust with foil to prevent overbrowning.

Prep: 30 minutes **Bake:** 45 minutes
Stand: 15 minutes **Oven:** 450°F/325°F
Makes: 6 servings

  1 recipe Pastry for Single-Crust Pie
  1 12-ounce package frozen spinach
      soufflé, thawed
  ¾ cup milk
  3 eggs, lightly beaten
  ¼ cup dairy sour cream
  4 ounces bulk pork sausage
  1 4-ounce can mushroom stems and
      pieces, drained
  ⅓ cup finely chopped onion
  ¾ cup shredded Swiss cheese (3 ounces)
  ¾ cup shredded mozzarella cheese
      (3 ounces)

1. Preheat oven to 450°F. Prepare and roll out Pastry for Single-Crust Pie. Line the unpricked pastry shell with a double thickness of foil. Bake for 8 minutes. Remove foil. Bake for 4 to 5 minutes more or until pastry is set and dry. Remove from oven. Reduce oven temperature to 325°F.

2. Meanwhile, for filling, in a large bowl stir together soufflé, milk, eggs, and sour cream; set aside. In a medium skillet cook sausage, mushrooms, and onion until meat is no longer pink; drain. Add sausage mixture to soufflé mixture; stir in cheeses.

3. Pour filling into the hot, baked pastry shell. Bake in the 325°F oven for 45 to 50 minutes or until a knife inserted near the center comes out clean. Let stand for 15 minutes.

Pastry for Single-Crust Pie: Stir together 1¼ cups all-purpose flour and ¼ teaspoon salt. Using a pastry blender, cut in ⅓ cup shortening until pieces are pea-size. Sprinkle 1 tablespoon cold water over part of the flour mixture; gently toss with a fork. Push moistened flour mixture to side of bowl. Repeat moistening, using 1 tablespoon water at a time, until all the flour mixture is moistened (4 to 5 tablespoons total water). Form dough into a ball. On a lightly floured surface, slightly flatten dough. Roll dough from center to edges into a 12-inch circle. Ease dough into a 9-inch pie plate. Trim dough to ½ inch beyond edge of pie plate. Fold under extra dough. Crimp edge. Do not prick pastry.

Per serving: 415 cal., 22 g total fat (9 g sat. fat), 206 mg chol., 826 mg sodium, 31 g carbo., 1 g fiber, 22 g pro.
Daily Values: 27% vit. A, 3% vit. C, 34% calcium, 12% iron

Scrambled Up!

Scrambled eggs are extremely easy to prepare—and are a perfect accompaniment to many breakfast dishes, such as bacon or ham, cinnamon rolls, pancakes, and more. For 3 servings, in a bowl combine 6 eggs, ⅓ cup milk, and a dash of both salt and black pepper. In a skillet melt 1 tablespoon butter over medium heat and pour in egg mixture. Cook, without stirring, until mixture begins to set on the bottom and around the edges. Add any of the desired fillings (below). With a spatula, lift and fold the partially cooked eggs so that the uncooked portion flows underneath. Continue to cook for 2 to 3 minutes or until egg mixture is cooked through.

• Blanched vegetables, such as broccoli, asparagus, or sugar snap peas
• A variety of sweet bell peppers: red, yellow, green, and purple
• Diced ham and shredded Swiss cheese
• Crumbled cooked bacon and cubed cheddar cheese
• Smoked salmon, capers, and boursin cheese
• Sliced cooked sausage links and shredded provolone cheese
• Chopped canned artichokes, diced prosciutto, and shredded Parmesan cheese

Baked Brie Strata

Make this strata the night before and pop it in the oven the next morning.

Prep: 25 minutes **Chill:** 4 hours
Bake: 55 minutes **Stand:** 10 minutes
Oven: 325°F **Makes:** 6 servings

- 2 small zucchini, cut crosswise into ¼-inch slices (about 2 cups)
  Nonstick cooking spray
- 6 cups crusty sourdough bread torn into bite-size pieces (6 ounces)
- 1 4.4-ounce package Brie cheese, cut into ½-inch cubes
- 1 cup halved cherry tomatoes
- 1 cup refrigerated or frozen egg product, thawed, or 4 eggs, beaten
- ⅔ cup evaporated fat-free milk
- ⅓ cup sliced green onion
- 3 tablespoons snipped fresh dillweed
- ½ teaspoon salt
- ⅛ teaspoon ground black pepper

1. In a saucepan cook zucchini, covered, in a small amount of boiling lightly salted water for 2 to 3 minutes or just until tender. Drain zucchini. Set aside.

2. Meanwhile, coat a 2-quart rectangular baking dish with cooking spray. Arrange 4 cups of the bread pieces in the prepared baking dish. If desired, remove and discard rind from cheese. Sprinkle cheese evenly over bread in baking dish. Arrange zucchini and tomatoes on top. Sprinkle with remaining 2 cups bread pieces.

3. In a medium bowl combine egg product, milk, green onion, dillweed, salt, and pepper. Pour evenly over mixture in baking dish. Lightly press down layers with back of a spoon. Cover with plastic wrap; chill for at least 4 hours or up to 24 hours.

4. Preheat oven to 325°F. Remove plastic wrap; cover dish with foil. Bake for 30 minutes. Uncover and bake for 25 to 30 minutes more or until a knife inserted near the center comes out clean. Let stand for 10 minutes before serving.

Per serving: 206 cal., 6 g total fat (4 g sat. fat), 22 mg chol., 596 mg sodium, 24 g carbo., 1 g fiber, 14 g pro.
Daily Values: 14% vit. A, 15% vit. C, 14% calcium, 11% iron

Baked Brie Strata

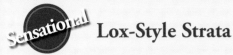

Lox-Style Strata

Bagels, cream cheese, and lox are a favorite morning meal—now enjoy them all together in a casserole!

Prep: 30 minutes **Chill:** 4 hours
Bake: 45 minutes **Stand:** 10 minutes
Oven: 350°F **Makes:** 12 servings

- 4 to 6 plain bagels, cut into bite-size pieces (8 cups)
- 1 3-ounce package thinly sliced smoked salmon (lox-style), cut into small pieces
- 2 3-ounce packages cream cheese, cut into ½-inch pieces
- ¼ cup finely diced red onion
- 4 teaspoons dried chives, crushed
- 8 eggs, beaten
- 2 cups milk
- 1 cup cottage cheese
- ½ teaspoon dried dillweed, crushed
- ¼ teaspoon ground black pepper

1. In a lightly greased 3-quart rectangular baking dish spread half of the bagel pieces. Top with salmon, cream cheese, onion, and chives. Spread remaining bagel pieces over salmon mixture.

2. In a large bowl whisk together eggs, milk, cottage cheese, dillweed, and pepper. Pour evenly over layers in dish. Lightly press down layers with the back of a spoon. Cover with plastic wrap and chill for at least 4 hours or up to 24 hours.

3. Preheat oven to 350°F. Remove plastic wrap. Bake, uncovered, for 45 to 50 minutes or until set and edges are puffed and golden. Let stand for 10 minutes before serving.

Per serving: 207 cal., 11 g total fat (5 g sat. fat), 164 mg chol., 424 mg sodium, 15 g carbo., 1 g fiber, 13 g pro.
Daily Values: 10% vit. A, 2% vit. C, 11% calcium, 13% iron

Rum and Chile Spiked Fruit Cocktails

Fresh jalapeño chile peppers add a mild, interesting kick to these colorful cocktails.

Prep: 25 minutes **Chill:** 1 hour
Makes: 8 servings

- 1 cup sugar
- 1 cup water
- 1 small fresh jalapeño chile pepper, seeded and quartered*
- 1 teaspoon finely shredded lime peel
- 1 tablespoon lime juice
- 1 tablespoon rum or ½ teaspoon rum extract
- 6 cups assorted cubed fruit, such as pineapple, red seedless grapes, mango, papaya, seedless orange sections, and/or seedless tangerine sections
- ½ cup coconut, toasted (see tip, page 63)

1. In a small saucepan combine sugar, water, jalapeño chile, lime peel, lime juice, and rum, if using. Bring to boiling, stirring to dissolve sugar. Place saucepan in a large bowl of ice water and stir occasionally until syrup is cooled. Remove and discard jalapeño. Stir in rum extract, if using.

2. In a large bowl toss fruit with syrup mixture. Cover and chill for 1 to 24 hours. Using a slotted spoon, transfer fruit to eight martini glasses. Sprinkle each serving with toasted coconut.

*Note: Because chile peppers contain oils that can burn skin and eyes, avoid direct contact with them as much as possible. When working with chile peppers, wear plastic or rubber gloves. If bare hands do touch the peppers, wash them well with soap and warm water.

Per serving: 193 cal., 2 g total fat (2 g sat. fat), 0 mg chol., 4 mg sodium, 45 g carbo., 2 g fiber, 1 g pro.
Daily Values: 8% vit. A, 53% vit. C, 2% calcium, 2% iron

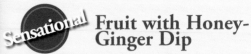 **Fruit with Honey-Ginger Dip**

Fresh, unpeeled ginger that is tightly wrapped can be stored in the refrigerator for up to 3 weeks or in the freezer for up to 3 months.

Prep: 30 minutes **Chill:** 24 hours
Makes: 12 servings

- 1 **32-ounce carton plain low-fat yogurt***
- ¼ **cup honey**
- 2 **to 3 teaspoons grated fresh ginger**
   Honey
   Crystalized ginger, chopped
- 3 **cups assorted fruit, such as red seedless grapes, mango slices, persimmon wedges, pineapple wedges, and/or desired fresh fruit**

1. For yogurt cheese, line a large sieve or colander with three layers of 100-percent-cotton cheesecloth or a clean paper coffee filter. Suspend lined sieve or colander over a bowl. Spoon in the yogurt. Cover with plastic wrap. Refrigerate at least 24 hours. Remove from refrigerator. Discard liquid. Transfer curd to a medium bowl. Stir in ¼ cup honey and grated fresh ginger. If desired, cover and store in refrigerator for up 3 days. Stir before serving.

2. To serve, spoon some of the yogurt mixture into a glass or serving bowl. Drizzle with additional honey and sprinkle with chopped crystalized ginger. Cover and chill until ready to use. Place glass filled with dip on a serving platter and arrange the fresh fruit around the glass.

***Note:** Use a brand of yogurt that contains no gums, gelatin, or fillers. These ingredients may prevent the whey from separating from the curd to make yogurt cheese.

Per serving: 108 cal., 1 g total fat (1 g sat. fat), 5 mg chol., 54 mg sodium, 21 g carbo., 1 g fiber, 4 g pro.
Daily Values: 3% vit. A, 18% vit. C, 14% calcium, 1% iron

Fruit with Honey-Ginger Dip

Fruit and Caramel Oatmeal

Forget those preseasoned packets of instant oatmeal. This homemade version is just as quick and healthful.

Start to Finish: 10 minutes **Makes:** 2 servings

- 2 1-ounce envelopes instant oatmeal (plain)
- 1 medium banana, peeled and sliced
  Desired fresh fruit, such as blueberries, sliced strawberries, and/or sliced peaches
- 2 tablespoons chopped pecans, toasted (see tip, page 63)
- 2 teaspoons caramel-flavored ice cream topping
  Milk (optional)

1. In two microwave-safe bowls prepare oatmeal according to package directions. Top each serving with banana slices, desired fresh fruit, and pecans. Drizzle with ice cream topping. If desired, heat in microwave on 100 percent power (high) for 30 seconds. If desired, serve with milk.

Per serving: 231 cal., 7 g total fat (1 g sat. fat), 0 mg chol., 302 mg sodium, 39 g carbo., 6 g fiber, 6 g pro.
Daily Values: 31% vit. A, 11% vit. C, 17% calcium, 37% iron

Baked Oatmeal

Baked Oatmeal

This breakfast dish gets a double-dose of oats—regular rolled oats and steel oats. Steel oats are not rolled and provide a distinctive chewy texture.

Prep: 20 minutes **Bake:** 40 minutes
Oven: 400°F **Makes:** 6 to 8 servings

- 2½ cups regular rolled oats
- ¼ cup oat bran
- ¼ cup steel-cut oats
- 2 teaspoons baking powder
- ½ teaspoon salt
- ½ teaspoon ground cinnamon
- 2 cups milk
- 1 egg, beaten
- ⅓ cup applesauce
- ¼ cup cooking oil
- ¼ cup granulated sugar
- ¼ cup packed brown sugar
- 2 cups fresh fruit, such as blueberries, chopped apples, or chopped strawberries
  Vanilla low-fat yogurt, milk, or cream

1. Preheat oven to 400°F. Lightly grease a 2-quart soufflé dish or casserole; set aside. In a large bowl stir together rolled oats, oat bran, steel-cut oats, baking powder, salt, and cinnamon; set aside.

2. In a bowl stir together milk, egg, applesauce, oil, granulated sugar, and brown sugar. Add to oat mixture; stir until combined. Turn into prepared dish.

3. Bake, uncovered, for 20 minutes. Stir mixture. Gently fold in fruit. Bake, uncovered, about 20 minutes more or until top is lightly browned. To serve, spoon into bowls and serve with yogurt.

Per serving: 533 cal., 17 g total fat (4 g sat. fat), 48 mg chol., 447 mg sodium, 82 g carbo., 7 g fiber, 18 g pro.
Daily Values: 5% vit. A, 18% vit. C, 46% calcium, 15% iron

Breads
for the
Holiday

Hot and crusty or soft and tender—nothing goes with Christmas dinner like a heaping basket of bread. Surprise everyone this year with some yummy yeasty and quick breads that will take this part of a holiday dinner from ho-hum to wow! Olive Focaccia with Grape Chutney will capture the attention of everyone's taste buds. So will Cobblestone Ranch Dinner Rolls—which surprisingly starts with a package of frozen white roll dough. Looking for a sweet bread to go with a breakfast or brunch? Try Pumpkin-Sour Cream Coffee Cake with Pecan Streusel and every last crumb will be gone from the platter. Pumpkin Raisin Scones are another sure-fire morning winner for the big holiday meal. If you're running really short on time, purchase some crusty bread and personalize it by checking out the creative ideas for jazzing up butter.

Multigrain Rolls, page 66

Olive Bread

For variety, use pitted sliced kalamata olives in this cheese bread. Serve with pizza sauce as an appetizer or with olive oil for dipping at dinner.

Prep: 20 minutes **Bake:** 18 minutes
Oven: 400°F **Makes:** 12 servings

- ½ cup grated Parmesan cheese
- 1 2.25-ounce can sliced pitted ripe olives, drained
- 4 to 5 cloves garlic, minced
- 1 13.8-ounce package refrigerated pizza dough
   Water
   Pizza sauce (optional)

1. Preheat oven to 400°F. Set aside 1 tablespoon of the Parmesan cheese. In a small bowl combine the remaining Parmesan cheese, olives, and garlic.

2. On a lightly floured surface, roll pizza dough into a 14×10-inch rectangle. Sprinkle ⅓ cup of the olive mixture along one 10-inch side of the dough in a 2-inch wide band. Fold dough over filling, allowing about two-thirds of the dough to extend beyond the filling. Add another ⅓ cup of the olive mixture on top of the filled layer, pressing filling lightly into the dough. Fold dough back over filling, making about a 3-inch pleat. Repeat filling and folding dough accordion-style once more with remaining filling. Gently pat sides of the loaf to form a 10½×3-inch rectangle; seal ends. Place shaped dough on a lightly greased baking sheet. Brush top of loaf with water and sprinkle with reserved Parmesan cheese.

3. Bake for 18 to 20 minutes or until browned. If desired, serve warm with pizza sauce.

Per serving: 90 cal., 3 g total fat (1 g sat. fat), 3 mg chol., 202 mg sodium, 13 g carbo., 1 g fiber, 3 g pro.
Daily Values: 1% vit. A, 1% vit. C, 5% calcium, 6% iron

 ## Olive Focaccia with Fresh Grape Chutney

The herby, yeasty aroma that wafts through the kitchen when this bread is baking is so tempting. If time is limited, substitute purchased focaccia. Simply warm it in the oven for a few minutes before serving with the chutney.

Prep: 40 minutes **Rise:** 1½ hours **Bake:** 20 minutes
Cool: 20 minutes **Oven:** 425°F **Makes:** 24 servings

- 1⅛ cups warm water (105° to 115°F)
- 1 package active dry yeast
- 4 tablespoons extra-virgin olive oil
- 1 teaspoon sugar
- 4¼ to 4¾ cups all-purpose flour
- 1 tablespoon chopped fresh rosemary or 1 teaspoon dried rosemary, crushed
- 1 teaspoon dried oregano, crushed
- 2 teaspoons coarse sea salt or kosher salt
- 1 cup pitted kalamata olives, sliced
- 1 recipe Fresh Grape Chutney (optional)

1. In a small bowl combine warm water, yeast, 3 tablespoons of the olive oil, and the sugar. Let stand about 5 minutes until bubbly and yeast is dissolved. In a large bowl combine 4 cups of the flour, the rosemary, oregano, and 1 teaspoon of the salt. Add olives and yeast mixture to flour mixture. Stir with a spoon until a dough forms. Turn dough out onto lightly floured surface. Knead in enough of the

Olive Focaccia with Fresh Grape Chutney

remaining flour to make a moderately stiff dough (5 to 8 minutes total). Shape dough into a ball. Place dough in a lightly oiled bowl, turning once to grease dough surface. Cover; let rise in a warm place until double in size (1 to 1½ hours).

2. Turn dough out onto a lightly oiled 15×10×1-inch baking pan. Press dough to fit pan. Brush dough with remaining 1 tablespoon olive oil. Sprinkle with remaining 1 teaspoon salt. Cover and let rise in a warm place for 30 minutes.

3. Meanwhile, if desired, prepare Fresh Grape Chutney. Preheat oven to 425°F. Bake focaccia for 20 to 25 minutes or until golden. Remove to wire rack; cool at least 20 minutes. Cut into squares. If desired, serve with Fresh Grape Chutney.

Per serving focaccia: 105 cal., 3 g total fat (0 g sat. fat), 0 mg chol., 197 mg sodium, 16 g carbo., 1 g fiber, 2 g pro.
Daily Values: 6% iron

Fresh Grape Chutney: Place 4 cups red seedless grapes (about 1¼ pounds) in a food processor. Process with three or four on-and-off pulses until chopped; set aside. (If you do not have a food processor, you may finely chop the grapes.) In a large skillet cook ½ cup chopped red onion in 1 tablespoon butter or margarine just until tender. Add 1 teaspoon snipped fresh rosemary or ¼ teaspoon dried rosemary, crushed, and ¼ teaspoon dried oregano, crushed. Cook for 1 minute. Add chopped grapes and 2 tablespoons red wine vinegar. Cook for 1 to 2 minutes more or until heated through. Transfer to a serving bowl. Serve with a slotted spoon. Makes 24 (2-tablespoon) servings.

 Pesto Swirl Bread

Watch pine nuts carefully when toasting them because they burn much more quickly than other nuts.

Prep: 15 minutes **Rise:** 2 hours **Bake:** 25 minutes
Chill: 1 hour **Oven:** 350°F
Makes: 1 loaf (16 servings)

- 1 16-ounce loaf frozen bread dough, thawed
- ½ cup purchased basil pesto
- 3 tablespoons pine nuts, toasted (see tip, right)

- ½ cup butter, softened
- 1 tablespoon oil-packed dried tomatoes, drained and finely chopped
- 1 tablespoon kalamata olives, pitted and finely chopped
- ¼ teaspoon ground black pepper

1. On a lightly floured surface, roll bread dough into a 12×8-inch rectangle. Spread pesto on dough to within ½ inch of the edges. Sprinkle with pine nuts. Starting from a short side, roll up tightly, sealing the seam by pinching dough together.

2. Place the shaped dough, seam side down, in a greased 9×5×3-inch loaf pan. Cover and let rise in a warm place for 2 to 3 hours or until nearly double in size. Preheat oven to 350°F. Bake loaf for 25 to 30 minutes or until bread sounds hollow when lightly tapped.

3. For tomato-olive butter, in a small mixing bowl beat butter, tomatoes, olives, and pepper with an electric mixer on low speed until combined. Cover and chill for 1 to 24 hours. Serve pesto bread with tomato-olive butter.

Per serving: 167 cal., 10 g total fat (5 g sat. fat), 18 mg chol., 118 mg sodium, 14 g carbo., 0 g fiber, 3 g pro.
Daily Values: 5% vit. A, 1% vit. C, 5% calcium, 2% iron

Toasting Nuts or Coconut

Spread nuts or coconut in a single layer in a shallow baking pan. Bake in a 350°F oven for 5 to 10 minutes or until the pieces are golden brown. Check the pieces frequently to make sure they do not brown too quickly. If they start to burn, they will go quickly and generally cannot be salvaged. Stir once or twice.

½ teaspoon dried dillweed
¼ teaspoon dried thyme, crushed
¼ teaspoon celery seeds (optional)

1. In a bowl dissolve yeast in ½ cup warm water; set aside. In a large bowl combine all-purpose flour, whole wheat flour, mashed potatoes, cottage cheese, ¼ cup potato water, oil, salt, dillweed, thyme, and if desired, celery seeds, stirring until well mixed. Add the yeast mixture; stir until combined.

2. Turn dough out onto a lightly floured surface. Knead until dough is soft, smooth, and elastic (3 to 5 minutes). Shape dough into a ball. Place dough in a lightly greased bowl, turning once to grease the dough surface. Cover; let rise in a warm place until double in size (45 to 60 minutes).

3. Punch down dough. Turn out onto a lightly floured surface. Cover; let rest for 10 minutes. Lightly grease a 1½-quart casserole or a 9×5×3-inch loaf pan.

4. Shape dough into a round or rectangular loaf. Place round loaf in prepared casserole or place rectangular loaf in prepared loaf pan. Cover and let rise in a warm place until nearly double in size (30 to 40 minutes). Preheat oven to 350°F.

5. Bake for 35 to 40 minutes or until bread sounds hollow when tapped on the top. Immediately remove from casserole or pan. Cool on a wire rack.

Per serving: 105 cal., 2 g total fat (0 g sat. fat), 1 mg chol., 187 mg sodium, 19 g carbo., 2 g fiber, 4 g pro.
Daily Values: 1% vit. A, 1% vit. C, 1% calcium, 6% iron

Herb Dinner Bread

Herb Dinner Bread

Use leftover mashed potatoes or purchased refrigerated mashed potatoes in this perfect-with-soup bread.

Prep: 30 minutes **Rise:** 1¼ hours **Rest:** 10 minutes
Bake: 35 minutes **Oven:** 350°F
Makes: 1 loaf (16 servings)

  1 package active dry yeast
  ½ cup warm water (105°F to 115°F)
  2 cups all-purpose flour
  1 cup whole wheat flour
  ⅔ cup mashed cooked potatoes
  ⅓ cup cream-style cottage cheese
  ¼ cup potato water or water
  1 tablespoon cooking oil
  1 teaspoon salt

Hurry-Up Biscuits

Add cheese or a teaspoon of basil or oregano to jazz up these 30-minute biscuits.

Prep: 15 minutes **Bake:** 15 minutes per batch
Oven: 375°F **Makes:** about 16 biscuits

  3 cups all-purpose flour
  4 teaspoons sugar
  4 teaspoons baking powder
  1 teaspoon salt
  2 cups whipping cream

1. Preheat oven to 375°F. Lightly grease two baking sheets or line with parchment paper; set aside. In a large bowl use a fork to stir together flour, sugar, baking powder, and salt until well combined. Add whipping cream all at once. Using a fork, stir just until mixture is combined.

2. Drop dough into about 16 mounds 1 inch apart on prepared baking sheets using an ice cream scoop (#16 size) or 2 large spoons. (If necessary, shape into mounds with hands.)

3. Bake biscuits for 15 to 17 minutes or until golden. Serve warm.

Per biscuit: 193 cal., 11 g total fat (7 g sat. fat), 41 mg chol., 217 mg sodium, 20 g carbo., 1 g fiber, 3 g pro.
Daily Values: 9% vit. A, 4% calcium, 6% iron

Cheesy Hurry-Up Biscuits: Prepare as above, except add 1 cup finely shredded or grated Parmesan cheese to the flour mixture in Step 1.

Per cheesy biscuit: 214 cal., 13 g total fat (8 g sat. fat), 46 mg chol., 294 mg sodium, 20 g carbo., 1 g fiber, 5 g pro.
Daily Values: 9% vit. A, 10% calcium, 6% iron

Herbed Cheese and Bacon Biscuits

Semisoft cheese with garlic and herbs does double-duty in these flaky biscuits. First it takes the place of traditional butter; second, it provides a tasty herb seasoning.

Prep: 20 minutes Bake: 10 minutes
Oven: 450°F Makes: 10 to 12 biscuits

  2 slices bacon
  ½ cup chopped red onion
  3 cups all-purpose flour
  1 tablespoon baking powder
  1 teaspoon sugar
  ½ teaspoon salt
  ¼ teaspoon ground black pepper
  1 5.2-ounce package semisoft cheese
      with garlic and herbs
  1 cup half-and-half or light cream

1. Preheat oven to 450°F. In a large skillet cook bacon until crisp. Remove bacon from skillet and drain on paper towels; reserve drippings in skillet. Crumble bacon and set aside. Cook onion in bacon drippings over medium heat until tender and beginning to brown. Remove from heat; set aside.

2. In a large bowl combine flour, baking powder, sugar, salt, and pepper. Using a pastry blender, cut in cheese until mixture resembles coarse crumbs. Stir in bacon and onion. Make a well in the center of the mixture. Add half-and-half all at once. Using a fork, stir just until mixture is moistened.

3. Turn dough out onto a lightly floured surface. Knead dough by folding and gently pressing for 4 to 6 strokes or just until dough holds together. Pat or lightly roll dough until ¾ inch thick. Cut dough with a floured 2½-inch biscuit cutter; reroll scraps as necessary and dip cutter in flour between cuts. Place dough circles 1 inch apart on an ungreased baking sheet.

4. Bake about 10 minutes or until golden. Serve warm.

Per biscuit: 261 cal., 11 g total fat (6 g sat. fat), 28 mg chol., 262 mg sodium, 31 g carbo., 1 g fiber, 7 g pro.
Daily Values: 2% vit. A, 1% vit. C, 7% calcium, 10% iron

Flavored Butters

Adding pizzazz to butter is so simple you will wonder why you never tried it before. To a softened ½ cup of unsalted butter (1 stick), add any of the following ingredients. To prepare, combine well and pack into a ramekin or a plastic dish. Store covered in the refrigerator for at least an hour and up to 3 days. Slather on bread or slice onto cooked vegetables, pasta, or meat.

• 2 teaspoons snipped fresh herbs (such as rosemary, thyme, basil, oregano, or dillweed)
• 1 teaspoon fresh minced garlic
• 1 tablespoon Dijon-style or other mustard
• 1 small jalapeño pepper, finely chopped
• ½ to 1 teaspoon wasabi powder
• 1 teaspoon lemon zest
• 2 teaspoons grated Parmesan cheese

Cobblestone Ranch Dinner Rolls

Frozen white roll dough is pre-shaped into balls, ready to thaw and bake.

Prep: 40 minutes **Rise:** 30 minutes
Bake: 20 minutes **Stand:** 15 minutes
Oven: 350°F **Makes:** 12 rolls

- ⅓ cup butter or margarine, melted
- ⅓ cup finely shredded Parmesan cheese
- 1 0.4-ounce envelope ranch dry salad dressing mix
- 1 16-ounce package frozen white roll dough (12 rolls), thawed
- 1 tablespoon yellow cornmeal

1. Coat a 9×1½-inch round baking pan with *nonstick cooking spray*; set aside. In a small bowl combine 3 tablespoons of the melted butter, Parmesan cheese, and dressing mix; set aside.

2. On a lightly floured surface, roll each thawed roll into a 3- to 4-inch circle. Place 1 rounded teaspoon of the Parmesan mixture in the center of each dough circle; pull edges to center and pinch to seal, shaping into a round ball. Place balls in prepared pan. Drizzle rolls with remaining melted butter. Sprinkle with cornmeal. Cover; let rise in a warm place until rolls are nearly double in size (30 to 45 minutes).

3. Preheat oven to 350°F. Bake for 20 to 25 minutes or until golden. Carefully invert to remove rolls. Invert again onto a serving platter. Let stand for 15 minutes before serving.

Per roll: 157 cal., 8 g total fat (4 g sat. fat), 15 mg chol., 235 mg sodium, 19 g carbo., 1 g fiber, 4 g pro.
Daily Values: 3% vit. A, 3% calcium, 7% iron

Multigrain Rolls

These good-for-you rolls have a nice sweetness thanks to the honey. To reinforce that flavor, serve with whipped honey butter.

Prep: 45 minutes **Rise:** 1½ hours
Rest: 10 minutes **Bake:** 12 minutes
Oven: 375°F **Makes:** 18 rolls

- 3¾ to 4¼ cups all-purpose flour
- 2 packages active dry yeast
- 1½ cups milk
- ⅓ cup honey
- ¼ cup butter or margarine
- 2 teaspoons salt
- 2 eggs
- ⅔ cup whole wheat flour
- ½ cup rye flour
- ½ cup quick-cooking rolled oats
- ⅓ cup toasted wheat germ
- 1 tablespoon cornmeal
  Cornmeal or quick-cooking rolled oats
- 1 egg, lightly beaten
- 1 tablespoon water
  Sesame seeds, poppy seeds, and/or cornmeal

1. In a large mixing bowl combine 2 cups of the all-purpose flour and yeast; set aside. In a medium saucepan heat and stir milk, honey, butter, and salt just until warm (120°F to 130°F) and butter almost melts; add to flour mixture along with 2 eggs. Beat with an electric mixer on medium speed for 30 seconds, scraping bowl frequently. Beat on high speed for 3 minutes, scraping bowl occasionally. Using a wooden spoon, stir in whole wheat and rye flours, ½ cup oats, wheat germ, and the 1 tablespoon cornmeal. Stir in as much of the remaining all-purpose flour as possible.

2. Turn dough out onto a lightly floured surface. Knead in enough of the remaining all-purpose flour to make a moderately stiff dough that is smooth and elastic (6 to 8 minutes total). Shape dough into a ball. Place in a lightly greased large bowl; turn once to grease the dough surface. Cover; let rise in a warm place until double in size (1 to 1½ hours).

3. Punch down dough. Turn dough out onto a lightly floured surface. Divide dough into six portions. Cover; let rest 10 minutes. Meanwhile, lightly grease two large baking sheets and sprinkle with additional cornmeal or oats.

4. To shape, divide each portion of dough into thirds. Shape each third of dough into a ball by pulling dough and pinching underneath. Flatten and pull each ball to form a 4×2-inch oval. Place on prepared baking sheets. Using kitchen shears, make three slanted cuts about ¾ inch deep on both long sides of each oval, creating a feathered look.

Multigrain Rolls

5. Cover and let rise in a warm place until nearly double in size (30 to 45 minutes). Preheat oven to 375°F. In a small bowl combine beaten egg and water. Brush tops of ovals with the egg mixture. Sprinkle each with sesame seeds, poppy seeds, and/or additional cornmeal. Bake for 12 to 15 minutes or until golden. Remove rolls from pans. Cool on wire racks.

Per roll: 212 cal., 5 g total fat (2 g sat. fat), 44 mg chol., 298 mg sodium, 36 g carbo., 2 g fiber, 7 g pro.
Daily Values: 3% vit. A, 5% calcium, 12% iron

 **Pumpkin Raisin Scones**

Crystalized ginger gives these scones a lovely zip. Find the ginger in the spice aisle of most supermarkets.

Prep: 10 minutes   Bake: 12 minutes
Oven: 375°F   Makes: 8 scones

2   cups packaged biscuit mix
⅓   cup raisins or dried cranberries
¼   cup granulated sugar
2   teaspoons pumpkin pie spice
½   cup canned pumpkin
¼   cup milk
1   tablespoon coarse or granulated sugar
1   tablespoon very finely snipped
     crystallized ginger

1. Preheat oven to 375°F. Grease a baking sheet; set aside. In a large bowl combine biscuit mix, raisins, ¼ cup granulated sugar, and pumpkin pie spice. In a small bowl combine pumpkin and 3 tablespoons of the milk. Add pumpkin mixture all at once to dry mixture; stir until combined.

2. Turn dough out onto a lightly floured surface. Knead dough by folding and gently pressing dough for 10 to 12 strokes or until dough is nearly smooth. Pat or lightly roll the dough into a ½-inch circle. Cut into 8 wedges. Place wedges 1 inch apart on prepared baking sheet.

3. In a small bowl combine 1 tablespoon sugar and the crystallized ginger. Brush dough wedges with remaining 1 tablespoon milk; sprinkle with ginger mixture.

4. Bake for 12 to 15 minutes or until a wooden toothpick inserted near center comes out clean. Cool on wire rack. Serve warm.

Per scone: 183 cal., 5 g total fat (1 g sat. fat), 1 mg chol., 376 mg sodium, 35 g carbo., 1 g fiber, 3 g pro.
Daily Values: 48% vit. A, 2% vit. C, 5% calcium, 7% iron

Goat Cheese and Onion Scones

Sweet scones may be queen of the tea table, but this savory version rules at dinnertime. Substitute feta cheese, if you like, and add a favorite herb.

Prep: 20 minutes **Bake:** 15 minutes
Oven: 400°F **Makes:** 12 scones

- 2 **cups all-purpose flour**
- 2 **tablespoons finely chopped green onion (1)**
- 2 **teaspoons baking powder**
- ¼ **teaspoon baking soda**
- ¼ **teaspoon salt**
- ¼ **teaspoon freshly ground black pepper**
- 1 **egg, beaten**
- 4 **ounces semisoft goat cheese (chèvre), crumbled or cut into small cubes**
- ½ **cup buttermilk or sour milk***

1. Preheat oven to 400°F. In a medium bowl combine flour, green onion, baking powder, baking soda, salt, and pepper. Make a well in the center of flour mixture; set aside.

2. In a small bowl stir together egg, goat cheese, and buttermilk. Add egg mixture all at once to flour mixture. Using a fork stir just until moistened.

Goat Cheese and Onion Scones

3. Turn dough out onto a lightly floured surface. Knead dough by folding and gently pressing dough for 10 to 12 strokes or until dough is nearly smooth. Divide dough in half. Pat or lightly roll half of the dough into a 5-inch circle. Cut into six wedges. Repeat with remaining dough. Place wedges 1 inch apart on an ungreased baking sheet.

4. Bake scones for 15 to 18 minutes or until golden. Serve warm.

***Note:** To make ½ cup sour milk, place 1½ teaspoons lemon juice or vinegar in a glass measuring cup. Add enough milk to make ½ cup total liquid; stir. Let mixture stand for 5 minutes before using.

Per scone: 106 cal., 3 g total fat (2 g sat. fat), 22 mg chol., 193 mg sodium, 15 g carbo., 1 g fiber, 5 g pro.
Daily Values: 1% vit. A, 1% vit. C, 7% calcium, 6% iron

Creamy Caramel-Pecan Rolls

These deliciously gooey rolls require only one rising time.

Prep: 25 minutes **Rise:** 1 hour **Bake:** 20 minutes
Oven: 375°F **Makes:** 24 rolls

- 1¼ **cups powdered sugar**
- ⅓ **cup whipping cream**
- 1 **cup coarsely chopped pecans**
- ½ **cup packed brown sugar**
- 1 **tablespoon ground cinnamon**
- 2 **16-ounce loaves frozen white bread dough or sweet roll dough, thawed**
- 3 **tablespoons butter or margarine, melted**
- ¾ **cup raisins (optional)**

1. Generously grease two 9×1½-inch round baking pans. Line bottoms with a circle of parchment paper or nonstick foil; set pans aside. For topping, in a small bowl stir together powdered sugar and whipping cream; divide evenly between prepared baking pans, gently spreading mixture. Sprinkle pecans evenly over sugar mixture.

2. In another small bowl stir together brown sugar and cinnamon; set aside. On a lightly floured surface, roll each loaf of dough into a 12×8-inch rectangle. Brush with melted butter; sprinkle with brown sugar-cinnamon mixture. If desired, sprinkle with raisins. Roll each rectangle starting from a long side. Seal seams. Slice each rolled rectangle into 12 pieces. Place, cut sides down, on topping in pans.

3. Cover; let rise in a warm place until nearly double in size (about 1 hour). Preheat oven to 375°F. Break surface bubbles of dough with a greased toothpick.

4. Bake for 20 to 25 minutes or until rolls sound hollow when gently tapped. (If necessary, cover rolls with foil the last 10 minutes of baking to prevent overbrowning). Cool in pans on wire racks for 5 minutes. Loosen edges and carefully invert rolls onto a serving platter. Spoon on any nut mixture that may remain in pan. Serve warm.

Per roll: 183 cal., 6 g total fat (2 g sat. fat), 8 mg chol., 13 mg sodium, 27 g carbo., 1 g fiber, 3 g pro.
Daily Values: 2% vit. A, 5% calcium, 2% iron

 ## Apple Harvest Cinnamon Rolls

To easily cut the dough, place a piece of heavy-duty thread under the roll where you want to make your cut. Bring the thread up around the sides, cross it at the top, and pull the ends in opposite directions.

Prep: 45 minutes **Rise:** 1¼ hours
Rest: 10 minutes **Bake:** 35 minutes
Oven: 350°F **Makes:** 12 rolls

  6 to 6½ cups all-purpose flour
  2 packages active dry yeast
  2 cups milk
  ¼ cup granulated sugar
  ¼ cup butter or margarine
 1½ teaspoons salt
  1 egg
  1 cup packed brown sugar
  ½ cup butter or margarine, melted
  2 teaspoons ground cinnamon
  2 cups chopped, peeled apple
  ¾ cup apple butter
  1 cup powdered sugar
  ¼ teaspoon ground cinnamon
     Apple juice

1. In a large mixing bowl combine 3 cups of the flour and yeast; set aside. In a medium saucepan heat and stir milk, granulated sugar, ¼ cup butter, and salt just until warm (120°F to 130°F) and butter almost melts. Add milk mixture to flour mixture. Add egg. Beat with an electric mixer on low to medium speed for 30 seconds, scraping the sides of the bowl. Beat on high speed for 3 minutes. Using a wooden spoon, stir in as much of the remaining flour as possible.

2. Turn dough out onto a lightly floured surface. Knead in enough of the remaining flour to make a moderately soft dough that is smooth and elastic (3 to 5 minutes total). Shape dough into a ball. Place dough in a lightly greased bowl, turning once to grease dough surface. Cover and let rise in a warm place until double in size (45 to 60 minutes).

3. For filling, in a medium bowl combine brown sugar, the ½ cup melted butter, and the 2 teaspoons cinnamon. Stir in chopped apple and apple butter. Set aside.

4. Punch down dough. Turn dough out onto a lightly floured surface. Divide dough in half. Cover and let rest 10 minutes. Grease a 13×9×2-inch baking pan. Roll each half of dough into a 16×12-inch rectangle. Spread half of the filling evenly over each rectangle to within 1 inch of the short sides. Roll each rectangle, starting from one of the short sides. Pinch dough to seal seams. Cut each roll into six 2-inch pieces. Place pieces, cut side down, in prepared pan. Cover and let rise in a warm place until nearly double in size (30 to 40 minutes).

5. Preheat oven to 350°F. Bake for 35 to 40 minutes or until golden brown. (If necessary, cover rolls with foil to prevent overbrowning.) Cool in pans on a wire rack for 10 minutes; remove rolls from pan and cool slightly on wire rack.

6. Meanwhile, for icing, in a small bowl combine powdered sugar and the ¼ teaspoon cinnamon. Add 1 tablespoon apple juice. Stir in additional apple juice, 1 teaspoon at a time, to reach drizzling consistency. Drizzle over rolls. Serve warm.

Per roll: 589 cal., 14 g total fat (8 g sat. fat), 51 mg chol., 431 mg sodium, 108 g carbo., 3 g fiber, 9 g pro.
Daily Values: 10% vit. A, 3% vit. C, 9% calcium, 22% iron

Coffee Cake with Streusel

If desired, substitute whatever nuts are available—walnuts, almonds, or even macadamia nuts.

Prep: 35 minutes **Stand:** 15 minutes
Bake: 65 minutes **Cool:** 15 minutes
Oven: 325°F **Makes:** 12 servings

  4 **eggs**
  6 **tablespoons butter or margarine, softened**
1½ **cups chopped pecans**
  1 **recipe Streusel**
2¼ **cups all-purpose flour**
1½ **teaspoons baking powder**
  ½ **teaspoon salt**
  ¾ **cup butter or margarine, softened**
  1 **8-ounce package cream cheese, softened**
1½ **cups sugar**
  2 **teaspoons vanilla**

1. Let eggs stand at room temperature for 30 minutes. Preheat oven to 325°F. Generously spread the inside of a 10-inch tube pan or 10-inch fluted tube pan with 6 tablespoons butter. Coat the inside of the pan with pecans, pressing the nuts into the butter as necessary; set aside. Prepare Streusel; set aside. In a medium bowl combine flour, baking powder, and salt; set aside.

2. In a large mixing bowl beat ¾ cup butter and cream cheese with an electric mixer on medium to high speed for 30 seconds. Add sugar and vanilla and beat about 4 to 5 minutes or until light and fluffy. Add eggs, one at a time, beating for 10 to 20 seconds after each addition and scraping sides of bowl thoroughly. Beat in flour mixture, one-third at a time, just until combined.

3. Spoon one-third to one-half of the batter into the prepared pan, spreading evenly. Sprinkle with half of the Streusel. Spoon remaining batter over the Streusel, spreading evenly. Sprinkle evenly with remaining Streusel.

4. Bake for 65 to 70 minutes or until cake pulls away from sides of pan and top springs back when lightly touched and/or a wooden toothpick inserted near the center comes out clean. Cool in pan on a wire rack for 15 to 20 minutes. Remove from pan. Turn upright and cool completely on rack.

Streusel: In a small bowl combine ½ cup chopped pecans, ¼ cup sugar, 1 tablespoon unsweetened cocoa powder, and 1½ teaspoons ground cinnamon.

Per serving: 568 cal., 40 g total fat (17 g sat. fat), 141 mg chol., 411 mg sodium, 48 g carbo., 2 g fiber, 8 g pro.
Daily Values: 22% vit. A, 8% calcium, 12% iron

Pumpkin-Sour Cream Coffee Cake with Pecan Streusel

For a pretty presentation use both dried cranberries and golden raisins in this delicious breakfast delight.

Prep: 45 minutes **Bake:** 1 hour **Cool:** 10 minutes
Oven: 325°F **Makes:** 12 servings

  1 **recipe Pecan Streusel**
  1 **cup canned pumpkin**
  ⅓ **cup packed brown sugar**
  ⅓ **cup dried cranberries or golden raisins**
  1 **tablespoon all-purpose flour**
  2 **cups all-purpose flour**
  2 **teaspoons baking powder**
  ½ **teaspoon baking soda**
  ½ **teaspoon salt**
  ¼ **teaspoon ground nutmeg**
  ½ **cup butter or margarine, softened**
  1 **cup granulated sugar**
1½ **teaspoons vanilla**
  2 **eggs**
  1 **8-ounce carton dairy sour cream**

1. Preheat oven to 325°F. Grease and flour a 9-inch springform pan; set aside. Prepare Pecan Streusel; set aside. For filling, in a small bowl stir together pumpkin, brown sugar, cranberries, and 1 tablespoon flour; set aside.

2. In a medium bowl combine 2 cups flour, baking powder, baking soda, salt, and nutmeg; set aside. In a large mixing bowl beat butter with an electric mixer on medium to high speed for 30 seconds. Add granulated sugar and vanilla. Beat on medium to high speed until combined, scraping sides of bowl occasionally. Add eggs, one at a time, beating after each addition. Add flour mixture and sour cream alternately to beaten mixture, beating just until combined after each addition. (The batter will be stiff.)

Pumpkin-Sour Cream Coffee Cake with Pecan Streusel

3. Spread 3 cups of the batter into the prepared pan, building up a 1-inch rim of batter around pan edges. Spoon pumpkin mixture into center of pan, spreading to make an even layer. Carefully spoon remaining batter in small mounds over the pumpkin mixture; gently spread batter to cover pumpkin mixture. Sprinkle Pecan Streusel over batter.

4. Bake for 60 to 65 minutes or until a wooden toothpick inserted near the center comes out clean. Cool in pan on a wire rack for 10 minutes. Loosen and remove sides of springform pan. Cool completely on wire rack.

Pecan Streusel: In a medium bowl stir together ⅓ cup all-purpose flour, ⅓ cup packed brown sugar, and ⅛ teaspoon ground nutmeg. Using a pastry blender, cut in 3 tablespoons butter until mixture resembles coarse crumbs. Stir in ⅓ cup chopped pecans. Makes about 1½ cups.

Per serving: 385 cal., 18 g total fat (10 g sat. fat), 74 mg chol., 357 mg sodium, 52 g carbo., 2 g fiber, 5 g pro.
Daily Values: 103% vit. A, 2% vit. C, 9% calcium, 10% iron

Cookie Tray

What would Christmas be without a bountiful assortment of cookies? Cookies certainly make the holiday sweeter. This year, make a day out of cookie baking—gather all the kids or grandkids, pick three to four of your favorite recipes, and set to work. Create the warmest traditions in delectable aromas wafting from the oven, laughter heard and shared, and of course, the irresistible temptation of a stolen cookie or two. When all is said and done, you'll have plenty of memories and dozens of cookies—just enough to make gifts for all the special people in your life. To make a festive cookie tray, present cookies on a brightly colored holiday plate wrapped securely in plastic wrap and tied with a bow. Nothing says "Merry Christmas" like a plate filled with holiday sweets!

Pecan-Cinnamon Tassies in a Snap, page 78

Piecrust Cookies

Bypass the pie-making and go for the extra crust reward we love most—pie-spiced, melt-in-your-mouth squares of crust.

Prep: 15 minutes **Bake:** 8 minutes
Oven: 400°F **Makes:** about 25 cookies

- ½ of a 15-ounce package rolled refrigerated unbaked piecrust (1 crust)
- 1 tablespoon butter or margarine, melted
- 2 tablespoons packed brown sugar
- ½ to 1 teaspoon pumpkin pie spice or apple pie spice

1. Preheat oven to 400°F. Unroll piecrust according to package directions using the microwave method. Place on a lightly floured surface. Brush piecrust with melted butter. Sprinkle with brown sugar and pumpkin pie spice. Use a pastry wheel or pizza cutter to cut dough into 1½- to 2-inch square cookies (some of the edges may be smaller). Place on an ungreased large baking sheet, leaving a small space between cookies.

2. Bake about 8 minutes or until golden brown. Serve warm or let cool.

Christmas Sugar Cookies

To store: Place cookies in layers separated by waxed paper in an airtight container; cover. Store at room temperature for up to 3 days or freeze for up to 3 months.

Per cookie: 46 cal., 3 g total fat (1 g sat. fat), 3 mg chol., 38 mg sodium, 5 g carbo., 0 g fiber, 0 g pro.

Christmas Sugar Cookies

Get out the Christmas cookie cutters and have little ones help make and decorate these traditional holiday cookies. Almond extract adds a boost of flavor but substitute vanilla extract if that is what you have on hand.

Prep: 25 minutes **Bake:** 5 minutes per batch
Chill: 30 minutes **Oven:** 375°F
Makes: about 36 cookies

- ⅔ cup butter, softened
- ¾ cup granulated sugar
- 1 teaspoon baking powder
- ¼ teaspoon salt
- 1 egg
- 1 tablespoon milk
- ½ teaspoon almond extract
- 2 cups all-purpose flour
- 1 recipe Powdered Sugar Glaze (optional)
- Edible glitter (optional)

1. Preheat oven to 375°F. In a large mixing bowl beat butter with an electric mixer on medium to high speed for 30 seconds. Add sugar, baking powder, and salt. Beat until combined, scraping sides of bowl occasionally. Beat in egg, milk, and almond extract until combined. Beat in as much of the flour as possible with the mixer. Stir in any remaining flour with a wooden spoon. Divide dough in half. If necessary, cover and chill dough about 30 minutes or until easy to handle.

2. On a lightly floured surface, roll half of dough at a time until ⅛ inch thick. Using a 2½- to 3-inch cookie cutter, cut dough into desired shapes. Place cutouts 1 inch apart on an ungreased cookie sheet.

3. Bake for 5 to 7 minutes or until edges are firm and bottoms are barely light brown. Transfer to

Gingersnap Sandwich Cookies

a wire rack and let cool. If desired, frost with Powdered Sugar Glaze and decorate as desired.

To store: Place cookies in layers separated by waxed paper in an airtight container; cover. Store at room temperature for up to 3 days or freeze unfrosted cookies for up to 3 months. Thaw cookies and if desired, frost.

Per cookie: 73 cal., 4 g total fat (2 g sat. fat), 16 mg chol., 66 mg sodium, 9 g carbo., 0 g fiber, 1 g pro.
Daily Values: 3% vit. A, 1% calcium, 2% iron

Powdered Sugar Glaze: Combine 6 cups sifted powdered sugar and ⅓ cup milk in a mixing bowl. Stir in additional milk, 1 teaspoon at a time, to make mixture of glazing consistency. If desired, divide mixture into portions and tint with desired food coloring.

Gingersnap Sandwich Cookies

Start with packaged cookies—a favorite crunchy or soft variety—and top them with a delicious flourish.

Start to Finish: 25 min. **Makes:** 15 cookies

⅓ cup purchased lemon curd or orange curd
2 tablespoons butter, softened
¾ cup powdered sugar
  Several drops yellow food coloring
    (optional)
30 purchased gingersnap cookies
  Powdered sugar

1. In a medium mixing bowl beat lemon curd and butter with an electric mixer on medium to high speed for 30 seconds. Add ¾ cup powdered sugar. If desired, add several drops yellow food coloring. Beat until smooth and fluffy.

2. Spread mixture on the bottom side of half of the cookies. Top with the remaining cookies, flat sides down. Sprinkle tops of cookies with powdered sugar.

To store: Since cookies are so easy to make and will soften when stored, prepare the sandwich cookies just before serving.

Per cookie: 119 cal., 3 g total fat (1 g sat. fat), 9 mg chol., 108 mg sodium, 22 g carbo., 1 g fiber, 1 g pro.
Daily Values: 1% vit. A, 1% calcium, 5% iron

Festive Gingerbread Cookies

For icing buy meringue powder in a store that sells cake-decorating supplies.

Prep: 45 minutes **Bake:** 6 minutes per batch
Chill: 1 hour **Oven:** 350°F
Makes: about 42 (3-inch) cookies

⅓ cup butter
⅓ cup shortening
1 cup granulated sugar
½ cup packed brown sugar
1 teaspoon baking soda
1 teaspoon ground ginger
½ teaspoon ground cinnamon
½ teaspoon ground nutmeg
1 egg
¼ cup mild-flavor molasses
2 tablespoons milk
2¼ cups all-purpose flour
1 recipe Meringue Icing
   Colored sugar or edible glitter (optional)

1. In a large mixing bowl beat butter and shortening with an electric mixer on medium speed for 30 seconds. Add granulated sugar, brown sugar, baking soda, ginger, cinnamon, and nutmeg; beat until combined, scraping sides of bowl occasionally. Beat in egg, molasses, and milk until combined. Beat in as much of the flour as possible with the mixer. Stir in any remaining flour with a wooden spoon. Divide dough in half. Cover dough and chill for 1 hour or until easy to handle.

2. Preheat oven to 350°F. Grease cookie sheets; set aside. On a lightly floured surface, roll half of the dough at a time to slightly less than ¼ inch thick. Cut dough with desired cutters. Place cutouts 1 inch apart on prepared cookie sheet.

3. Bake for 6 to 8 minutes or until edges are lightly browned. Cool on cookie sheet for 1 minute. Transfer to wire racks; let cool. Decorate as desired with Meringue Icing, using a clean, fine-tip brush to paint icing onto cookies or pipe icing onto cookies. If desired, sprinkle with colored sugar.

Meringue Icing: In a medium mixing bowl combine ⅓ cup warm water, 2 tablespoons meringue powder, and 1 tablespoon lemon juice. Beat lightly with a fork until combined. Add 3 to 3¼ cups powdered sugar. Beat with an electric mixer on high speed until the icing is the consistency of soft whipped cream. If desired, divide icing and color each portion with a different food coloring. Store tightly covered in the refrigerator. Makes 2½ cups.

To store: Place cookies in layers separated by waxed paper in an airtight container; cover. Store at room temperature for up to 3 days or freeze unfrosted cookies for up to 3 months. Thaw cookies, then frost.

Per cookie: 119 cal., 3 g total fat (1 g sat. fat), 9 mg chol., 44 mg sodium, 22 g carbo., 0 g fiber, 1 g pro.
Daily Values: 1% vit. A, 1% calcium, 3% iron

Shortcut Candy Cane Cookies

Twist two different colored ropes of dough to form these cookies. Flavored with a touch of peppermint, the treats will draw applause at any holiday gathering. Be sure to save a couple for Santa!

Prep: 55 minutes **Bake:** 5 minutes per batch
Chill: 30 minutes **Oven:** 375°F
Makes: about 22 cookies

½ cup butter, softened
1 cup powdered sugar
1 egg
½ teaspoon peppermint extract
1½ cups all-purpose flour
6 drops red food coloring
¼ cup finely crushed striped round
   peppermint candies

1. In a medium mixing bowl beat butter with an electric mixer on medium speed for 30 seconds. Add powdered sugar. Beat until combined, scraping sides of bowl often. Beat in egg and peppermint extract. Beat in as much of the flour as possible with the mixer. Stir in any remaining flour with a wooden spoon. Divide dough in half.

2. Knead red food coloring and crushed peppermint candies into one portion of the dough. Leave the remaining dough plain. Cover dough and chill about 30 minutes or until easy to handle.

3. Preheat oven to 375°F. Line cookie sheet with foil or parchment paper; set aside. To make candy canes, on a lightly floured surface, shape a ¾-inch ball of the plain cookie dough into a 5-inch rope. Repeat with a ¾-inch ball of pink cookie dough. Place the ropes side by side and twist together. Pinch ends to seal. Form into a cane shape. Place 2 inches apart on prepared cookie sheet.

4. Bake for 5 to 7 minutes or until edges are lightly browned. Transfer cookies to a wire rack; let cool.

To store: Place cookies in layers separated by waxed paper in an airtight container; cover. Store at room temperature for up to 3 days or freeze for up to 3 months.

Per cookie: 98 cal., 5 g total fat (3 g sat. fat), 21 mg chol., 34 mg sodium, 13 g carbo., 0 g fiber, 1 g pro.
Daily Values: 3% vit. A, 2% iron

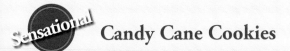

Candy Cane Cookies

Prep: 30 minutes **Chill:** 1 hour
Bake: 7 minutes per batch **Stand:** 30 minutes
Oven: 375°F **Makes:** about 36 cookies

- ⅓ cup shortening
- ⅓ cup butter, softened
- ¾ cup sugar
- 1 teaspoon baking powder
- 1 egg
- 2 tablespoons milk
- 1 teaspoon vanilla
- ⅓ cup unsweetened cocoa powder
- 1¾ cups all-purpose flour
- 4 ounces white baking chocolate
- 2 to 4 teaspoons shortening
- ½ to ⅔ cup crushed peppermint candy canes

1. In a medium mixing bowl beat ⅓ cup shortening and the butter with an electric mixer on medium speed for 30 seconds. Beat in sugar and baking powder. Beat in egg, milk, and vanilla. Beat in cocoa powder and as much of the flour as possible with the mixer. Stir in any remaining flour with a wooden spoon. Divide dough in half. Cover dough and chill at least 1 hour.

2. Preheat oven to 375°F. Working with one portion of dough at a time, on a lightly floured surface roll dough to slightly less than ¼ inch thick. Use a 4-inch candy-cane-shape cutter or trace around a cardboard pattern to cut dough. Place cutouts 1 inch apart on an ungreased cookie sheet. Bake for 7 to 9 minutes or until firm and light brown. Transfer cookies to a wire rack; let cool.

3. For drizzle, in a small saucepan heat white baking chocolate and 2 teaspoons shortening over low heat until melted, stirring often. Add more shortening, if necessary, to make a drizzle of desired consistency. Drizzle a few cookies with mixture; sprinkle with crushed candy canes. Repeat with remaining cookies. Let cookies stand until set.

To store: Place cookies in layers separated by waxed paper in an airtight container; cover. Store drizzled cookies at room temperature for up to 3 days or freeze undrizzled cookies for up to 3 months. Thaw cookies, then drizzle.

Per cookie: 102 cal., 5 g total fat (2 g sat. fat), 11 mg chol., 25 mg sodium, 13 g carbo., 0 g fiber, 1 g pro.
Daily Values: 1% vit. A, 2% calcium, 2% iron

Candy Cane Cookies

Pecan-Cinnamon Tassies in a Snap

1. Preheat oven to 350°F. Let piecrust stand according to package directions. Unroll piecrusts. Use a 2½-inch round cookie cutter to cut 12 rounds from each piecrust. Gently ease dough rounds into 24 ungreased 1¾-inch muffin cups, pressing dough evenly on the bottom and up the sides of the cups.

2. For filling, in a bowl stir together egg, brown sugar, and butter. Stir in pecans and cinnamon.

3. Spoon about 1 heaping teaspoon of the filling into each pastry-lined muffin cup. Bake for 20 to 25 minutes or until pastry is golden and filling is puffed. Cool 5 minutes in pan. Remove from pan and transfer to a wire rack; let cool completely. If desired, drizzle tassies with chocolate and/or caramel ice cream topping before serving.

To store: Place mini-tarts in an airtight container without ice cream topping drizzle; cover. Store in the refrigerator for up to 3 days or freeze for up to 3 months. If desired, drizzle before serving.

Per mini-tart: 137 cal., 8 g total fat (3 g sat. fat), 15 mg chol., 84 mg sodium, 15 g carbo., 0 g fiber, 1 g pro.
Daily Values: 1% vit. A, 1% calcium, 1% iron

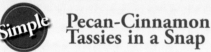

Pecan-Cinnamon Tassies in a Snap

Pecans have a higher fat content than any other nut, so take care when storing them as the high-fat content tends to make them go rancid more quickly. You can store unshelled pecans, wrapped, in a cool, dry place up to 6 months. Shelled pecans can be refrigerated for up to 3 months or frozen for up to 6 months.

Prep: 20 minutes **Bake:** 20 minutes
Oven: 350°F **Makes:** 24 tarts

- 1 **15-ounce package rolled refrigerated unbaked piecrust (2 crusts)**
- 1 **egg**
- ⅔ **cup packed brown sugar**
- 2 **tablespoons butter, melted**
- ¾ **cup coarsely chopped pecans, toasted (see tip, page 63)**
- ½ **teaspoon ground cinnamon**
   Chocolate-flavored ice cream topping, warmed (optional)
   Caramel-flavored ice cream topping (optional)

Chocolate-Drizzled Honey-Pecan Triangles

If you like pecan pie, you will enjoy these nut-filled gems. They make a stunning presentation on a cookie tray.

Prep: 25 minutes **Bake:** 40 minutes
Oven: 350°F **Makes:** 48 triangles

   Nonstick cooking spray
- 1 **cup butter, softened**
- ⅓ **cup granulated sugar**
- ¼ **teaspoon baking powder**
- ⅛ **teaspoon salt**
- 2 **eggs**
- ½ **teaspoon vanilla**
- 2¼ **cups all-purpose flour**
- 1 **cup butter**
- 1 **cup packed brown sugar**
- ½ **cup honey**

1½ cups pecan pieces
1 teaspoon finely shredded lemon peel
3 ounces bittersweet chocolate, chopped
1½ teaspoons shortening

1. Preheat oven to 350°F. Line a 13×9×2-inch baking pan with foil, extending foil over edges of pan; lightly coat foil with cooking spray. Set pan aside.

2. For crust, in a large mixing bowl beat 1 cup softened butter with an electric mixer on medium to high speed for 30 seconds. Add granulated sugar, baking powder, and salt. Beat until combined. Add eggs and vanilla; beat until combined. Beat in as much of the flour as possible with the mixer. Stir in any remaining flour with a wooden spoon. Spread or pat mixture into prepared pan. Bake for 15 minutes or until crust is set and lightly browned. Set aside on a wire rack.

3. For filling, in a medium saucepan combine 1 cup butter, brown sugar, and honey. Heat over medium heat until boiling, stirring to dissolve sugar. Boil gently, uncovered, for 3 minutes. Remove from heat. Stir in pecans and lemon peel. Pour over warm crust. Bake about 25 minutes more or until filling is bubbly over entire surface. Remove; cool in pan on a wire rack.

4. When cool, use foil to lift bars from pan. Place on a cutting board. Cut into 24 squares. Cut each square diagonally to form triangles.

5. In a medium saucepan heat the chocolate and shortening over low heat until melted, stirring frequently. Place triangles on a waxed paper-lined tray or cookie sheet. Drizzle chocolate over triangles; let stand until set.

To store: Place triangles in layers separated by waxed paper in an airtight container; cover. Store in the refrigerator for up to 3 days or freeze without the chocolate drizzle for up to 3 months. Thaw cookies, then drizzle.

Per triangle: 159 cal., 11 g total fat (6 g sat. fat), 29 mg chol., 67 mg sodium, 15 g carbo., 1 g fiber, 1 g pro.
Daily Values: 5% vit. A, 1% calcium, 3% iron

Spritz-Style Peppermint Cookies

Red paste food coloring can be found in the baking aisle of most grocery stores near the liquid food coloring.

Prep: 20 minutes **Bake:** 9 minutes per batch
Oven: 375°F **Makes:** 30 to 36 cookies

1 16.5- to 18-ounce roll refrigerated sugar cookie dough
½ cup all-purpose flour
½ teaspoon peppermint extract
  Red paste food coloring (optional)
4 ounces white baking chocolate, chopped
2 teaspoons shortening
¼ cup finely crushed striped round peppermint candies (about 11 candies)

1. Preheat oven to 375°F. In a large bowl stir together the cookie dough, flour, and peppermint extract. If desired, divide dough in half and tint half of the dough with red paste food coloring. Pack dough into a cookie press fitted with the star plate. Force dough through the press about 1 inch apart onto ungreased cookie sheets.

2. Bake about 9 minutes or until edges are firm and just beginning to brown. Transfer cookies to wire racks; let cool.

3. In a heavy small saucepan melt white chocolate and shortening over low heat, stirring frequently. Dip half of each cookie into white chocolate, allowing excess to drip off. Place on waxed paper-lined trays or cookie sheets. Sprinkle with crushed peppermint candies. Let stand until set.

To store: Place cookies in layers separated by waxed paper in an airtight container; cover. Store at room temperature for up to 3 days or freeze undipped cookies for up to 3 months. Thaw cookies, then dip.

Per cookie: 106 cal., 5 g total fat (2 g sat. fat), 5 mg chol., 71 mg sodium, 15 g carbo., 0 g fiber, 1 g pro.
Daily Values: 2% calcium, 2% iron

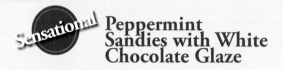

Peppermint Sandies with White Chocolate Glaze

To crush the peppermint candies, place them in a plastic resealable bag. Lay on the counter and use a rolling pin to crush.

Prep: 25 minutes **Bake:** 15 minutes per batch
Stand: 48 minutes **Oven:** 325°F
Makes: about 48 cookies

- 1 cup butter, softened
- ⅓ cup powdered sugar
- ¼ cup finely crushed striped round peppermint candies (about 11 candies)
- 1 tablespoon water
- ½ teaspoon vanilla
- ½ teaspoon peppermint extract
- 2 cups all-purpose flour
- 1 cup whipping cream
- 6 ounces white baking chocolate
  Crushed striped round peppermint candies

1. Preheat oven to 325°F. In a large mixing bowl beat butter with an electric mixer on medium to high speed for 30 seconds. Add powdered sugar and ¼ cup crushed peppermint candies. Beat until combined, scraping sides of bowl occasionally. Beat in water, vanilla, and peppermint extract until combined. Beat in as much of the flour as possible with the mixer. Stir in any remaining flour with a wooden spoon.

2. Shape dough into 1-inch balls. Place 1 inch apart on an ungreased cookie sheet. Bake about 15 minutes or until bottoms are lightly browned. Transfer cookies to a wire rack; let cool.

3. Meanwhile, for white chocolate glaze, in a medium saucepan bring whipping cream just to simmering. Remove from heat. Add white chocolate. Let stand for 3 minutes. Stir until smooth. Let stand for 45 to 60 minutes or until glaze starts to thicken.

4. Spoon glaze on top of each cooled cookie. Sprinkle with additional crushed peppermint candies. Let stand until set.

To store: Place cookies in layers separated by waxed paper in an airtight container; cover. Store at room temperature for up to 3 days. Freeze unglazed cookies for up to 3 months. Thaw cookies; glaze.

Per cookie: 102 cal., 7 g total fat (4 g sat. fat), 18 mg chol., 34 mg sodium, 9 g carbo., 0 g fiber, 1 g pro.
Daily Values: 4% vit. A, 1% calcium, 1% iron

Peppermint Sandies with White Chocolate Glaze

 ## Raspberry-Oatmeal Bars

Be sure to find preserves that are seedless for these pretty, simple, and tasty bars.

Prep: 15 minutes **Bake:** 20 minutes
Oven: 375°F **Makes:** 40 bars

- 1 package 2-layer-size yellow or white cake mix
- 2½ cups quick-cooking rolled oats
- ¾ cup butter, melted
- 1 12-ounce jar seedless raspberry jam, seedless blackberry jam, or apricot preserves (about 1 cup)
- 1 tablespoon water

1. Preheat oven to 375°F. Line a 13×9×2-inch baking pan with foil. Grease foil and set pan aside.

2. In a very large bowl stir together cake mix and oats; stir in melted butter until crumbly. Press half (about 3 cups) of the crumb mixture evenly into prepared pan. In a small bowl combine jam and water; spread over crust to within ½ inch of the edges. Sprinkle evenly with remaining crumb mixture.

3. Bake for 20 to 25 minutes or until golden brown. Cool in pan on a wire rack. Use foil to lift bars from pan. Cut into bars.

To store: Place bars in layers separated by waxed paper in an airtight container; cover. Store in the refrigerator for up to 2 days.

Per bar: 133 cal., 5 g total fat (3 g sat. fat), 9 mg chol., 110 mg sodium, 20 g carbo., 1 g fiber, 2 g pro.

Daily Values: 2% vit. A, 1% vit. C, 1% calcium, 3% iron

Pecan Shortbread Raspberry Cookies

Pecan Shortbread Raspberry Cookies

Any flavor of preserves, such as strawberry, blueberry, cherry, or apricot, will work in this nutty cookie—though seedless varieties work best. Use whatever flavor you have on hand or try an assortment of different preserves for a selection.

Prep: 40 minutes   **Chill:** 1 hour
Bake: 7 minutes per batch   **Oven:** 350°F
Makes: about 40 cookies

- 1 **cup butter, softened**
- ⅔ **cup granulated sugar**
- 1 **teaspoon vanilla**
- ½ **teaspoon almond extract**
- 2 **cups all-purpose flour**
- 1 **cup ground pecans**
     Powdered sugar
- ⅓ **cup seedless raspberry preserves**

1. In a large mixing bowl beat butter with an electric mixer on medium to high speed for 30 seconds. Add granulated sugar, vanilla, and almond extract; beat until fluffy, scraping bowl often. Beat in flour and pecans until combined. Wrap dough in plastic wrap; chill for 1 to 2 hours or until dough is easy to handle.

2. Preheat oven to 350°F. On a lightly floured surface, roll half of the dough at a time until ⅛ inch thick. Using a 2-inch round scalloped cookie cutter, cut rounds from dough. Place 1 inch apart on ungreased cookie sheets. Using a 1-inch round cutter, cut centers from half of the unbaked cookies. Remove centers; reroll dough to make more cookies. Bake for 7 to 9 minutes or until edges are firm and bottoms are lightly browned. Transfer to wire racks; let cool.

3. To assemble, sift powdered sugar over tops of cookies with holes; set aside. Spread about ½ teaspoon preserves onto bottom of each cookie without a hole. Top with a cookie with a hole, placing the sugar side up.

To store: Place cooled cookies, without preserves, in an airtight container; cover. Store at room temperature for up to 3 days or freeze for up to 3 months. Assemble as above before serving.

Per cookie: 101 cal., 7 g total fat (3 g sat. fat), 12 mg chol., 34 mg sodium, 10 g carbo., 0 g fiber, 1 g pro.

Daily Values: 3% vit. A, 2% iron

Chocolate-Coconut Mint Bars

Prep: 20 minutes **Bake:** 25 minutes
Oven: 350°F **Makes:** 24 bars

> Nonstick cooking spray
> 1½ cups finely crushed chocolate
>   sandwich cookies with white filling
>   (about 16 cookies)
> 2 tablespoons butter, melted
> 1 cup chopped walnuts
> 1 cup flaked coconut
> ¾ cup semisweet chocolate and mint swirled
>   pieces or semisweet chocolate pieces
> 1 14-ounce can sweetened condensed milk

1. Preheat oven to 350°F. Line an 11×7×1½-inch baking pan with foil, extending foil over all edges of pan. Lightly coat foil with cooking spray; set pan aside. In a small bowl mix crushed cookies with melted butter; press mixture into the bottom of the prepared pan. Sprinkle crumb mixture with nuts, coconut, and chocolate pieces. Drizzle sweetened condensed milk evenly over all.

2. Bake about 25 minutes or until bubbly around edges and top is lightly browned. Cool in pan on a wire rack. Use foil to lift bars from pan. Pull foil away from sides. Invert; remove foil completely. Invert onto a cutting board; cut into bars.

To store: Place bars in layers separated by waxed paper in an airtight container; cover. Store in the refrigerator for up to 3 days or freeze for 3 months.

Per bar: 179 cal., 11 g total fat (5 g sat. fat), 8 mg chol., 81 mg sodium, 21 g carbo., 1 g fiber, 3 g pro.
Daily Values: 1% vit. A, 1% vit. C, 5% calcium, 3% iron

Buttery Mint Slices

These melt-in-your-mouth cookies take on two different looks, depending on whether you use the white baking pieces with mint extract and green food coloring or the chocolate swirled pieces.

Prep: 25 minutes **Chill:** 2 hours
Bake: 10 minutes per batch **Oven:** 350°F
Makes: about 72 cookies

Buttery Mint Slices

- ½ cup butter, softened
- ⅔ cup sugar
- 1 teaspoon baking powder
- ½ teaspoon salt
- 1 egg
- 1 tablespoon milk
- 1 teaspoon vanilla
- 2 cups all-purpose flour
- ⅓ cup white baking pieces plus ¼ teaspoon mint extract plus a few drops green food coloring or semisweet chocolate and mint swirled pieces, melted and slightly cooled
- ⅓ cup white baking pieces, melted and slightly cooled

1. In a large mixing bowl beat butter with an electric mixer on medium to high speed for 30 seconds. Add sugar, baking powder, and salt. Beat until combined, scraping sides of bowl occasionally. Beat in egg, milk, and vanilla until combined. Beat in as much of the flour as possible with the mixer. Stir in any remaining flour with a wooden spoon. Divide dough in half.

2. For green colored dough, in a medium bowl stir or knead together half of the dough and ⅓ cup melted white baking pieces plus extract and food coloring. (Or use half of dough to make brown colored dough using the chocolate swirled pieces.) Divide mint dough (green or brown) into thirds. In a second bowl stir or knead together remaining dough and ⅓ cup melted white baking pieces, making a white dough; divide dough in half.

3. Line an 8×4×2-inch loaf pan with plastic wrap. Press one-third of the mint dough (green or choco-late) evenly into pan. Press one-half of the white dough evenly on top of mint layer. Repeat the layers, finishing with mint dough on top. Cover with plastic wrap. Chill for at least 2 hours or until firm.

4. Preheat oven to 350°F. Remove dough brick from pan and unwrap; place on cutting board. Using a sharp knife, cut brick crosswise into ⅛-inch slices. Cut each slice in half crosswise. Place slices 2 inch-es apart on an ungreased cookie sheet.

5. Bake about 10 minutes or until edges are set. Transfer cookies to a wire rack; let cool.

To store: Place cookies in layers separated by waxed paper in an airtight container; cover. Store at room temperature for up to 3 days or freeze for up to 3 months.

Per cookie: 42 cal., 2 g total fat (1 g sat. fat), 6 mg chol., 31 mg sodium, 6 g carbo., 0 g fiber, 0 g pro.
Daily Values: 1% vit. A, 1% iron

Easy Fudgy Brownie Cookies

Use any variety of nut (or leave them out) in this cookie-brownie combination.

Prep: 20 minutes **Bake:** 10 minutes per batch
Oven: 350°F **Makes:** about 48 cookies

- 1 18- to 21-ounce package brownie mix
- ½ cup butter, melted
- 1 egg
- 1 cup semisweet chocolate pieces
- 2 ounces white baking chocolate, chopped
- ½ cup chopped walnuts
- 1 16-ounce can chocolate frosting (optional)

1. Preheat oven to 350°F. Line cookie sheets with parchment paper; set aside. In a large bowl stir together brownie mix, butter, and egg until well combined. Stir in chocolate pieces, chopped white baking chocolate, and walnuts.

2. Drop dough by rounded teaspoons (or use a small cookie scoop) 2 inches apart onto prepared cookie sheets. Bake for 10 minutes or until edges are set (centers will be slightly soft). Let cool on cookie sheets for 2 minutes. Transfer cookies to a wire rack; let cool. If desired, spread each cooled cookie with about 2 teaspoons of the frosting.

To store: Place cookies in layers separated by waxed paper in an airtight container; cover. Store at room temperature for up to 3 days or freeze unfrosted cookies for up to 3 months.

Per cookie: 96 cal., 6 g total fat (2 g sat. fat), 10 mg chol., 49 mg sodium, 11 g carbo., 0 g fiber, 1 g pro.
Daily Values: 1% vit. A, 1% calcium, 2% iron

Decadent Mocha Fudge Cookies

Instant espresso powder is the secret ingredient in these divine cookies. Serve with a cup of espresso or coffee for dipping.

Prep: 35 minutes **Bake:** 12 minutes per batch
Stand: 30 minutes **Oven:** 350°F
Makes: about 42 cookies

- 2 6-ounce packages bittersweet chocolate, chopped
- ½ cup butter
- 1½ cups sugar
- 4 eggs
- 1 tablespoon instant espresso coffee powder or instant coffee crystals
- ⅓ cup all-purpose flour
- ¼ teaspoon baking powder
- ⅛ teaspoon salt
- 1 cup semisweet chocolate pieces
- ¾ cup chopped almonds
- 1¼ cups white baking pieces
- ¾ teaspoon shortening

1. In a medium saucepan combine chopped chocolate and butter. Heat and stir over low heat until mixture is melted and smooth. Remove from heat. Cool for 10 minutes.

2. In a large bowl combine sugar, eggs, and espresso powder. Beat with an electric mixer on medium to high speed for 2 to 3 minutes or until well mixed and color lightens slightly. Add cooled chocolate mixture; beat until combined. In a small bowl stir together flour, baking powder, and salt. Add to chocolate mixture; beat until combined. Stir in chocolate pieces, nuts, and ½ cup of the white baking pieces.

3. Cover bowl and let stand about 20 minutes or until mixture thickens slightly. Preheat oven to 350°F. Line two cookie sheets with parchment paper or foil.

4. Using a rounded tablespoon measure, drop dough about 2 inches apart onto prepared cookie sheets. Bake for 12 to 13 minutes or until tops are cracked and appear set. Let cool on cookie sheets for 1 minute. Transfer to a wire rack; let cool.

5. For drizzle, in a small saucepan heat remaining ¾ cup white baking pieces and shortening over low heat until melted, stirring often. Cool slightly. Place in a small resealable plastic bag. Snip a very small piece from one corner of the bag. Pipe a thin drizzle over each cookie. Let stand until set.

To store: Place cookies in layers separated by waxed paper in an airtight container; cover. Store at room temperature for up to 3 days or freeze undrizzled cookies for up to 3 months. Thaw cookies, then drizzle.

Per cookie: 171 cal., 10 g total fat (6 g sat. fat), 26 mg chol., 44 mg sodium, 20 g carbo., 1 g fiber, 2 g pro.
Daily Values: 2% vit. A, 1% calcium, 4% iron

Decadent Mocha Fudge Cookies

Candy-Topped Brownies

These brownies feature an assortment of ooey-gooey toppings. Select red and green candy-coated chocolate pieces for a festive holiday presentation.

Prep: 20 minutes **Bake:** 24 minutes
Oven: 350°F **Makes:** 24 brownies

- 1 19.5- to 21.5-ounce package brownie mix
- 1½ cups tiny marshmallows
- ½ cup miniature semisweet chocolate pieces

½ cup miniature candy-coated semisweet
 chocolate pieces
⅓ cup toffee pieces
⅓ cup caramel ice cream topping

1. Preheat oven to 350°F. Grease the bottom of a 13×9×2-inch baking pan; set aside.

2. Prepare brownie mix according to package directions. Spread batter into prepared pan.

3. Bake for 24 to 27 minutes or until edges are firm. Remove pan from oven. Top with marshmallows, chocolate pieces, candy pieces, and toffee pieces. Drizzle with the caramel topping. Bake for 1 to 2 minutes more or until marshmallows are puffy. Cool in pan on wire rack. Cut into bars.

To store: Place bars in a single layer in an airtight container; cover. Store in the refrigerator for up to 2 days.

Per brownie: 223 cal., 11 g total fat (3 g sat. fat), 19 mg chol., 101 mg sodium, 31 g carbo., 0 g fiber, 2 g pro.
Daily Values: 1% vit. A, 1% calcium, 5% iron

Cream Cheese Brownies

Create a sumptuous brownie with a haunting combination of silken cream cheese, macadamia nuts, and chocolate.

Prep: 30 minutes **Bake:** 45 minutes **Chill:** 1 hour
Oven: 350°F **Makes:** 32 brownies

8 ounces semisweet chocolate, chopped
3 tablespoons butter
4 eggs
1¼ cups sugar
⅓ cup water
1 teaspoon vanilla
1 cup all-purpose flour
¾ cup chopped macadamia nuts, toasted
 (see tip, page 63)
1 teaspoon baking powder
¼ teaspoon salt
1 8-ounce package cream cheese, softened
⅔ cup sugar
2 tablespoons all-purpose flour

1 tablespoon lemon juice
1 teaspoon vanilla
1 recipe Chocolate Glaze
32 whole macadamia nuts (optional)

1. Preheat oven to 350°F. Line a 13×9×2-inch baking pan with foil, extending foil over edges of pan. Grease foil; set aside. In a large heavy saucepan stir chocolate and butter over low heat until chocolate is melted. Set aside to cool.

2. In a large mixing bowl beat 2 of the eggs with an electric mixer on medium speed until foamy. Add 1¼ cups sugar, water, and 1 teaspoon vanilla; beat about 5 minutes or until mixture is thick and lemon-colored. Beat in cooled chocolate mixture. Stir in 1 cup flour, ¾ cup nuts, baking powder, and salt. Spread half of the chocolate batter in prepared baking pan; set pan and remaining batter aside.

3. In a medium mixing bowl beat cream cheese, ⅔ cup sugar, remaining 2 eggs, 2 tablespoons flour, lemon juice, and 1 teaspoon vanilla with an electric mixer until smooth. Spread evenly over batter in pan. Spoon remaining chocolate batter evenly over cream cheese mixture. Swirl batter with a knife to make a marble pattern.

4. Bake for 45 minutes. Cool in pan on a wire rack. Spread Chocolate Glaze over cooled brownies or if desired, cut into bars and top each with a small amount of glaze and a whole macadamia nut. Chill 1 hour or until glaze is set.

Chocolate Glaze: In a small saucepan stir ⅓ cup whipping cream and 6 ounces finely chopped semisweet chocolate over low heat until chocolate is melted.

To store: Place bars in layers separated by waxed paper in an airtight container; cover. Store in the refrigerator for up to 3 days or freeze unglazed bars for up to 3 months. Thaw in refrigerator, then glaze.

Per brownie: 200 cal., 11 g total fat (6 g sat. fat), 40 mg chol., 64 mg sodium, 23 g carbo., 1 g fiber, 3 g pro.
Daily Values: 4% vit. A, 2% calcium, 6% iron

Shortcut Baklava

Preparing the Greek dessert baklava is usually an all-day process. With this easy version, the delicious results can be enjoyed in under an hour.

Prep: 15 minutes **Bake:** 25 minutes
Cool: 10 minutes **Oven:** 375°F **Makes:** 16 servings

- 1 **15-ounce package rolled refrigerated unbaked piecrusts (2 crusts)**
- 1 **cup finely chopped walnuts**
- ⅓ **cup sugar**
- 2 **tablespoons honey**
- 1 **teaspoon ground cinnamon**
- 1 **teaspoon lemon juice**
- 1 **tablespoon honey**
- 1 **teaspoon water**
  Cinnamon-sugar*

1. Preheat oven to 375°F. Let piecrusts stand according to package directions. Unfold; place one crust on an ungreased cookie sheet.

2. For filling, in a small bowl stir together walnuts, sugar, 2 tablespoons honey, cinnamon, and lemon juice. Spread over piecrust on cookie sheet, leaving about a ½-inch border. Top with remaining piecrust. Seal edges of piecrusts by pressing with the tines of a fork, or pinch and flute the edges. Prick top piecrust all over with a fork. In a small bowl stir together the remaining 1 tablespoon honey and water. Brush mixture over top piecrust. Sprinkle lightly with cinnamon-sugar.

Baklava

3. Bake about 25 minutes or until golden. Cool on cookie sheet on a wire rack for 10 minutes. Cut into 16 wedges. Cool completely.

***Note:** If you can't find cinnamon-sugar in your supermarket, in a small bowl stir together 1 tablespoon sugar and ½ teaspoon ground cinnamon.

To store: Place baklava pieces in layers separated by waxed paper in an airtight container; cover. Store in the refrigerator for up to 3 days or freeze for up to 3 months.

Per serving: 198 cal., 12 g total fat (3 g sat. fat), 5 mg chol., 109 mg sodium, 22 g carbo., 1 g fiber, 2 g pro.
Daily Values: 1% vit. C, 1% calcium, 2% iron

Baklava

Be sure to keep phyllo dough covered with plastic wrap while working to keep it from drying out.

Prep: 50 minutes **Bake:** 40 minutes
Cook: 30 minutes **Oven:** 325°F **Makes:** 35 servings

- 1¼ **cups sugar**
- 1 **cup water**
- 2 **to 3 inches stick cinnamon**
- ½ **teaspoon finely shredded lemon peel**
- ½ **cup honey**
- 2 **tablespoons brandy (or 1 tablespoon brandy and 1 tablespoon rum) (optional)**
- 1 **tablespoon fresh lemon juice**
- 16 **ounces walnuts, very finely ground (3 cups)**
- ½ **cup sugar**
- 2 **tablespoons ground cinnamon**
- ½ **teaspoon ground nutmeg**
- 1½ **cups unsalted butter, melted**
- 1 **16-ounce package frozen phyllo dough (14x9-inch sheets), thawed**

1. For syrup, in a medium saucepan stir together 1¼ cups sugar, water, cinnamon stick, and lemon peel. Bring to boiling; reduce heat. Simmer, uncovered, over medium heat for 30 minutes, stirring occasionally. Remove from heat. Stir in honey, brandy (if desired), and lemon juice. Strain syrup to remove lemon peel and cinnamon. Let syrup cool to room temperature (do not refrigerate).

2. Preheat oven to 325°F. For filling, in a large bowl stir together walnuts, ½ cup sugar, ground cinnamon, and nutmeg; set aside.

3. Brush the bottom of a 3-quart baking dish with some of the melted butter. Unfold phyllo dough. With kitchen shears or a knife cut through the entire stack of phyllo dough sheets at one time to make a 13×9-inch rectangle. Discard extra pieces. Keep phyllo covered with plastic wrap, removing sheets as needed. One layer at a time, layer 10 phyllo sheets in the dish, generously brushing each sheet with melted butter. Sprinkle one-third (about 1⅓ cups) of the filling on the phyllo layers. Repeat layering the phyllo sheets and filling twice. Layer remaining phyllo sheets on the third layer of filling, brushing each sheet with butter before layering the next sheet. Drizzle any remaining butter on the top layer.

4. Using a sharp knife, make four straight cuts through all the layers the length of the dish to make five rows. Then make eight diagonal cuts through all layers, making diamonds. (Do not remove the pieces from dish.) Bake for 40 to 50 minutes or until golden. Slightly cool in baking dish on a wire rack. Spoon syrup over hot baklava. Cool completely or let stand overnight at room temperature before serving.

To store: Place baklava pieces in layers separated by waxed paper in an airtight container; cover. Store in the refrigerator for up to 3 days or freeze for up to 3 months. Thaw in refrigerator.

Per serving: 294 cal., 20 g total fat (7 g sat. fat), 26 mg chol., 75 mg sodium, 26 g carbo., 1 g fiber, 3 g pro.
Daily Values: 7% vit. A, 1% vit. C, 3% calcium, 6% iron

Biscotti

This recipe can easily be varied. Substitute orange peel for the lemon peel and chopped pecans for the almonds for another version of this delicious, perfect-with-coffee cookie.

Prep: 20 minutes **Bake:** 38 minutes **Cool:** 1 hour
Oven: 375°/325°F **Makes:** about 40 biscotti

- ⅔ cup sugar
- 2 tablespoons finely shredded lemon peel
- 2 eggs
- ½ cup cooking oil
- 1½ teaspoons vanilla
- 2 cups sliced almonds
- 1¾ cups all-purpose flour
- 1 teaspoon baking powder
- ¼ teaspoon baking soda
- ¼ teaspoon salt
  All-purpose flour (optional)

1. Preheat oven to 375°F. Line cookie sheets with parchment paper; set aside.

2. In a food processor or medium mixing bowl combine sugar and lemon peel; add eggs. Process or beat with an electric mixer about 30 seconds. Slowly add oil and vanilla and process or beat until combined. Add 1⅔ cups of the sliced almonds and mix until chopped.

3. In a medium bowl combine flour, baking powder, baking soda, and salt; gradually add flour mixture to the almond mixture, processing or beating just until combined. With a wooden spoon, stir in remaining ⅓ cup almonds and up to ¼ cup more flour, if needed, to form a soft dough. Divide dough in half; shape each half into a 12-inch roll. Place the rolls on prepared cookie sheets.

4. Bake for 20 to 25 minutes or until light brown and a wooden toothpick inserted near center comes out clean (rolls will spread slightly). Cool on cookie sheet for 1 hour. (If desired, wrap cooled rolls in plastic wrap and let stand overnight at room temperature.)

5. Reduce oven temperature to 325°F. Transfer rolls to a cutting board. Use a serrated knife to diagonally cut each roll into ½-inch slices. Place slices, cut sides down, on lightly buttered cookie sheets. Bake for 10 minutes. Turn slices over and bake for 8 to 10 minutes more or until dry and crisp (do not overbake). Transfer to a wire rack; let cool.

To store: Place biscotti in layers separated by waxed paper in an airtight container; cover. Store at room temperature for up to 3 days or freeze for up to 3 months.

Per biscotti: 98 cal., 6 g total fat (0 g sat. fat), 10 mg chol., 35 mg sodium, 8 g carbo., 1 g fiber, 2 g pro.
Daily Values: 1% vit. C, 3% calcium, 3% iron

Mocha-Hazelnut Biscotti

Melted chocolate chips in a dough accented with golden cappuccino chips make these biscotti perfect holiday coffee dippers.

Prep: 25 minutes **Bake:** 1 hour **Cool:** 1 hour
Oven: 350°/300°F **Makes:** about 36 biscotti

- 2¾ cups all-purpose flour
- 2½ teaspoons baking powder
- ½ teaspoon salt
- ⅔ cup butter, softened
- 1 cup sugar
- 2 cups bittersweet or semisweet chocolate pieces, melted and cooled
- 3 eggs
- 1 teaspoon vanilla
- ¾ cup cappuccino-flavored baking pieces or milk chocolate pieces
- ½ cup finely chopped toasted hazelnuts (filberts) (see tip, page 63)
- 1 recipe Chocolate and Cappuccino Glazes

1. Preheat oven to 350°F. Grease a large cookie sheet; set aside. In a medium bowl combine flour, baking powder, and salt; set aside. In a large mixing bowl beat butter with an electric mixer on medium to high speed for 30 seconds. Add sugar; beat until combined, scraping sides of bowl occasionally. Beat in melted chocolate, eggs, and vanilla until combined. Beat in as much of the flour mixture as possible with the mixer. Stir in any remaining flour mixture with a wooden spoon. Stir in cappuccino baking pieces and hazelnuts. (Dough will be soft.)

2. With lightly floured hands shape dough into two 9×3-inch loaves. Place loaves 4 inches apart on prepared cookie sheet; flatten slightly. Bake for 30 minutes or until a wooden toothpick inserted near center comes out clean. Cool loaves on cookie sheet for 1 hour.

3. Reduce oven temperature to 300°F. Transfer loaves to a cutting board. Cut each loaf into ½-inch slices. Carefully place slices, cut sides down, on the cookie sheet. Bake for 15 minutes; gently turn slices over and bake 15 minutes more or until dry and crisp. Transfer biscotti to a wire rack; let cool. Drizzle Chocolate and Cappuccino Glazes over cooled biscotti. Let set before serving or storing.

Chocolate and Cappuccino Glazes: In saucepan combine ½ cup bittersweet or semisweet chocolate pieces and 2 teaspoons shortening. Stir over low heat until melted and smooth. Set aside. Repeat with ½ cup cappuccino-flavored baking pieces or milk chocolate pieces and 2 teaspoons shortening.

To store: Place biscotti in layers separated by waxed paper in an airtight container; cover. Store at room temperature for up to 1 week or freeze undrizzled cookies for up to 3 months. Thaw cookies; drizzle glazes over top.

Per biscotti: 206 cal., 12 g total fat (6 g sat. fat), 28 mg chol., 85 mg sodium, 24 g carbo., 1 g fiber, 3 g pro.
Daily Values: 3% vit. A, 3% calcium, 6% iron

Cranberry-Cashew Clusters

For another version of this simple treat, substitute macadamia nuts for the cashews and dried cherries for the cranberries.

Prep: 15 minutes **Stand:** 30 minutes
Makes: about 24 clusters

- 12 ounces vanilla-flavored candy coating, chopped
- ¾ cup dry roasted cashews, coarsely chopped
- ¾ cup dried cranberries

1. Line a cookie sheet with waxed paper; set aside. In a medium saucepan melt candy coating over low heat, stirring frequently. Remove from heat. Stir in nuts and cranberries.

2. Drop mixture from slightly rounded teaspoons onto prepared cookie sheets. Let stand for 30 to 60 minutes or until set.

To store: Place clusters in layers separated by waxed paper in an airtight container; cover. Store at room temperature for up to 1 week or freeze for up to 3 months.

Per cluster: 116 cal., 7 g total fat (4 g sat. fat), 0 mg chol., 1 mg sodium, 14 g carbo., 0 g fiber, 1 g pro.
Daily Values: 1% calcium, 2% iron

White Cranberry-Cashew Truffles

 **White Cranberry-Cashew Truffles**

Because the cashews will be ground anyway, save money by purchasing those labeled "pieces" rather than whole nuts.

Prep: 1 hour **Chill:** 3 hours plus 10 minutes
Freeze: 15 minutes **Makes:** about 60 truffles

- 1 cup lightly salted roasted cashews
- ½ cup dried cranberries
- 4 6-ounce packages white baking chocolate, chopped
- ½ cup whipping cream
- 1 tablespoon butter
- 2 tablespoons brandy or orange juice
- 2 tablespoons shortening
  Flaked coconut (optional)
  Snipped dried cranberries (optional)
  White baking chocolate, melted (optional)

1. For filling, in a food processor place cashews and ½ cup cranberries; cover and process until finely chopped. Remove to a medium bowl; set aside. In a food processor, place 12 ounces of the chopped white baking chocolate. Cover and process until finely chopped. In a small saucepan heat and stir whipping cream and butter over low heat until hot but not boiling. Remove from heat. With the food processor running, carefully pour hot cream mixture through the feed tube into chopped white chocolate. Process until smooth, scraping down bowl if necessary. Transfer white chocolate mixture to bowl with

the cranberry mixture. Add brandy; stir to combine. Cover; chill filling about 3 hours or until firm. Shape filling into ¾-inch balls; freeze for 15 minutes.

2. Meanwhile, for coating, in a 4-cup glass measuring cup combine the remaining 12 ounces white chocolate and the shortening. In a large glass bowl pour very warm tap water (100°F to 110°F) to a depth of 2 inches. Place measuring cup containing the white chocolate inside the large bowl. (Water should cover bottom half of the glass measuring cup.) Stir white chocolate constantly with a rubber spatula until chocolate is completely melted and smooth. (This takes about 20 minutes; don't rush. If water cools, remove glass measure. Discard cool water; add warm water. Return glass measure to bowl of water.)

3. Line a baking sheet with waxed paper. Use a fork to dip frozen balls into melted white chocolate, allowing excess chocolate to drip back into the measuring cup. If desired, sprinkle tops of truffles with coconut or snipped dried cranberries. If desired, drizzle with additional melted white chocolate. Chill for 10 minutes or until set.

To store: Place truffles in layers separated by waxed paper in an airtight container; cover. Store in refrigerator for up to 2 weeks. Freeze for up to 3 months.

Per truffle: 95 cal., 6 g total fat (3 g sat. fat), 5 mg chol., 29 mg sodium, 8 g carbo., 0 g fiber, 1 g pro.
Daily Values: 1% vit. A, 2% calcium, 1% iron

Peanut Butter Cup Fudge

Easy Bittersweet Chocolate-Orange Fudge

Orange and chocolate are a tasty flavor match and this recipe shows off the duo at its best.

Prep: 15 minutes **Chill:** 2 hours
Makes: about 2 pounds (64 pieces)

    Butter
16 ounces bittersweet chocolate, chopped
 1 14-ounce can sweetened condensed milk
 2 tablespoons orange liqueur or orange juice
 1 teaspoon vanilla
 1 cup chopped pecans or almonds, toasted
    (see tip, page 63)

1. Line a 9×9×2-inch baking pan with foil, extending foil over edges. Butter foil; set pan aside.

2. In a large saucepan heat and stir the chocolate and sweetened condensed milk over low heat until chocolate is melted and mixture is smooth. Remove from heat. Stir in orange liqueur and vanilla until combined. Stir in nuts. Spread mixture into prepared pan. Cover and chill for 2 hours or until firm. Use foil to lift candy from pan. Transfer to a cutting board. Cut into squares.

To store: Place candy in an airtight container; cover. Store in the refrigerator for up to 2 weeks or freeze for up to 3 months.

Per piece: 69 cal., 5 g total fat (2 g sat. fat), 3 mg chol., 10 mg sodium, 8 g carbo., 1 g fiber, 1 g pro.
Daily Values: 1% vit. A, 2% calcium, 2% iron

Peanut Butter Cup Fudge

This candy is a guaranteed hit of the party.

Prep: 45 minutes **Chill:** 5 hours
Makes: about 4½ pounds (96 pieces)

    Butter
 4 cups sugar
 2 5-ounce cans evaporated milk
    (1⅔ cups total)
 1 cup butter
 1 10-ounce package peanut butter-flavored
    pieces (1¾ cups)
 1 7-ounce jar marshmallow creme
 1 cup finely chopped peanuts
 1 teaspoon vanilla
 ⅔ cup whipping cream
 6 ounces semisweet chocolate, chopped
24 miniature peanut butter cups, quartered*

1. Line a 13×9×2-inch baking pan with foil, extending foil over edges. Butter foil; set aside.

2. Butter sides of a heavy 3-quart saucepan. Add sugar, evaporated milk, and 1 cup butter. Cook over medium-high heat until boiling (bubbly over entire surface), stirring to dissolve sugar. Reduce heat to medium and boil, uncovered, for 10 minutes.

3. Remove saucepan from heat. Add peanut butter pieces, marshmallow creme, peanuts, and vanilla; stir until peanut butter pieces are melted. Spread into prepared pan; set aside until surface is set.

4. For chocolate layer, in a small saucepan heat cream over low heat just until tiny bubbles appear around edge of pan. Remove from heat. Add chocolate; let stand for 5 minutes. Stir until smooth. Pour chocolate over peanut butter layer, spreading to cover completely. Chill until almost firm, about 1 hour.

5. Score fudge into squares. Place a peanut butter cup quarter on each piece. Chill until very firm, about 4 hours. Use foil to lift candy from pan. Place on a cutting board. Cut into pieces. Store in the refrigerator. If desired, serve in candy wrappers.

*Note: When cutting peanut butter cups, place the cup, top side down, on a cutting board. Using a serrated knife, cut each cup into quarters.

To store: Place candy in an airtight container; cover. Store in the refrigerator for up to 2 weeks or freeze for up to 3 months.

Per piece: 111 cal., 6 g total fat (3 g sat. fat), 9 mg chol., 34 mg sodium, 14 g carbo., 0 g fiber, 1 g pro.
Daily Values: 2% vit. A, 1% calcium, 1% iron

Dessert Dazzlers

When dinner is over, everyone looks forward to that sweet piece of pie, cake, or other decadently divine dessert. Use the flavors of the season to enliven your desserts: maple, apple, ginger, pumpkin, pear, cranberry, or orange. Definitely remember chocolate—everyone's year-round favorite. A dessert party is a fun-filled and delicious way to celebrate the season. Whip up a variety of desserts and cut them into small portions so guests can sample some of everything. Offer a varied selection from rich and decadent to light yet oh-so-satisfying. How about a table filled with Cranberry Chocolate Layer Cake with Chocolate Buttercream and White Russian Cake next to Apple-Candied Ginger Pie and Miniature Fruit Tarts? Brew some coffee, pour some sparkling wine, and everyone will make an appearance at this sweet soirée.

Double Chocolate Mascarpone Raspberry Pie, page 96

Easy Apple Pie

Simple to make, this pie is perfect for young bakers to assist in preparation.

Prep: 35 minutes **Bake:** 65 minutes
Oven: 375°F **Makes:** 8 servings

    1 recipe No-Roll Piecrust
    ½ cup sugar
    2 tablespoons all-purpose flour
    1 teaspoon ground cinnamon
    6 cups peeled and sliced apples
       Sugar

1. Preheat oven to 375°F. Prepare No-Roll Piecrust; set aside. In a very large bowl stir together ½ cup sugar, flour, and cinnamon. Add apples. Stir to combine.

2. Transfer apple mixture to prepared piecrust. Top with dough circles. Sprinkle with additional sugar. Place a baking sheet on the oven rack; place pie plate on baking sheet.

3. Bake for 65 minutes or until filling is bubbly in the center. If necessary, cover top of pie with foil the last 10 to 15 minutes of baking to prevent over-browning. Remove pie from oven and remove foil. Cool completely on wire rack before serving.

No-Roll Piecrust: In a bowl stir together 2½ cups all-purpose flour, 2 tablespoons sugar, and ½ teaspoon salt. In a small bowl stir together ½ cup cooking oil and ⅓ cup milk; add all at once to flour mixture. Stir with a fork until mixture comes together. With floured hands form into a ball. Divide into three equal balls. Using your hands, firmly press two of the dough balls onto bottom and up the sides of a 9-inch pie plate. Continue pressing to form an edge at the rim of the pie plate; set aside. Divide remaining dough portion into six equal parts. On waxed paper, pat each dough portion into a 3-inch circle; set aside.

Per serving: 368 cal., 14 g total fat (2 g sat. fat), 1 mg chol.,
152 mg sodium, 57 g carbo., 3 g fiber, 4 g pro.
Daily Values: 1% vit. A, 5% vit. C, 3% calcium, 11% iron

 **Apple-Candied Ginger Pie**

Ginger makes its way into this company-special pie in two versions: crystallized ginger in the filling and gingersnaps in the topping. For a twist, serve with cinnamon ice cream.

Prep: 40 minutes **Bake:** 60 minutes
Oven: 375°F **Makes:** 10 servings

    1 recipe Pastry for Single-Crust Pie
    1 recipe Coconut-Almond Crumb Topping
    ¾ cup sugar
    3 tablespoons all-purpose flour
    2 tablespoons finely chopped
       crystallized ginger
    1 teaspoon ground cinnamon or
       apple pie spice
    6 cups sliced, peeled, tart cooking apples,
       such as Granny Smith (6 apples)
       Vanilla ice cream

1. Preheat oven to 375°F. Prepare and roll out Pastry for Single-Crust Pie; set aside. Prepare the Coconut-Almond Crumb Topping; set aside.

2. For filling, in a very large bowl stir together sugar, flour, ginger, and cinnamon. Add apples; gently toss until apples are coated with sugar mixture. Transfer apple mixture to pastry-lined pie plate. Sprinkle evenly with Coconut-Almond Crumb Topping, pressing down as necessary. Cover entire pie surface loosely with foil.

3. Place pie on the middle rack of oven. Place a baking sheet on the rack below the pie plate to catch any juices that bubble over. Bake for 40 minutes. Remove foil. Bake for 20 to 30 minutes more or until fruit is tender and filling is bubbly. Cool on wire rack for at least 2 hours before serving. Serve with scoops of vanilla ice cream.

Pastry for Single-Crust Pie: In a medium bowl stir together 1¼ cups all-purpose flour and ¼ teaspoon salt. Using a pastry blender, cut in ⅓ cup shortening until pieces are pea size. Sprinkle 1 tablespoon cold water over part of the flour mixture; gently toss with a fork. Push moistened dough to side of bowl. Repeat moistening flour mixture, using 1 tablespoon water at a time, until flour mixture is moistened (4 to 5 tablespoons total water). Form dough into

Apple-Candied Ginger Pie

a ball. On a lightly floured surface, use your hands to slightly flatten dough. Roll dough from center to edges into a circle about 13 inches in diameter. Ease pastry into a 10-inch pie plate. Trim pastry to ½ inch beyond edge of pie plate. Fold under extra pastry. Crimp edge. Do not prick pastry.

Coconut-Almond Crumb Topping: In a small bowl combine ⅓ cup finely crushed gingersnaps, ⅓ cup finely crushed vanilla wafers (or ⅔ cup of either finely crushed gingersnaps or vanilla wafers), ½ cup chopped almonds or pecans, ⅓ cup flaked coconut, and 3 tablespoons butter or margarine, melted. Toss until coated.

Per serving: 338 cal., 17 g total fat (6 g sat. fat), 10 mg chol., 137 mg sodium, 46 g carbo., 4 g fiber, 4 g pro.
Daily Values: 3% vit. A, 6% vit. C, 3% calcium, 9% iron

Apples for Baking

An apple is just an apple, right? Not true when it comes to baking. Texture and ability to hold flavor determine which apples are most delicious eaten out of hand and which are best for baking. The most delicious apple pie is made with a combination of both sweet and tart apples. Some of the best cooking apples are:

Sweet varieties:	Tart varieties:
Jonagold	Granny Smith
Golden Delicious	Jonathon
Braeburn	Cortland
Fuji	Winesap
Ida Red	

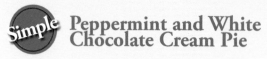 ## Peppermint and White Chocolate Cream Pie

This lovely, easy-to-prepare pie has the perfect combination of chocolate and mint flavors.

Prep: 40 minutes **Chill:** 15 minutes plus 8 hours
Makes: 8 servings

- 1⅓ cups crushed chocolate wafer cookies (about 28 wafers)
- ¼ cup butter, melted
- ½ cup chopped layered chocolate-mint candies
- 1 4-serving size package white chocolate instant pudding and pie filling mix
- 1½ cups milk
- 1 cup whipping cream
- 2 tablespoons powdered sugar
- ¼ teaspoon peppermint extract

1. In a medium bowl combine cookie crumbs and melted butter tossing to mix well. Stir in 3 tablespoons of the chopped chocolate-mint candies. Transfer crumb mixture to a well-greased 9-inch pie plate. Press onto bottom and sides to form a firm, even crust. Cover and chill at least 15 minutes.

2. Meanwhile, prepare pudding mix according to package directions for traditional pudding pie, using the 1½ cups milk. Spread filling into chilled crust. Cover and chill for 8 to 24 hours.

3. Before serving, in a chilled mixing bowl combine cream, powdered sugar, and peppermint extract. Beat with chilled beaters of an electric mixer on medium speed until stiff peaks form. Pipe or spoon whipped cream in dollops on top of pie. Sprinkle with remaining chocolate-mint candies.

Per serving: 377 cal., 24 g total fat (15 g sat. fat), 60 mg chol., 376 mg sodium, 38 g carbo., 1 g fiber, 4 g pro.
Daily Values: 14% vit. A, 1% vit. C, 10% calcium, 5% iron

 ## Double Chocolate-Mascarpone Raspberry Pie

Be sure to cool the melted jam so that the berries will not wilt when spreading the topping over them.

Prep: 45 minutes **Bake:** 13 minutes **Chill:** 3 hours
Oven: 450°F **Makes:** 10 servings

- 1 recipe Pastry for Single-Crust Pie (page 94) or ½ of a 15-ounce package rolled refrigerated unbaked piecrust (1 crust)
- 6 ounces bittersweet chocolate, chopped
- 1 8-ounce carton mascarpone cheese
- ½ cup powdered sugar
- 2 tablespoons raspberry liqueur
- 1 cup whipping cream
- 1½ cups fresh red raspberries
- ⅓ cup seedless red raspberry jam, melted and cooled slightly
- 1 recipe White Chocolate Topping
  Fresh red raspberries (optional)
  Bittersweet and/or white chocolate shavings or curls (optional)

1. Preheat oven to 450°F. Prepare Pastry for Single-Crust Pie. On a lightly floured surface, roll dough from center to edges into a circle about 12 inches in diameter. (Or let refrigerated piecrust stand according to package directions.) Ease pastry into a 9-inch pie plate. Trim pastry to ½ inch beyond edge of pie plate. Fold under extra pastry. Crimp edge. Prick bottom and sides of pastry with a fork. Line with a double thickness of foil. Bake for 8 minutes. Remove foil. Bake for 5 to 6 minutes more or until golden. Cool piecrust on a wire rack.

2. For filling, in a medium saucepan combine bittersweet chocolate, mascarpone cheese, and powdered sugar. Cook and stir over medium-low heat until chocolate is melted and mixture is smooth. Remove from heat. Stir in liqueur. Set filling aside to cool to room temperature.

3. In a medium chilled mixing bowl beat whipping cream with an electric mixer on medium speed until soft peaks form. Stir about ½ cup of the whipped cream into the cooled filling to lighten the mixture. Fold in remaining whipped cream just until combined.

4. Carefully spoon bittersweet chocolate mixture into baked piecrust, spreading evenly. Cover and chill for 3 to 24 hours or until set.

5. Just before serving, add 1½ cups raspberries to melted jam and toss gently to coat. Spoon raspberry mixture over bittersweet chocolate mixture. Spoon White Chocolate Topping into a pastry bag fitted with a large star tip. Pipe topping in small mounds or a swirled border around pie edge. If desired, garnish with additional fresh raspberries and chocolate shavings.

White Chocolate Topping: In a heavy small saucepan heat and stir 2 ounces chopped white baking chocolate with ¼ cup whipping cream until chocolate is melted and mixture is smooth; cool. In a chilled medium mixing bowl beat ⅔ cup whipping cream with an electric mixer on medium speed until mixture mounds but does not form peaks; turn off mixer. Add white chocolate mixture. Beat on low speed just until stiff peaks form (tips stand straight). Watch carefully so you don't overbeat mixture.

Per serving: 559 cal., 42 g total fat (23 g sat. fat), 93 mg chol., 100 mg sodium, 44 g carbo., 3 g fiber, 9 g pro.
Daily Values: 14% vit. A, 11% vit. C, 6% calcium, 9% iron

Double Chocolate-Mascarpone Raspberry Pie

Pumpkin Gingerbread Pie

Simple

To make your own pumpkin pie spice, in a small bowl combine ½ teaspoon cinnamon, ¼ teaspoon ground ginger, ¼ teaspoon ground allspice, and ⅛ teaspoon ground nutmeg.

Prep: 25 minutes **Bake:** 50 minutes
Oven: 350°F **Makes:** 8 servings

　　Nonstick cooking spray
　1　cup canned pumpkin
　⅓　cup sugar
　1　teaspoon pumpkin pie spice
　1　egg, lightly beaten
　½　cup half-and-half or light cream
　1　14½-ounce package gingerbread mix
　　Whipped cream (optional)

1. Preheat oven to 350°F. Coat a 10-inch deep-dish pie plate or an 8×8×2-inch baking dish with cooking spray; set aside. In a small bowl stir together pumpkin, sugar, and pumpkin pie spice. Add egg; beat lightly with a rotary beater or fork just until combined. Gradually add half-and-half, stirring until combined.

2. Prepare gingerbread mix according to package directions. Pour batter into prepared pie plate or dish. Lightly spoon pumpkin mixture over gingerbread batter; swirl gently using a table knife.

3. Bake for 50 minutes for pie plate or 60 minutes for baking dish or until a wooden toothpick inserted in gingerbread portion comes out clean. Cool slightly on a wire rack. Serve warm or at room temperature. If desired, serve with whipped cream.

Per serving: 304 cal., 10 g total fat (3 g sat. fat), 58 mg chol., 364 mg sodium, 50 g carbo., 2 g fiber, 5 g pro.
Daily Values: 98% vit. A, 3% vit. C, 8% calcium, 17% iron

Toffee-Almond Crunch Pumpkin Pie

2. For filling, in a large bowl stir together pumpkin, granulated sugar, 1 teaspoon cinnamon, salt, ginger, nutmeg, and cloves. Add eggs; beat lightly with a wooden spoon just until combined. Gradually add half-and-half, stirring until combined.

3. Carefully pour filling in pastry shell. To prevent overbrowning, cover edge of pie crust with foil. Bake for 30 minutes. Remove foil. Bake for 15 minutes more. Sprinkle Toffee-Almond Crunch evenly over pie. Bake 15 to 20 minutes more or until pie is set and topping is golden. Cool on wire rack. Cover and refrigerate within 2 hours. If desired, top each serving with Sweetened Whipped Cream. If desired, sprinkle with cinnamon.

Toasted Almond Pastry: In a medium bowl stir together 1¼ cups all-purpose flour, ¼ cup ground toasted almonds (see tip, page 63), and ¼ teaspoon salt. Using a pastry blender, cut in ⅓ cup shortening until pieces are pea size. Sprinkle 1 tablespoon cold water over part of the flour mixture; gently toss with a fork. Push moistened dough to side of bowl. Repeat moistening flour mixture, using 1 tablespoon of cold water at a time (4 to 5 tablespoons water total), until flour mixture is moistened. Form dough into a ball. On a lightly floured surface, use hands to slightly flatten dough. Roll dough from center to edges into a circle about 12 inches in diameter. Ease pastry into a 9-inch pie plate. Trim pastry to 1 inch beyond edge of pie plate. Fold under extra pastry. Crimp and form a high edge to keep filling from bubbling over. Do not prick pastry.

Toffee-Almond Crunch: In a small bowl stir together 3 tablespoons all-purpose flour and 3 tablespoons packed brown sugar. Stir in 2 tablespoons softened butter. Stir in ¾ cup coarsely chopped sliced almonds and ½ cup toffee pieces.

Per serving: 505 cal., 28 g total fat (10 g sat. fat), 111 mg chol., 346 mg sodium, 57 g carbo., 4 g fiber, 9 g pro.
Daily Values: 172% vit. A, 5% vit. C, 11% calcium, 17% iron

Sweetened Whipped Cream: Combine 1 cup whipping cream, 2 tablespoons granulated sugar, and ½ teaspoon vanilla. Beat with an electric mixer on medium speed until soft peaks form.

Sensational Toffee-Almond Crunch Pumpkin Pie

Pumpkin pie is tops for the holiday table, but why not give it an extra punch of flavor? Try this decadent Toffee-Almond Crunch topping—it gives a wonderful texture to this twist on traditional pumpkin pie.

Prep: 45 minutes **Bake:** 1 hour
Oven: 375° F **Makes:** 8 servings

1	recipe Toasted Almond Pastry
1	15-ounce can pumpkin
¾	cup granulated sugar
1	teaspoon ground cinnamon
½	teaspoon salt
½	teaspoon ground ginger
½	teaspoon ground nutmeg
¼	teaspoon ground cloves
3	eggs, lightly beaten
1¼	cups half-and-half or light cream
1	recipe Toffee-Almond Crunch
	Sweetened Whipped Cream (optional)
	Ground cinnamon (optional)

1. Preheat oven to 375°F. Prepare and roll out Toasted Almond Pastry.

Apple-Walnut Cake

Starting with a cake mix makes this delicious dessert supersimple to whip up. Thanks to the addition of apple, brandy, and walnuts, everyone will think you made it from scratch.

Prep: 30 minutes **Bake:** according to package directions **Makes:** 12 servings

- 1 package 2-layer-size spice cake mix
- 1 cup finely chopped, peeled apples
- 2 tablespoons apple brandy (such as Calvados) or apple juice
- ¾ cup chopped black walnuts
- 1 16-ounce can vanilla frosting
  Apple slices and/or chopped black walnuts (optional)

1. Prepare cake mix according to package directions, except stir finely chopped apples, brandy, and black walnuts into batter. Use desired pan size. Cool completely on wire rack.

2. Spread cake with vanilla frosting. Just before serving, if desired, garnish with apple slices and/or black walnuts.

Per serving: 411 cal., 17 g total fat (5 g sat. fat), 0 mg chol., 372 mg sodium, 60 g carbo., 1 g fiber, 3 g pro.
Daily Values: 1% vit. C, 9% calcium, 5% iron

 ## Chipotle Apple Pecan Cake

Chipotle chile pepper in a cake? You bet! One teaspoon of chipotle powder teams with cinnamon, nutmeg, and ginger to create an intriguingly delicious dessert.

Prep: 40 minutes **Bake:** 1¼ hours
Oven: 325°F **Makes:** 16 servings

    Nonstick cooking spray
    Flour
- 3 cups all-purpose flour
- 2 teaspoons ground cinnamon
- 1½ teaspoons ground nutmeg
- 1 teaspoon baking soda
- 1 teaspoon ground chipotle chile pepper
- ¾ teaspoon ground ginger
- ½ teaspoon ground white pepper
- ¼ teaspoon salt
- ⅛ teaspoon ground cloves
- 1½ cups cooking oil
- 1¾ cups sugar
- 3 eggs
- 1 tablespoon vanilla
- 3 large (1¼ pounds) sweet-tart apples peeled, cored, and diced (3 cups)
- 1 cup chopped pecans, toasted (see tip, page 63)
- 1 recipe Spicy Caramel Glaze

1. Preheat oven to 325°F. Lightly coat a 10-inch fluted tube pan with cooking spray. Lightly sprinkle with flour; set aside. In a bowl combine 3 cups flour, cinnamon, nutmeg, baking soda, chipotle pepper, ginger, white pepper, salt, and cloves; set aside.

2. In a mixing bowl beat oil and sugar with an electric mixer on medium speed until combined. Add eggs, one at a time; beat well after each addition. Beat in vanilla and as much flour mixture as possible with the mixer. Stir in remaining flour mixture, apples, and pecans. Spoon batter into prepared pan.

3. Bake for 1¼ hours until a wooden toothpick inserted near center comes out clean. Meanwhile, prepare Spicy Caramel Glaze. Cool cake in pan 10 minutes; invert on rack. Place rack over baking sheet. Drizzle warm cake with Spicy Caramel Glaze, respooning glaze that drips on baking sheet over cake. Cool completely before serving.

Spicy Caramel Glaze: In a saucepan combine ½ cup packed brown sugar, ¼ cup butter, ¼ cup whipping cream, and ½ teaspoon ground chipotle chile pepper. Bring to boiling, stirring occasionally. Boil gently 2 minutes. Remove from heat. Stir in 1 teaspoon vanilla. Let stand for 1¼ hours until slightly thickened. Drizzle glaze over warm cake.

Per serving: 490 cal., 31 g total fat (7 g sat. fat), 53 mg chol., 165 mg sodium, 50 g carbo., 2 g fiber, 4 g pro.
Daily Values: 7% vit. A, 3% vit. C, 3% calcium, 9% iron

Snow Angel Cake

This luscious dessert—angel food cake topped with whipped dessert topping and coconut—provides an energy boost after a long day of sledding or shopping. Serve it along with a small mug of spiced cider.

Start to Finish: 20 minutes **Makes:** 12 servings

- 1 8- to 9-inch purchased angel food cake
- ¼ cup lemon curd
- ¼ cup seedless raspberry jam
- 1 8-ounce container frozen light whipped
      dessert topping, thawed

- ¼ cup flaked coconut
      Fresh raspberries
      Powdered sugar

1. Split cake in half horizontally. Place bottom half of cake on a serving plate. In a small bowl combine lemon curd and raspberry jam. Spread jam mixture on bottom half of cake. Add top half of cake. Spread top and sides of cake with whipped topping. Sprinkle with coconut. Garnish with fresh raspberries. Sprinkle top of cake with powdered sugar.

Per serving: 157 cal., 3 g total fat (3 g sat. fat), 5 mg chol., 188 mg sodium, 30 g carbo., 2 g fiber, 2 g pro.
Daily Values: 4% vit. C, 4% calcium, 1% iron

Snow Angel Cake

Orange-Blueberry Angel Food Cake

Flecked with blueberries and orange peel, this feather-light cake is capped with a drizzle of orange glaze. Now that's a little bit of heaven!

Prep: 20 minutes **Bake:** 40 minutes
Stand: 30 minutes **Oven:** 350°F
Makes: 12 servings

1½ cups egg whites (10 to 12 large)
1½ cups powdered sugar
1 cup sifted cake flour or
     sifted all-purpose flour
1½ teaspoons cream of tartar
1 teaspoon vanilla
1 cup granulated sugar
1½ cups freeze-dried blueberries*
1 tablespoon finely shredded orange peel
1 cup powdered sugar
3 to 5 teaspoons frozen orange juice
     concentrate, thawed

1. In a very large mixing bowl allow egg whites to stand at room temperature for 30 minutes. Meanwhile, sift 1½ cups powdered sugar and flour together three times; set aside.

2. Preheat oven to 350°F. Add cream of tartar and vanilla to egg whites. Beat with an electric mixer on medium speed until soft peaks form (tips curl). Add granulated sugar, about 2 tablespoons at a time, beating until stiff peaks form (tips stand straight).

3. Sift one-fourth of the powdered sugar mixture over beaten egg whites; fold in gently. Repeat, folding in remaining powdered sugar mixture by fourths. Gently fold in freeze-dried blueberries and orange peel. Pour into an ungreased 10-inch tube pan. Gently cut through batter to remove air pockets.

4. Bake cake on the lowest oven rack for 40 to 45 minutes or until top springs back when lightly touched. Immediately invert cake in pan; cool completely in pan. Loosen cake from pan; remove cake.

5. In a small bowl combine 1 cup powdered sugar and 3 teaspoons of the orange juice concentrate. Stir in enough of the remaining orange juice concentrate, 1 teaspoon at a time, to reach a drizzling consistency. Drizzle over cooled cake.

*Note: Look for freeze-dried blueberries in the produce section of the supermarket. Do not substitute dried blueberries.

Per serving: 208 cal., 0 g total fat (0 g sat. fat), 0 mg chol., 48 mg sodium, 48 g carbo., 0 g fiber, 4 g pro.
Daily Values: 6% vit. C, 4% iron

Cranberry Cake

Fresh cranberries and chopped pecans add festive touches to this perfect holiday cake. If desired, serve with ample spoonfuls of whipped cream.

Prep: 20 minutes **Bake:** 40 minutes
Cool: 30 minutes **Oven:** 350°F
Makes: 12 servings

3 cups fresh cranberries
1 cup chopped pecans
2 cups sugar
2 eggs
1 cup all-purpose flour
½ cup butter, melted
2 tablespoons milk
   Sweetened Whipped Cream (see recipe,
     page 98) (optional)

1. Preheat oven to 350°F. Generously grease a 2-quart rectangular baking dish. Spread cranberries and pecans over bottom of the dish. Sprinkle with 1 cup of the sugar.

2. In a medium mixing bowl beat eggs with an electric mixer on high speed until foamy. Add remaining 1 cup sugar, flour, melted butter, and milk; beat on low speed just until combined (batter will be thick). Carefully spread batter over cranberries and nuts.

3. Bake for 40 to 45 minutes or until top is brown and a wooden toothpick inserted near the center comes out clean. Cool on wire rack at least 30 minutes. To serve, spoon warm cake into dessert dishes, cranberry side up. If desired, top with Sweetened Whipped Cream.

Per serving: 319 cal., 16 g total fat (5 g sat. fat), 57 mg chol., 71 mg sodium, 44 g carbo., 2 g fiber, 3 g pro.
Daily Values: 6% vit. A, 6% vit. C, 2% calcium, 5% iron

Cranberry Chocolate Layer Cake

 **Cranberry Chocolate Layer Cake**

Cake flour differs from all-purpose flour in that cake flour has a higher starch content resulting in incredibly tender cakes. Find it near the all-purpose flour in the supermarket.

Prep: 25 minutes **Bake:** 30 minutes
Oven: 350°F **Makes:** 12 to 16 servings

　　Unsalted butter
　　Unsweetened cocoa powder
1¾ cups cake flour
1 cup unsweetened cocoa powder
2 teaspoons baking soda
½ teaspoon salt
½ cup unsalted butter, softened
2 cups sugar
2 teaspoons vanilla
2 eggs
1¾ cups buttermilk*
¼ cup strong brewed coffee
½ cup dried cranberries or coarsely
　　chopped dried tart cherries

½ cup cranberry jelly
1 recipe Chocolate Buttercream
　Sugared cranberries (optional)

1. Preheat oven to 350°F. Butter two 9-inch round baking pans. Add about 1 tablespoon cocoa powder to one pan. Tilt and roll the pan to evenly distribute cocoa; shake out excess cocoa into second baking pan. Repeat to coat bottom and sides of second pan with cocoa. Shake out any excess cocoa powder; set pans aside. In a medium bowl stir together flour, 1 cup cocoa powder, baking soda, and salt; set aside.

2. In a large mixing bowl beat ½ cup butter with an electric mixer on medium to high speed for 30 seconds. Add sugar and vanilla; beat until well combined. Add eggs, one at a time, beating well after each. In a small bowl stir together buttermilk and coffee. Add flour mixture and buttermilk mixture alternately to beaten mixture, beating on low speed after each addition just until combined. Fold in cranberries. Divide batter evenly between prepared pans.

3. Bake for 30 to 35 minutes or until a wooden toothpick inserted near the center comes out clean. Cool on wire racks for 10 minutes. Remove cakes from pans. Cool thoroughly on wire racks.

4. Place one cake layer on a serving plate. Using a thin metal spatula, spread jelly on the cake to within ½ inch of the edges. Top with a layer of Chocolate Buttercream (about ⅓ cup). Place second cake layer on top. Frost the top and sides with remaining Chocolate Buttercream. Chill in the refrigerator to firm buttercream. If desired, top wedges of cake with sugared cranberries.

Chocolate Buttercream: In a small saucepan melt 5 ounces semisweet chocolate and 1 ounce unsweetened chocolate over low heat, stirring occasionally. Remove from heat and cool. In a medium mixing bowl combine melted chocolates; ¼ cup sugar, if desired; ¼ cup refrigerated or frozen egg product, thawed; 1 to 2 tablespoons instant espresso coffee powder or instant coffee crystals; 1 tablespoon cognac, orange liqueur, Kirsch, or cherry brandy; and 1 teaspoon vanilla. Beat until smooth. Gradually add 1 cup unsalted butter that is room temperature and cut into 1-inch pieces, beating until mixture is fluffy and ingredients are well combined. Makes about 2½ cups frosting.

*Note: For a buttermilk substitution, mix 1¼ cups milk with ½ cup dairy sour cream and use in place of the 1¾ cups buttermilk.

Per serving: 603 cal., 31 g total fat (18 g sat. fat), 99 mg chol., 374 mg sodium, 76 g carbo., 2 g fiber, 8 g pro.
Daily Values: 17% vit. A, 1% vit. C, 14% calcium, 20% iron

White Russian Cake

Based on the famous cocktail, this cake gets its punch from the drink's main flavors: coffee, chocolate, and cream.

Prep: 20 minutes **Bake:** according to package directions **Makes:** 12 servings

1 **package 2-layer-size chocolate cake mix**
¼ **cup coffee liqueur**
¾ **of an 8-ounce container frozen whipped dessert topping, thawed**

2 **tablespoons coffee liqueur**
3 **ounces semisweet chocolate, melted and cooled**
 Chocolate-covered coffee beans (optional)

1. Prepare cake mix according to package directions, except replace ¼ cup of the water with ¼ cup coffee liqueur. Bake batter in two 8- or 9-inch round baking pans according to package directions. Remove from pans and cool completely on wire racks.

2. In a medium bowl fold together whipped dessert topping and 2 tablespoons liqueur. Spread one of the cake layers with half of the whipped topping mixture. Top with second cake layer. Spread with remaining whipped topping mixture. Drizzle with melted chocolate. If desired, garnish with chocolate-covered coffee beans.

Per serving: 359 cal., 16 g total fat (6 g sat. fat), 35 mg chol., 281 mg sodium, 47 g carbo., 1 g fiber, 4 g pro.
Daily Values: 2% calcium, 5% iron

White Russian Cake

One-Layer Chocolate Cake

Strong brewed coffee and bourbon combine to make this chocolate cake a masterpiece to remember.

Prep: 20 minutes **Bake:** 35 minutes
Stand: 10 minutes **Oven:** 325°F
Makes: 8 servings

- 2 ounces unsweetened chocolate, chopped
- 2 ounces bittersweet chocolate, chopped
- ¾ cup strong brewed coffee
- 6 tablespoons butter, cut up
- 2 tablespoons bourbon or
   strong brewed coffee
- 1 egg, lightly beaten
- ½ teaspoon vanilla
- 1 cup all-purpose flour
- 1 cup sugar
- ½ teaspoon baking soda
- ⅛ teaspoon salt
  Whipped cream
  Fresh red raspberries

1. Preheat oven to 325°F. Grease the bottom of a 9×1½-inch round baking pan. Line the bottom with waxed paper. Grease and flour the waxed paper; set aside.

2. In a medium saucepan heat unsweetened and bittersweet chocolates with coffee and butter over medium-low heat, stirring occasionally until chocolate is melted. Remove from heat and cool for 10 minutes. Using a wooden spoon beat in the bourbon, egg, and vanilla. Add flour, sugar, baking soda, and salt; mix well. Pour batter into prepared pan.

3. Bake for 35 minutes or until a wooden toothpick inserted near the center comes out clean. Cool cake in pan on a wire rack for 10 minutes. Remove from pan. Remove waxed paper. Cool thoroughly on wire rack. Invert cake onto a serving platter and garnish individual servings with whipped cream and raspberries.

Per serving: 382 cal., 21 g total fat (13 g sat. fat), 70 mg chol.,
194 mg sodium, 46 g carbo., 3 g fiber, 4 g pro.
Daily Values: 11% vit. A, 10% vit. C, 4% calcium, 14% iron

Crustless Cheesecake

To boost the flavor of this supersimple dessert favorite, add 1 teaspoon finely shredded lemon peel or 1 teaspoon vanilla to the cheesecake batter along with the eggs. If you like, skip the Cranberry Sauce and sugared cranberries and top the cake with cut-up fresh fruit.

Prep: 25 minutes **Bake:** 70 minutes **Cool:** 1 hour
Chill: overnight **Oven:** 275°F **Makes:** 10 servings

- 4 8-ounce packages cream cheese, softened
- 1 cup sugar
- 3 eggs
- 1 recipe Cranberry Sauce (optional)
  Sugared cranberries (optional)

1. Preheat oven to 275°F. Line the outside of an 8-inch springform pan with heavy foil. Grease the bottom and sides inside the pan; set aside.

2. In a very large mixing bowl beat cream cheese and sugar with a sturdy handheld or freestanding electric mixer on medium to high speed for 8 to 10 minutes, scraping twice, until mixture is smooth and sugar is dissolved. Stir in eggs just until combined. Pour batter into prepared pan. Place springform pan in a shallow roasting pan. Place roasting pan on the oven rack. Carefully pour enough hot water into the roasting pan to come halfway up the outer sides of springform pan. Bake for 70 to 75 minutes or until center appears nearly set when gently shaken.

3. Carefully remove springform pan from water and let cheesecake cool on a wire rack for 15 minutes. Run a thin metal spatula around the edge of the cheesecake to loosen from sides of pan. Cool for 45 minutes more. Cover and chill overnight. To serve, remove sides of the pan and cut into wedges. If desired, top with Cranberry Sauce and sugared cranberries.

Per serving: 417 cal., 33 g total fat (20 g sat. fat), 163 mg chol.,
290 mg sodium, 23 g carbo., 0 g fiber, 9 g pro.
Daily Values: 26% vit. A, 8% calcium, 8% iron

Cranberry Sauce: In a blender puree 1 cup of whole cranberry sauce. To serve, pour sauce over top of cheesecake or drizzle sauce over individual slices.

Sensational Eggnog Cheesecake

Eggnog Cheesecake

This scrumptious cheesecake makes any holiday occasion more festive. The crust contains cashews and the filling includes eggnog, rum (if you like), and nutmeg.

Prep: 25 minutes **Bake:** 40 minutes **Cool:** 2 hours
Chill: 6 hours **Oven:** 350°F **Makes:** 16 servings

- 1 cup ground cashews*
- 1 cup finely crushed graham crackers (14 squares)
- ½ cup sugar
- 2 tablespoons all-purpose flour
- ½ cup butter, melted
- 4 8-ounce packages cream cheese, softened
- 1 cup sugar
- 1 tablespoon rum (optional)
- 1 teaspoon vanilla
- ½ teaspoon ground nutmeg
- 3 eggs
- 1½ cups dairy or canned eggnog
  Purchased cashew brittle (optional)

1. Preheat oven to 350°F. For crust, in a medium bowl stir together ground cashews, crushed graham crackers, ½ cup sugar, and flour. Drizzle melted butter over the cashew mixture. Toss until well mixed. Press cashew mixture onto the bottom and about 1½ inches up the sides of a 10-inch springform pan.

2. For filling, in a very large mixing bowl beat cream cheese with electric mixer on medium-high speed until fluffy. Gradually beat in 1 cup sugar until smooth. Reduce speed to medium; beat in rum (if desired), vanilla, and nutmeg. Add eggs all at once; beat on low speed just until combined (do not overbeat). Stir in eggnog (batter will be thin). Pour filling into the crust-lined pan. Place springform pan in a shallow baking pan in case springform pan leaks.

3. Bake for 40 to 45 minutes or until center appears nearly set when gently shaken.

4. Cool in springform pan on wire rack for 15 minutes. Using a small sharp knife, loosen crust from sides of pan. Cool for 30 minutes more. Remove side of springform pan. Cool completely. Cover and chill at least 6 hours or up to 24 hours. If desired, garnish with cashew brittle.

*Note: Use a grinder, blender, or food processor to grind the nuts, watching carefully because nuts can form a paste if ground too much.

Per serving: 446 cal., 33 g total fat (18 g sat. fat), 131 mg chol., 286 mg sodium, 31 g carbo., 0 g fiber, 9 g pro.
Daily Values: 20% vit. A, 1% vit. C, 9% calcium, 9% iron

Simple Miniature Fruit Tarts

A few minutes is all it takes to transform purchased cookies into a special dessert. Let children help you "decorate" the tarts with coconut and fresh fruit.

Start to Finish: 15 minutes **Makes:** 4 tarts

- 4 purchased large (3-inch) soft sugar cookies or chocolate cookies
- ¼ cup tub-style cream cheese spread with strawberries, chocolate-hazelnut spread, or fudge ice cream topping
- 2 tablespoons coconut
- 1 cup sliced fresh fruit, such as kiwifruit, bananas, and/or strawberries

1. Spread flat side of each cookie with cream cheese spread; sprinkle with coconut. Top with fruit.

Per tart: 164 cal., 9 g total fat (4 g sat. fat), 23 mg chol., 114 mg sodium, 21 g carbo., 2 g fiber, 2 g pro.
Daily Values: 3% vit. A, 37% vit. C, 2% calcium, 2% iron

Crescent Fruit Pizza

Use a variety of colorful fresh fruit to top this dessert pizza. Be sure to let the crust cool completely before adding the pudding layer.

Prep: 35 minutes **Bake:** 11 minutes
Chill: 1 hour **Oven:** 375°F **Makes:** 8 servings

- 1 8-ounce package (8) refrigerated crescent rolls
- 1 tablespoon butter or margarine, melted
- ½ teaspoon almond extract
- 4 teaspoons sugar
- 1 4-serving package vanilla instant pudding and pie filling mix
- 1½ cups milk
- 1 teaspoon finely shredded orange peel
- ¼ of an 8-ounce container frozen whipped dessert topping, thawed
- 3 cups fresh fruit, such as blueberries, sliced kiwifruit, sliced strawberries, raspberries, and/or peeled peach slices

1. Preheat oven to 375°F. Press rolls into the bottom of a 12-inch pizza pan or a 13×9×2-inch baking pan. In a small bowl combine butter and almond extract; brush over dough. Sprinkle with sugar.

2. Bake for 11 to 13 minutes or until golden. Cool completely in pan on wire rack.

3. In a medium mixing bowl combine pudding mix and milk. Beat with an electric mixer on low speed for 1 minute. Stir in orange peel. Cover and chill for 10 minutes. Fold in dessert topping.

4. Spread pudding mixture over crust. Arrange fruit over pudding. Cover and chill for at least 1 hour or up to 3 hours before serving.

Per serving: 238 cal., 10 g total fat (4 g sat. fat), 8 mg chol., 439 mg sodium, 35 g carbo., 2 g fiber, 4 g pro.
Daily Values: 3% vit. A, 55% vit. C, 7% calcium, 3% iron

Crepes with Maple-Pear Sauce

Sweet and tender slices of juicy pear simmered with maple syrup make a glorious crepe filling. Toasted pecans sprinkled on top are a crunchy final touch.

Start to Finish: 10 minutes **Makes:** 5 servings

- 1 15.25-ounce can pear slices, drained
- 1 cup pure maple syrup or maple-flavored syrup
- 1 4- to 4.5-ounce package ready-to-use crepes (10 crepes)
- ½ cup chopped pecans, toasted (see tip, page 63)

1. In a small saucepan combine pear slices and maple syrup; heat through.

2. Meanwhile, fold crepes into quarters. Place two crepes on each of five dessert plates. Pour hot pear mixture over crepes. Sprinkle with pecans.

Per serving: 349 cal., 11 g total fat (1 g sat. fat), 35 mg chol., 77 mg sodium, 64 g carbo., 3 g fiber, 3 g pro.
Daily Values: 2% vit. A, 2% vit. C, 7% calcium, 9% iron

Crescent Fruit Pizza

 Caramel Apple Crepes

If you want the flecks and flavor from vanilla beans, but don't want the work involved, try using vanilla bean paste. Substitute an equal amount of paste for vanilla extract in recipes where you want to see the flecks, such as in ice cream, custards, or whipped cream. Look for it in specialty food shops.

Prep: 15 minutes **Cook:** 20 minutes
Makes: 4 servings

- ¾ cup all-purpose flour
- ⅓ cup water
- ⅓ cup milk
- 2 eggs
- 2 tablespoons granulated sugar
- 4 teaspoons walnut oil or cooking oil
- 1 cup packed brown sugar
- 4 teaspoons cornstarch
- 1 cup whipping cream
- 2 tablespoons apple brandy or brandy
- 1 tablespoon butter or margarine
- 2 cups thinly sliced, peeled apples, such as Granny Smith, Rome Beauty, or Jonagold
- ½ cup purchased crème fraîche (optional)
- 1 teaspoon vanilla bean paste or vanilla (optional)
- ½ cup Candied Pecans

1. For crepes,* in a blender combine flour, water, milk, eggs, granulated sugar, and oil. Cover and blend until smooth, stopping and scraping sides of container as necessary. Heat a lightly greased 6-inch skillet over medium heat; remove from heat. Spoon 2 tablespoons batter into skillet; lift and tilt skillet to spread batter evenly. Return skillet to heat; brown on one side only. Invert skillet over paper towels; remove crepe from skillet. Repeat with remaining batter.

2. Fold 12 of the crepes into quarters with the browned side out. Place three crepes on each of four dessert plates. (To freeze remaining crepes, layer cooled crepes with sheets of waxed paper in an air-tight container; freeze for up to 4 months. Thaw at room temperature for 1 hour before using.)

3. For sauce, in a large saucepan stir together brown sugar and cornstarch. Stir in whipping cream, brandy, and butter. Add apples. Cook and stir over

Caramel Apple Crepes

medium heat until thickened and bubbly. Cook and stir for 2 minutes more.

4. If desired, for topping, in a small bowl stir together crème fraîche and vanilla bean paste. To serve, pour warm apple sauce over crepes. Sprinkle with Candied Pecans. If desired, serve with topping.

Candied Pecans: Line a baking sheet with foil. Butter the foil; set baking sheet aside. In a large heavy skillet combine 1½ cups raw or roasted pecan pieces, ½ cup granulated sugar, 2 tablespoons butter, and 1 teaspoon vanilla. Cook over medium-high heat, shaking skillet occasionally, until sugar begins to melt. Do not stir. Reduce heat to low. Continue cooking until sugar is golden brown, stirring occasionally. Remove skillet from heat. Pour nut mixture onto prepared baking sheet. Cool completely. Break into pieces. Store tightly covered in the refrigerator for up to 3 weeks.

*Note: For crepes in a hurry, skip Step 1 and substitute 12 ready-made crepes purchased from the supermarket.

Per serving: 766 cal., 45 g total fat (19 g sat. fat), 202 mg chol., 116 mg sodium, 83 g carbo., 3 g fiber, 9 g pro.
Daily Values: 25% vit. A, 5% vit. C, 13% calcium, 15% iron

Gifts Aplenty

Food is a gift that just keeps giving—
the first time when it's opened, the
second time when it's being savored!
Whether you're looking for something
savory or sweet, you're sure to find the
perfect match in this chapter. Asian
Pickled Carrots provide an intriguing
flavor and can be made start to finish
in less than an hour with no processing.
Presented in a pretty basket with a box
of crackers and some cheese, this is
one gift that wins for originality. Place
Chocolate-Orange Cakes and Little
Lemon Snowballs on a pretty platter
and you will have a gift any sweet tooth
will love. Whatever the gift and whoever
the recipient, giving food gifts is a
surefire way to wish important people in
your life a merry holiday season!

Chocolate-Orange Cakes, page 118

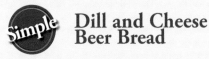

Dill and Cheese Beer Bread

Forget rising, kneading, punching, and all of that. Even if you rarely bake bread from scratch, you can make this savory loaf! Just stir and bake.

Prep: 20 minutes **Bake:** 45 minutes
Oven: 350°F **Makes:** 1 loaf (16 servings)

3 cups self-rising flour*
½ cup shredded cheddar cheese (2 ounces)
½ cup shredded Monterey Jack cheese with jalapeño peppers (2 ounces)
2 tablespoons sugar
1 tablespoon dillseed
1 teaspoon dried dillweed
1 12-ounce can beer

1. Preheat oven to 350°F. Grease the bottom and ½ inch up the sides of a 9×5×3-inch loaf pan; set aside.

2. In a large mixing bowl stir together flour, cheddar cheese, Monterey Jack cheese, sugar, dillseed, and dillweed. Add beer and stir until well combined. Spread batter in the prepared pan.

3. Bake about 45 minutes or until bread sounds hollow when lightly tapped. Cool in pan on a wire rack for 10 minutes; remove bread from pan and cool completely on wire rack. Serve or wrap and store in the refrigerator for up to 3 days.

*Note: If desired, substitute 3 cups all-purpose flour plus 1 tablespoon baking powder, 1 teaspoon salt, and ¾ teaspoon baking soda for the self-rising flour.

Per serving: 128 cal., 3 g total fat (2 g sat. fat), 7 mg chol., 344 mg sodium, 20 g carbo., 1 g fiber, 4 g pro.
Daily Values: 2% vit. A, 14% calcium, 7% iron

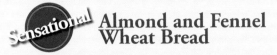

Almond and Fennel Wheat Bread

A chewy bread with a crisp crust, this rustic loaf teams chopped nuts and fennel seeds for old-world heartiness and taste.

Prep: 35 minutes **Rise:** 1½ hours **Bake:** 30 minutes
Oven: 375°F **Makes:** 1 loaf (12 servings)

1⅓ cups warm water (105°F to 115°F)
1 package active dry yeast
1 teaspoon sugar
1 tablespoon olive oil
2 teaspoons fennel seeds, crushed
1½ teaspoons salt
1 cup whole wheat flour
½ cup chopped almonds, toasted (see tip, page 63)
2¼ to 2¾ cups bread flour or all-purpose flour

1. In a large bowl stir together warm water, yeast, and sugar; let mixture stand for 5 minutes. Add olive oil, fennel seeds, and salt.

2. Using a wooden spoon, stir in whole wheat flour. Stir in nuts and as much of the bread flour as possible, stirring until the dough begins to form a ball. Turn dough out onto a lightly floured surface. Knead in enough of the remaining bread flour to make a moderately stiff dough that is smooth and elastic (6 to 8 minutes total). Shape the dough into a ball. Place dough in a lightly greased bowl, turning once to grease surface of the dough. Cover and let rise in a warm place until double in size (about 1 hour).

Almond and Fennel Wheat Bread

3. Punch down dough. Turn dough out onto a lightly floured surface. Cover and let rest 10 minutes. Meanwhile, lightly grease a baking sheet. Shape dough into an 8×4-inch oval loaf. Place on prepared baking sheet. Sprinkle lightly with additional bread flour. Cover and let rise in a warm place until almost double in size (30 to 45 minutes).

4. Preheat oven to 375°F. Using a sharp knife slash top of loaf several times, making each cut about ½ inch deep. For a crisp crust, spray or brush the loaf with cold water. Bake about 30 minutes or until bread sounds hollow when lightly tapped, brushing or spraying with water halfway through baking. Transfer to a wire rack; cool.

Per serving: 167 cal., 4 g total fat (0 g sat. fat), 0 mg chol., 293 mg sodium,

28 g carbo., 3 g fiber, 6 g pro.

Daily Values: 2% calcium, 10% iron

Herbed Crouton Sticks

These king-size croutons make terrific dunkers for soups or dips and a fine accompaniment to salads.

Prep: 15 minutes Bake: 25 minutes
Oven: 300°F Makes: about 24 sticks

1 **8-ounce thin loaf baguette-style French bread**
½ **cup butter**
1 **tablespoon snipped fresh basil or**
    ½ teaspoon dried basil, crushed
⅛ **teaspoon garlic powder**

1. Preheat oven to 300°F. Cut baguette in half horizontally. Cut bread into strips 3½ inches long by 1 inch wide or into a length that will fit into a gift container; set aside. In a 12-inch skillet melt butter. Stir in basil and garlic powder. Add half the crouton sticks, stirring until coated with butter mixture. Arrange crouton sticks in a single layer in a shallow baking pan. Repeat with remaining crouton sticks.

2. Bake for 25 to 30 minutes or until crouton sticks are dry and crisp, turning once. Cool completely.

To store: Place in an airtight container; cover. Store at room temperature for up to 3 days or freeze for up to 3 months.

Per stick: 60 cal., 4 g total fat (2 g sat. fat), 10 mg chol., 85 mg sodium,

5 g carbo., 0 g fiber, 1 g pro.

Daily Values: 2% vit. A, 1% calcium, 1% iron

Cornmeal Croutons

Coarse sea salt makes these croutons special. Give to guests along with your favorite homemade vinaigrette that you've put in a pretty bottle and wrapped with a festive ribbon.

Prep: 15 minutes Bake: 12 minutes
Oven: 350°F Makes: about 28 croutons

1 **egg**
1 **8.5-ounce package corn muffin mix**
⅔ **cup finely shredded Romano cheese or Parmesan cheese**
2 **tablespoons milk**
    Freshly ground black pepper
    Coarse sea salt (optional)

1. Preheat oven to 350°F. Grease a very large baking sheet or two large baking sheets; set aside.

2. In a medium bowl lightly beat the egg. Add muffin mix, cheese, and milk; stir until combined. Drop into small mounds by scant teaspoonfuls onto prepared baking sheet(s). Lightly sprinkle with pepper and if desired, sea salt.

3. Bake for 12 to 14 minutes or until golden. Remove from baking sheet; let cool completely on a wire rack.

To store: Place croutons in an airtight container; cover. Store at room temperature for up to 1 day, in the refrigerator for up to 3 days, or freeze for up to 1 month. If refrigerated, let stand at room temperature for 30 minutes before serving. If frozen, thaw in the refrigerator and let stand at room temperature for 30 minutes.

Per crouton: 46 cal., 2 g total fat (0 g sat. fat), 9 mg chol., 93 mg sodium,

6 g carbo., 0 g fiber, 2 g pro.

Daily Values: 2% calcium, 1% iron

Brownie Wreath

 Brownie Wreath

During the holiday season, keep the ingredients for this recipe on hand for last-minute school or bake-sale treats. The outer crust will soften and cut easier if you wrap and store the wreath overnight. If you like, make a "bow" for the wreath by cutting one from red construction paper.

Prep: 20 minutes **Bake:** 40 minutes
Oven: 325°F **Makes:** 24 servings

- 1 19- to 22-ounce package fudge
     brownie mix
     Purchased vanilla frosting
     Green paste food coloring
     Red, green, and white candies
      for decorating

1. Preheat oven to 325°F. Grease and flour a 10-inch fluted tube pan; set aside. Prepare brownie mix according to package directions for cake brownies; spread batter into prepared pan.

2. Bake for 40 to 45 minutes or until a wooden toothpick inserted near center of cake comes out clean. Cool in pan on a wire rack for 10 minutes. Remove from pan. Cool thoroughly on rack.

3. Tint frosting with green food coloring to desired color. Decorate cake with frosting and candies. Let stand until frosting dries.

To store: Wrap well and store in an airtight container at room temperature for up to 3 days.

Per serving: 207 cal., 9 g total fat (2 g sat. fat), 17 mg chol., 105 mg sodium, 30 g carbo., 0 g fiber, 2 g pro.
Daily Values: 2% calcium, 4% iron

 **Peanut Butter Brownie**

Know someone who is nuts about a particular kind of candy bar? Personalize this gift by sprinkling the favorite chopped bite-size bits on top.

Prep: 30 minutes **Bake:** 35 minutes
Oven: 350°F **Makes:** 12 servings

- ¼ cup butter
- 2 ounces unsweetened chocolate, chopped
- 3 tablespoons creamy peanut butter
- 1 egg, beaten
- ¾ cup sugar
- ½ cup all-purpose flour
- ½ teaspoon vanilla
- 1 recipe Peanut Butter Glaze
- ⅓ cup chopped assorted candies, such as bite-size chocolate-covered peanut butter cups, candy-coated chocolate and peanut butter pieces, and/or chocolate-coated caramel-topped nougat bars with peanuts

1. Preheat oven to 350°F. Grease a 6-inch springform pan; set aside.

2. In a small heavy saucepan melt butter and chocolate over low heat, stirring frequently. Stir in peanut butter. Cool about 10 minutes. In a medium bowl stir together egg, sugar, flour, and vanilla. Stir in cooled chocolate mixture. Pour mixture into the prepared baking pan.

3. Bake for 35 minutes. Cool in pan on a wire rack for 10 minutes. Loosen sides of springform pan. Cool thoroughly on rack. Remove sides of the springform pan. Using a thin metal spatula or knife, loosen bottom of brownie from bottom of pan and carefully transfer brownie to a flat plate or a 7- or 8-inch cardboard round covered with foil.

4. Prepare Peanut Butter Glaze. Pour warm glaze over cooled brownie, spreading evenly and allowing it to drip down sides. Top with assorted candies.

Peanut Butter Glaze: In a small heavy saucepan melt 2 tablespoons creamy peanut butter and 1 tablespoon butter over low heat. Remove from heat and stir in ¾ cup powdered sugar. Stir in 2 teaspoons very hot water. Stir in additional hot water, 1 teaspoon at a time, to make a glaze.

To store: Place in a tightly covered container in the refrigerator for up to 3 days or freeze unglazed brownie for up to 1 month. Thaw and glaze.

Per serving: 234 cal., 12 g total fat (6 g sat. fat), 30 mg chol., 82 mg sodium, 30 g carbo., 1 g fiber, 4 g pro.
Daily Values: 3% vit. A, 2% calcium, 7% iron

 Easy Flower Cookies on Sticks

Based on a roll of refrigerated sugar cookie dough, these cookies are simple enough to prepare that children could help make them—and be proud to give them to teachers or day care providers.

Prep: 40 minutes **Bake:** 8 minutes per batch
Cool: 1 minute per batch **Oven:** 375°F
Makes: 20 cookies

- 1 18-ounce roll refrigerated sugar cookie dough
- ¼ cup all-purpose flour
- ¼ cup fine or coarse colored sugar(s)
- 20 4½-inch craft sticks
- 20 milk chocolate stars

1. Preheat oven to 375°F. Knead together cookie dough and flour until combined. Shape dough into one hundred ¾-inch balls. Roll balls in colored sugar(s) to coat. For each flower cookie, place a craft stick on an ungreased cookie sheet. Place five balls in a circle around the tip of the stick so their sides are just touching; leave 2 inches between cookies on the cookie sheet.

2. Bake for 8 to 10 minutes or until edges are lightly browned. Press a chocolate star in the center of each flower shape. Cool for 1 minute on cookie sheet. Transfer cookies to a wire rack and let cool.

To store: Place cookies in layers separated by waxed paper in an airtight container; cover. Store at room temperature for up to 3 days or freeze for up to 3 months.

Per cookie: 148 cal., 7 g total fat (2 g sat. fat), 8 mg chol., 109 mg sodium, 21 g carbo., 0 g fiber, 1 g pro.
Daily Values: 3% calcium, 3% iron

Flower Cookie Pops

Ever hear the saying "too pretty to eat?" You sure will after you present these colorful garden-inspired cookie pops to your friends—but they're sure to gobble them up anyway!

Prep: 50 minutes **Chill:** 1 hour **Bake:** 8 minutes
Oven: 375°F **Makes:** about 24 cookies

⅔ cup butter, softened
½ of an 8-ounce can almond paste, crumbled (½ cup)
⅓ cup sugar
2 teaspoons finely shredded orange peel or lemon peel
1 teaspoon baking powder
½ teaspoon salt
¼ teaspoon almond extract
1 egg
2½ cups all-purpose flour
Paste and liquid food coloring (optional)
Short wooden dowels
1 egg white, beaten
Sugar

1. In a large mixing bowl beat butter and almond paste with an electric mixer on medium to high speed about 1 minute or until combined. Add ⅓ cup sugar, orange peel, baking powder, salt, and almond extract. Beat until combined, scraping sides of bowl occasionally. Beat in egg. Beat in as much of the flour as possible with the mixer. Stir in any remaining flour with a wooden spoon.

2. Divide dough into several portions. If desired, work desired paste food coloring into each portion. Cover; chill dough 1 hour or until easy to handle.

3. Preheat oven to 375°F. Grease cookie sheets; set aside. On a lightly floured surface, roll half of the dough at a time until ⅜ inch thick. Using 2½- to 3½-inch cutters, cut dough into desired shapes. (Or if desired, shape flower cookies and leaves from dough.) Place cutouts 1 inch apart on prepared cookie sheets, staggering rows of cookies so that wooden dowels can be inserted into flower shapes. (If desired, stain dowels with green liquid food coloring.) Insert a wooden dowel ½ inch into the bottom edge of each cookie. Brush cookies with egg white and sprinkle lightly with additional sugar.

4. Bake for 8 to 10 minutes or until edges are firm and bottoms are very light brown. Cool on cookie sheet for 1 minute. Carefully transfer cookies to a wire rack and let cool.

To store: Place cookies in layers separated by waxed paper in an airtight container; cover. Store at room temperature for up to 3 days or freeze for up to 3 months.

Per cookie: 130 cal., 7 g total fat (3 g sat. fat), 22 mg chol., 106 mg sodium, 15 g carbo., 1 g fiber, 2 g pro.
Daily Values: 3% vit. A, 3% calcium, 4% iron

 Peanut Snowmen

Keep the oven off and the mixer covered! These quick cookies begin with a favorite purchased treat and end with candy decorations. Just one step comes between start and finish: a simple icing.

Prep: 40 minutes **Makes:** 15 snowmen

1 cup sifted powdered sugar
¼ teaspoon vanilla
3 to 4 teaspoons milk
15 peanut-shaped peanut butter sandwich cookies
15 large gumdrops
Granulated sugar
Candy decorations or decorator icing

Peanut Snowmen

Caramel-Nut Revel Bars

1. For icing, in a small bowl combine powdered sugar, vanilla, and enough milk to make a thin icing consistency. Spread about 1 teaspoon icing over the top and sides of each peanut butter cookie so that the texture of the cookie shows through the icing.

2. To make gumdrop hats, roll a large gumdrop into an oval in granulated sugar. Roll oval into a cone shape; press to seal ends. Curl up bottom edge of cone to form a brim. Attach hat to head of peanut butter snowman with icing. Add candy decorations or decorator icing to make dots for eyes and buttons.

To store: Place in a single layer in an airtight container; cover. Store in the refrigerator for up to 3 days.

Per snowman: 123 cal., 3 g total fat (1 g sat. fat), 0 mg chol., 66 mg sodium, 23 g carbo., 0 g fiber, 1 g pro.
Daily Values: 1% calcium, 2% iron

 **Caramel-Nut Revel Bars**

Oh so sweet and gooey, these chocolate, peanut, and marshmallow cookies will be a hit with everyone!

Prep: 30 minutes **Bake:** 30 minutes
Oven: 350°F **Makes:** about 36 bars

  ½ **cup butter, softened**
  1 **cup packed brown sugar**
  ½ **teaspoon baking soda**
  1 **egg**
  1 **teaspoon vanilla**
  1¼ **cups all-purpose flour**
  1½ **cups quick-cooking rolled oats**
  20 **vanilla caramels, unwrapped**
  2 **tablespoons milk**
  2 **cups tiny marshmallows**
  1 **cup dry roasted peanuts**
  1½ **cups semisweet chocolate pieces**
  1 **14-ounce can sweetened condensed milk**
  2 **tablespoons butter**
  2 **teaspoons vanilla**

1. Preheat oven to 350°F. Line a 13×9×2-inch baking pan with foil, extending foil over edges of pan; set pan aside. In a large mixing bowl beat ½ cup butter with an electric mixer on medium to high speed for 30 seconds. Add brown sugar and baking soda. Beat until combined, scraping sides of bowl occasionally. Beat in egg and 1 teaspoon vanilla. Beat in as much of the flour as possible with the mixer. Stir in any remaining flour with a wooden spoon. Stir in the oats. Reserve ⅔ cup of the oat mixture. With floured hands, press remaining oat mixture into bottom of prepared pan. Set aside.

2. In a small saucepan combine caramels and milk. Cook and stir over low heat just until caramels are melted. Drizzle caramel mixture over oatmeal mixture. Sprinkle with 1⅓ cups of the marshmallows and ⅔ cup of the peanuts; set aside.

3. In a medium saucepan combine chocolate pieces, sweetened condensed milk, and 2 tablespoons butter. Cook over low heat until chocolate melts, stirring occasionally. Remove from heat. Stir in 2 teaspoons vanilla. Pour chocolate mixture evenly over the marshmallows and nuts in pan. Spoon small mounds of reserved oat mixture evenly over chocolate mixture. Sprinkle evenly with remaining ⅔ cup marshmallows and ⅓ cup peanuts.

4. Bake about 30 minutes or until golden. Cool in pan on a wire rack. To serve, lift bars from pan using foil. Place on a cutting board and cut into bars.

To store: Place bars in a single layer in an airtight container; cover. Store at room temperature for up to 3 days or freeze for up to 3 months.

Per bar: 223 cal., 10 g total fat (5 g sat. fat), 18 mg chol., 78 mg sodium, 32 g carbo., 2 g fiber, 4 g pro.
Daily Values: 3% vit. A, 6% calcium, 6% iron

Berry Freezer Jam

Prepare this fresh jam when berries are in season and at their best.

Prep: 30 minutes **Stand:** 24 hours
Makes: about 5 half-pints

- 4 **cups fresh blackberries, raspberries, or hulled strawberries**
- 4 **cups sugar**
- ½ **teaspoon finely shredded lemon peel**
- 1 **1.75-ounce package regular powdered fruit pectin**
- ¾ **cup water**

1. In a bowl use a potato masher to crush the berries until there are 2 cups crushed berries. Mix berries, sugar, and lemon peel. Let stand for 10 minutes, stirring occasionally. In a small saucepan combine pectin and water. Bring to boiling over high heat; boil 1 minute, stirring constantly. Remove from heat and add to berry mixture; stir for 3 minutes or until sugar is dissolved and mixture is no longer grainy.

2. Ladle into half-pint freezer containers, leaving a ½-inch headspace. Seal and label with contents and date. Let stand at room temperature for 24 hours or until set. Store jam for up to 3 weeks in refrigerator or for up to 1 year in the freezer.

Per tablespoon: 49 cal., 0 g total fat (0 g sat. fat), 0 mg chol., 1 mg sodium, 13 g carbo., 0 g fiber, 0 g pro.
Daily Values: 3% vit. C

Brandied Cranberry-Orange Marmalade

Suggest that the recipient of this lovely red-hued marmalade spread it on toast, English muffins, bagels, or just about anything!

Prep: 65 minutes
Cook: 30 minutes plus process for 5 minutes
Stand: 3 days
Makes: about 6 half-pints (about 48 tablespoons)

Brandied Cranberry-Orange Marmalade

Asian Pickled Carrots

3 medium oranges
1½ cups water
⅛ teaspoon baking soda
2 cups fresh cranberries
4 inches stick cinnamon
4 cups sugar
½ of a 6-ounce package (1 foil pouch) liquid fruit pectin
2 tablespoons brandy

1. Cut peel of oranges lengthwise into quarters, cutting just through the peel to the surface of the fruit. Pry back the quartered peels with a spoon. Scrape off the bitter white portions inside the peel and discard. Cut peels into thin strips. In a medium saucepan bring peels, water, and baking soda to boiling; reduce heat. Simmer, covered, for 20 minutes. Do not drain. Section oranges, reserving juices; discard seeds. Add orange sections, juice, cranberries, and cinnamon to peels in saucepan; return to boiling. Cover and simmer for 10 minutes. Carefully remove stick cinnamon and discard.

2. In an 8- to 10-quart heavy kettle combine fruit mixture and sugar. Bring to a full rolling boil, stirring constantly. Quickly stir in pectin. Return to a full rolling boil; boil for 1 minute, stirring constantly. Remove from heat; skim off foam with a metal spoon. Stir in brandy.

3. Ladle into hot, sterilized half-pint canning jars, leaving a ¼-inch headspace. Wipe jar rims; adjust lids. Process the filled jars in a boiling-water canner for 5 minutes (start timing when water returns to boil). Remove jars from canner; cool on racks. Label jars with contents and date. Let marmalade stand for 3 to 5 days before serving.

Per tablespoon: 73 cal., 0 g total fat (0 g sat. fat), 0 mg chol., 4 mg sodium, 18 g carbo., 0 g fiber, 0 g pro.
Daily Values: 8% vit. C

Asian Pickled Carrots

Packaged baby carrots make creating this gift so convenient. Served alongside meats and cheeses, the carrots add color and crunch to an appetizer spread.

Start to Finish: 45 minutes
Makes: 3 half-pints (about 18 servings)

1 16-ounce package peeled baby carrots
1 teaspoon salt
¼ cup peeled and julienned fresh ginger
3 whole allspice
¾ cup water
¾ cup rice vinegar
⅓ cup packed brown sugar
4 whole cloves
4 whole peppercorns

1. In a saucepan cook carrots and salt, covered, in a small amount of boiling water for 3 minutes or until crisp-tender. Drain and place in three clean half-pint jars. Place some of the ginger and 1 whole allspice in each jar.

2. In a medium saucepan combine water, vinegar, brown sugar, cloves, and peppercorns. Bring mixture to boiling; reduce heat. Simmer, uncovered, for 5 minutes. Pour over carrots, ginger, and allspice in jars. Seal jars. Label jars with contents and date and store in the refrigerator for up to 3 months.

Per serving: 33 cal., 0 g total fat (0 g sat. fat), 0 mg chol., 149 mg sodium, 7 g carbo., 1 g fiber, 0 g pro.
Daily Values: 76% vit. A, 2% vit. C, 1% calcium, 1% iron

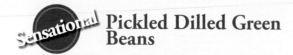 **Pickled Dilled Green Beans**

Prep: 45 minutes

Cook: 5 minutes plus process for 5 minutes

Makes: 5 pints (about 20 servings)

- 3 pounds fresh green beans
- 5 fresh red serrano chile peppers (optional)
- 3 cups white wine vinegar
- 1 tablespoon pickling salt
- 1 tablespoon sugar
- 3 tablespoons snipped fresh dill
- ½ teaspoon crushed red pepper
- 6 cloves garlic, minced
- 5 small heads fresh dill (optional)

1. Wash beans; drain. Trim ends, if desired. Place enough water to cover beans in an 8-quart Dutch oven or kettle. Bring to boiling. Add beans and fresh chile peppers, if desired, to the boiling water; return to boiling. Boil, uncovered, for 5 minutes. Drain. Immediately pack beans lengthwise into hot, sterilized pint canning jars, cutting beans to fit if necessary and leaving ½-inch headspace. Place one hot pepper (if using) into each jar so that it shows through the glass. Set aside.

2. In a large saucepan combine 3 cups *water*, vinegar, pickling salt, sugar, snipped dill, crushed red pepper, and garlic. Bring to boiling. Pour over beans in jars, leaving a ½-inch headspace. If desired, add small heads fresh dill to jars. Remove air bubbles, wipe jar rims, and adjust lids. Process filled jars in a boiling-water canner for 5 minutes (start timing when water begins to boil). Remove jars; cool on racks. Label jars with contents and date.

Per serving: 42 cal., 0 g total fat (0 g sat. fat), 0 mg chol., 357 mg sodium, 7 g carbo., 3 g fiber, 2 g pro.

Daily Values: 12% vit. A, 46% vit. C, 3% calcium, 6% iron

 **Little Lemon Snowballs**

Start to Finish: 30 minutes Makes: 12 cupcakes

- 12 purchased unfrosted white cupcakes*
- ½ cup purchased lemon curd or cranberry curd

- ⅛ cup butter, softened
- 3½ cups powdered sugar
- ¼ cup purchased unsweetened coconut milk or milk
  Purchased unsweetened coconut milk or powdered sugar
- 2 cups flaked coconut

1. Remove paper bake cups from cupcakes if present. Using a serrated knife, cut each cupcake in half horizontally. Spread 2 teaspoons of the lemon curd on cut side of bottom half of each cupcake. Reassemble cakes.

2. For frosting, in a medium bowl beat butter with an electric mixer on medium to high speed until fluffy. Gradually add 1 cup of the powdered sugar, beating well. Slowly beat in coconut milk. Gradually beat in the remaining powdered sugar. Beat in additional coconut milk or powdered sugar to reach spreading consistency.

3. Invert cupcakes (top sides down). Generously frost cupcake tops and sides. Coat tops and sides with coconut, pressing gently to stick.

*Note: Order unfrosted cupcakes from a local bakery or bake cupcakes from a favorite mix.

To store: Place cakes in an airtight container; cover. Store in the refrigerator for up to 3 days.

Per cupcake: 556 cal., 20 g total fat (10 g sat. fat), 24 mg chol., 321 mg sodium, 93 g carbo., 2 g fiber, 5 g pro.

Daily Values: 4% vit. A, 10% calcium, 8% iron

 **Chocolate-Orange Cakes**

Prep: 1½ hours Bake: 15 minutes

Stand: 1 hour 20 minutes Cool: 10 minutes

Oven: 350°F Makes: 12 cakes

- ½ cup butter
- 1 cup sugar
- ⅓ cup unsweetened cocoa powder
- 2 teaspoons finely shredded orange peel
- ½ teaspoon baking powder
- ¼ teaspoon baking soda

⅛ teaspoon salt
1 egg
1 teaspoon vanilla
1 cup all-purpose flour
¾ cup milk
1 recipe Chocolate-Orange Ganache
1 recipe Candied Orange Peel or curled
   orange peel strips
   Coarse sugar

1. Preheat oven to 350°F. Line twelve 2½-inch muffin cups with paper bake cups or lightly grease and flour muffin cups; set aside.

2. In a large saucepan melt butter over medium heat. Remove from heat. Let stand for 5 minutes. Stir in sugar, cocoa powder, orange peel, baking powder, baking soda, and salt until combined. Add egg and vanilla. Using a wooden spoon, beat lightly until combined.

3. Alternately add flour and milk to chocolate mixture, beating with the wooden spoon after each addition just until combined. Divide batter among prepared muffin cups, filling each about three-fourths full.

4. Bake for 15 to 20 minutes or until a wooden toothpick inserted near the centers comes out clean. Cool in muffin cups on a wire rack for 10 minutes. Using a knife, loosen the edges; remove cupcakes and invert onto wire racks (top sides down), leaving 2 inches between each cupcake. Cool completely.

5. Remove paper bake cups from cupcakes (if using); return to wire rack (top sides down). Place wire rack with cupcakes on a piece of waxed paper.

6. Prepare Chocolate-Orange Ganache. Using a spoon, slowly spoon ganache over cupcakes, allowing excess to run down the sides to completely coat the tops and sides of cupcakes. Top cupcakes with Candied Orange Peel and coarse sugar. Let stand at room temperature for 1 hour to allow ganache to set up slightly.

Chocolate-Orange Ganache: In a medium saucepan bring ¾ cup whipping cream just to boiling over medium heat. Remove from heat. Add 8 ounces bittersweet or semisweet chocolate, chopped; 2 tablespoons butter; and 2 teaspoons finely shredded orange peel (do not stir). Let stand for 5 minutes. Stir until very smooth. Let stand for 15 minutes before spooning over cupcakes.

Candied Orange Peel: Cut peels of 2 oranges lengthwise into quarters, cutting just through the peel to the surface of the fruit. Pry back the quartered peels with a spoon. Scrape off the bitter white part inside the peel and discard. Cut peels into ⅜-inch strips. Wrap and refrigerate peeled fruit for another use. In a 2-quart saucepan combine 1⅓ cups sugar and ⅓ cup water. Cover and bring to boiling, stirring occasionally. Add orange peel strips. Return to boiling, stirring constantly to dissolve sugar; reduce heat. Cook, uncovered, over medium-low heat for 15 minutes or until peel is translucent, stirring occasionally. Mixture should boil at a moderate, steady rate over entire surface. Using a slotted spoon, remove peel from syrup, allowing it to drain. Transfer peel to a wire rack set over waxed paper. Cool slightly just until cool enough to handle but still warm and slightly sticky. Roll peel in additional sugar to coat. If desired, dip one end of each piece in melted bittersweet or semisweet chocolate. Continue drying on the rack for 1 to 2 hours. Store, tightly covered, in a cool, dry place for up to 1 week. Makes 2 cups.

Per cake: 448 cal., 23 g total fat (14 g sat. fat), 65 mg chol., 154 mg sodium, 63 g carbo., 3 g fiber, 4 g pro.
Daily Values: 12% vit. A, 4% vit. C, 6% calcium, 9% iron

Chocolate-Orange Cakes

Luscious Leftover Luncheon

For some, leftovers bring as much anticipation as the actual Christmas feast during the holiday season. This year, do more than reheat and serve. Turn these pages to discover some creative ways to magically transform leftover turkey, mashed potatoes, stuffing, cranberries, and more! From Spicy Ham and Bean Soup to Sweet Potato Cheesecake, Stuffing Patties, and Turkey Manicotti, you will be amazed at how differently delicious your holiday meal can become. Let these recipes be a springboard for other inspiring leftover transformations. Experiment with other flavors—give that Turkey Salad Sandwich an Indian flavor by adding some curry instead of tarragon and chutney instead of mustard, or use pumpkin instead of sweet potatoes for a dazzling Pumpkin Cheesecake. The possibilities are endless!

Asian Turkey à la King, page 124

Turkey-Pesto Pockets

Pair these hearty pocket sandwiches with a green salad lightly dressed with balsamic vinegar. If you can't find dried tomato pesto, the basil counterpart works just as well.

Prep: 20 minutes **Bake:** 15 minutes
Cool: 5 minutes **Oven:** 375°F
Makes: 6 servings

 2 cups chopped cooked turkey (12 ounces)
 1 9-ounce package frozen artichoke hearts, thawed, drained, and coarsely chopped
 ¾ cup purchased dried tomato pesto
 ¾ cup finely shredded Parmesan or Romano cheese
 ¼ teaspoon ground black pepper
 2 13.8-ounce packages refrigerated pizza dough
 Milk
 1 8-ounce can pizza sauce, warmed

1. Preheat oven to 375°F. Lightly grease a very large baking sheet; set aside. For filling, in a large bowl combine turkey, artichokes, pesto, ½ cup of the cheese, and pepper.

2. On a lightly floured surface, gently stretch or roll one package of pizza dough into a 15×10-inch rectangle. Using a pizza cutter or sharp knife, cut crosswise into three 10×5-inch rectangles.

3. Place about ⅔ cup of the turkey mixture on half of each rectangle; spread to within about 1 inch of edges. Fold dough over filling, forming a square. Pinch or press with a fork to seal edges. Prick tops with a fork. Brush with milk and sprinkle with half of the remaining cheese. Repeat with remaining pizza crust, filling, and cheese.

4. Bake for 15 to 18 minutes or until golden. Cool 5 minutes before serving. Serve with pizza sauce for dipping.

Per serving: 553 cal., 20 g total fat (5 g sat. fat), 53 mg chol., 1,059 mg sodium, 60 g carbo., 6 g fiber, 31 g pro.
Daily Values: 10% vit. A, 11% vit. C, 24% calcium, 27% iron

Turkey Manicotti

Cook all the shells that come in the package as they tend to break as they boil.

Prep: 30 minutes **Bake:** 25 minutes
Cook: 30 minutes **Stand:** 10 minutes
Oven: 350°F **Makes:** 6 servings

 12 dried manicotti shells
 ½ cup chopped onion (1 medium)
 4 cloves garlic, minced
 2 tablespoons olive oil
 2 14.5-ounce cans fire-roasted diced tomatoes, undrained
 ⅓ cup dry red wine
 2 tablespoons tomato paste
 2 cups chopped cooked turkey (12 ounces)
 1 cup shredded mozzarella cheese (4 ounces)
 ½ of a 15-ounce carton ricotta cheese (¾ cup)
 ½ of an 8-ounce tub cream cheese spread with chive and onion
 ¼ cup grated Parmesan cheese
 1 teaspoon dried basil, crushed
 ½ teaspoon dried oregano, crushed
 ¼ teaspoon salt
 ¼ teaspoon ground black pepper

1. Cook manicotti according to package directions; drain. Rinse with cold water; drain again and set aside. Meanwhile, for sauce, in a medium saucepan cook onion and garlic in hot oil over medium-high heat until onion is tender. Stir in undrained tomatoes, wine, and tomato paste. Bring to boiling; reduce heat. Cover and simmer for 30 minutes.

2. Preheat oven to 350°F. For filling, in a large bowl combine turkey, ½ cup of the mozzarella cheese, ricotta, cream cheese spread, Parmesan, basil, oregano, salt, and pepper. Using a small spoon, carefully fill each manicotti shell with about ¼ cup filling. Arrange filled shells in a 3-quart rectangular baking dish. Pour sauce over shells. Sprinkle with remaining ½ cup mozzarella cheese.

3. Bake, covered, for 25 to 30 minutes or until heated through. Let stand, covered, for 10 minutes before serving.

Per serving: 503 cal., 22 g total fat (11 g sat. fat), 83 mg chol., 777 mg sodium, 42 g carbo., 2 g fiber, 30 g pro.
Daily Values: 23% vit. A, 31% vit. C, 30% calcium, 19% iron

Turkey Manicotti

Simple

Turkey Salad Sandwiches

This quick-to-fix sandwich provides so many choices for change. Vary the flavor by using basil instead of tarragon. Serve on a croissant or your favorite flavor of toasted bread. Lettuce, red onion, and/or tomato slices add crunch and color.

Start to Finish: 20 minutes **Makes:** 6 sandwiches

- 3 **cups finely chopped cooked turkey (18 ounces)**
- ½ **cup mayonnaise**
- ¼ **cup thinly sliced green onion (2)**
- 2 **tablespoons Dijon-style mustard**
- 1 **teaspoon dried tarragon, thyme, or basil, crushed**
- 6 **croissants, split, or 12 slices rye or wheat bread, toasted**
- 6 **slices provolone cheese (6 ounces) Lettuce leaves, red onion slices, and/or tomato slices (optional)**

1. For filling, in a large bowl combine turkey, mayonnaise, green onion, mustard, and tarragon. Divide filling among bottom halves of croissants. Add a slice of cheese to each. If desired, add lettuce, onion, and/or tomato slices. Add tops of croissants.

Per serving: 553 cal., 34 g total fat (11 g sat. fat), 96 mg chol., 733 mg sodium, 22 g carbo., 1 g fiber, 37 g pro.
Daily Values: 11% vit. A, 2% vit. C, 26% calcium, 17% iron

Asian Turkey à la King

To save a few steps, use puff pastry shells and bake according to package directions. Split in half and proceed as directed below.

Prep: 30 minutes **Bake:** 10 minutes
Oven: 400°F **Makes:** 6 servings

- 1 frozen puff pastry sheet (½ of a 17.3-ounce package), thawed
- 4 teaspoons cornstarch
- ⅛ teaspoon ground black pepper
- ¾ cup chicken broth
- 1 tablespoon dry sherry or chicken broth
- 1 tablespoon soy sauce
- 1 cup sliced carrots (2 medium)
- 1 cup chopped red sweet pepper (1 large)
- ¼ cup sliced green onion (2)
- 2 tablespoons cooking oil
- 1 15-ounce can whole straw mushrooms, drained
- 3 cups chopped cooked turkey (18 ounces)
- 1 8-ounce can sliced water chestnuts, drained
- ⅓ cup tub-style cream cheese spread with chive and onion
- ¼ cup chopped cashews

1. Preheat oven to 400°F. On a lightly floured surface, unfold puff pastry. Using a sharp knife cut pastry in half lengthwise and then into thirds crosswise, making six rectangles. Cut each rectangle diagonally in half to make two triangles, for a total of 12 triangles. Arrange pastry triangles on an greased baking sheet. Bake for 10 to 15 minutes or until puffed and golden. Transfer to a wire rack and let cool for 5 minutes.

2. Meanwhile, in a small bowl combine cornstarch and black pepper. Whisk in broth, sherry, and soy sauce; set aside. In a large skillet cook and stir carrots, sweet pepper, and green onion in hot oil over medium-high heat for 3 minutes. Add mushrooms. Cook and stir for 2 minutes more. Stir cornstarch mixture; stir into vegetable mixture in skillet. Cook and stir until thickened and bubbly; cook and stir for 2 minutes more. Stir in turkey and water chestnuts; heat through.

3. For each serving, place a baked pastry triangle in each shallow bowl. Place about 1 tablespoon cream cheese over each pastry. Place another pastry triangle on top of the cream cheese. Spoon turkey mixture over and sprinkle with cashews.

Per serving: 581 cal., 32 g total fat (10 g sat. fat), 78 mg chol., 804 mg sodium, 39 g carbo., 5 g fiber, 33 g pro.
Daily Values: 88% vit. A, 84% vit. C, 7% calcium, 24% iron

Cranberry-Cream Cheese Spread

To soften cream cheese, let the cheese stand at room temperature for 30 to 60 minutes.

Prep: 20 minutes **Chill:** 4 hours
Makes: 3 cups (twenty-four 2-tablespoon servings)

- 2 8-ounce packages cream cheese, softened
- 3 tablespoons packed brown sugar
- ½ cup chopped pecans, toasted (see tip, page 63)
- ½ cup whole cranberry sauce
- 1 teaspoon finely shredded orange peel
  Party rye bread, assorted crackers, and/or fresh fruit, such as pear or apple slices, grapes, and/or strawberries

1. In a medium mixing bowl beat the cream cheese and brown sugar with an electric mixer on medium speed until smooth. Stir in pecans, cranberry sauce, and orange peel. Cover and chill for 4 to 24 hours.

Asian Turkey à la King

Cranberry-Cream Cheese Spread

2. Meanwhile, in a large skillet melt butter over medium heat. Add turkey slices; cover and cook for 5 minutes or until heated through. Top toast slices with turkey. Place a scoop of mashed potatoes next to the toast on each plate. Cover and keep warm.

3. For sauce, carefully stir brown sugar and cornstarch into drippings in skillet; stir in cranberry sauce, orange peel, wine, orange juice, salt, and pepper. Cook and stir over medium-high heat until thickened and bubbly. Cook and stir for 1 minute more. Spoon sauce over turkey and potatoes.

Per serving: 629 cal., 10 g total fat (4 g sat. fat), 86 mg chol., 682 mg sodium, 96 g carbo., 4 g fiber, 32 g pro.
Daily Values: 4% vit. A, 62% vit. C, 6% calcium, 18% iron

2. To serve, transfer cheese mixture to a serving bowl. Serve with bread, crackers, and/or fruit.

Per serving spread: 97 cal., 8 g total fat (4 g sat. fat), 21 mg chol., 57 mg sodium, 5 g carbo., 0 g fiber, 2 g pro.
Daily Values: 5% vit. A, 2% calcium, 2% iron

Cranberry-Sauced Hot Turkey Sandwiches

Wine, orange juice and peel, and a bit of sugar, salt, and pepper add a lovely layer of flavor to traditional cranberry sauce in this knife-and-fork sandwich.

Start to Finish: 30 minutes Makes: 4 servings

- 4 ¾-inch diagonally cut slices Italian bread or Texas toast, toasted
- 1 24-ounce package refrigerated garlic mashed potatoes or 2⅔ cups leftover mashed potatoes, reheated
- 2 tablespoons butter or margarine
- 12 ounces cooked turkey breast, sliced
- 3 tablespoons packed brown sugar
- 1 tablespoon cornstarch
- 1 16-ounce can whole cranberry sauce
- ¼ teaspoon finely shredded orange peel
- ⅓ cup dry red wine or orange juice
- ¼ cup orange juice
- ¼ teaspoon salt
- ⅛ teaspoon ground black pepper

1. On each of four plates place one slice of toast. Prepare refrigerated mashed potatoes according to microwave package directions. Set aside.

Ham and Swiss on Ciabatta

Purchased basil pesto packs amazing flavor into these simple sandwiches. You also could make them easily with leftover turkey or roast beef.

Prep: 15 minutes Bake: 15 minutes (if desired)
Oven: 350°F Makes: 6 servings

- ⅓ cup mayonnaise or salad dressing
- 2 tablespoons purchased basil pesto
- 6 ciabatta rolls, split
- 12 ounces thinly sliced cooked ham
- 6 slices Swiss cheese (4 to 6 ounces)
- 6 thin slices tomato
- 6 lettuce leaves (optional)

1. In a small bowl combine mayonnaise and pesto. Spread mayonnaise mixture evenly on cut sides of ciabatta rolls. Divide ham, cheese, and tomatoes among roll bottoms. Add roll tops.

2. For hot sandwiches, preheat oven to 350°F. Wrap sandwiches individually in foil. Bake for 15 to 20 minutes or until heated through. Serve warm. For cold sandwiches, if desired, place lettuce leaves on top of tomato slices in sandwiches. Serve immediately.

Per serving: 399 cal., 24 g total fat (7 g sat. fat), 56 mg chol., 1,098 mg sodium, 26 g carbo., 2 g fiber, 19 g pro.
Daily Values: 6% vit. A, 6% vit. C, 24% calcium, 12% iron

125

2. Stir in broth, water, ham, drained black beans, kidney beans, cumin, thyme, cayenne pepper, and black pepper. If desired, stir in wine. Bring to boiling; reduce heat. Simmer, covered, for 25 to 30 minutes or until carrots are tender. If desired, serve with sour cream and garnish with cilantro.

Per serving: 204 cal., 6 g total fat (1 g sat. fat), 23 mg chol., 1,247 mg sodium, 21 g carbo., 7 g fiber, 19 g pro.

Daily Values: 58% vit. A, 35% vit. C, 6% calcium, 10% iron

Shepherd's Pie Diablo

Start to Finish: 25 minutes   Makes: 6 servings

 1   pound ground beef
 ½   cup chopped onion (1 medium)
 1   1.25-ounce envelope taco seasoning mix
 1   15-ounce can mixed vegetables, drained
 1   10¾-ounce can condensed fiesta nacho
       cheese soup
 2½ cups leftover mashed potatoes
 ½   cup shredded Monterey Jack cheese
       (2 ounces)
       Chopped green onion
       Dairy sour cream (optional)
       Bottled salsa (optional)

1. In a large skillet cook ground beef and onion over medium heat until meat is browned and onion is tender. Drain fat. Stir in taco seasoning mix and amount of water according to package directions. Prepare according to package directions.

2. Stir in drained mixed vegetables and soup. Return to boiling; reduce heat. Drop spoonfuls of mashed potatoes on top of the mixture. Sprinkle with cheese. Cover and simmer over low heat for 8 minutes or until heated through. Sprinkle with green onion. If desired, serve with sour cream and salsa.

Per serving: 481 cal., 33 g total fat (13 g sat. fat), 72 mg chol., 1,432 mg sodium, 30 g carbo., 5 g fiber, 17 g pro.

Daily Values: 84% vit. A, 23% vit. C, 16% calcium, 16% iron

Spicy Ham and Bean Soup

Spicy Ham and Bean Soup

Sour cream and cilantro are optional but adding them makes this recipe truly spectacular. Pass hot sauce for those who really like their food with a kick.

Prep: 30 minutes   Cook: 30 minutes
Makes: 8 servings

 1   cup chopped onion (1 large)
 1   cup sliced carrot (2 medium)
 ½   cup sliced celery (1 stalk)
 ½   cup chopped red and/or green
       sweet pepper (1 small)
 6   cloves garlic, minced
 2   tablespoons cooking oil
 4   cups beef broth
 2   cups water
 2   cups cubed cooked ham
 1   15-ounce can black beans,
       rinsed and drained
 1   15-ounce can red kidney beans,
       rinsed and drained
 2   teaspoons ground cumin
 1   teaspoon dried thyme, crushed
 ⅛   to ¼ teaspoon cayenne pepper
 ⅛   teaspoon ground black pepper
 ½   cup dry white wine (optional)
       Dairy sour cream (optional)
       Fresh cilantro sprigs (optional)

1. In a 4- to 6-quart Dutch oven cook onion, carrot, celery, sweet pepper, and garlic in hot oil over medium-high heat about 5 minutes or until onion is tender.

 **Mashed Potato Patties with Tapenade Cream**

Olive tapenade can be found with the relishes and other condiments in most supermarkets.

Start to Finish: 30 minutes **Makes:** 8 servings

2½ cups leftover mashed potatoes or one 24-ounce package refrigerated mashed potatoes
2 ounces smoked Gouda or smoked cheddar cheese, shredded; or crumbled feta cheese (⅛ cup)
1 tablespoon all-purpose flour
1 tablespoon snipped fresh cilantro, dill, tarragon, or chopped green onion
⅛ teaspoon freshly ground black pepper
1 egg
1 tablespoon water
½ cup fine dry bread crumbs
2 teaspoons olive oil
½ cup dairy sour cream
3 tablespoons purchased olive tapenade, 1 to 2 teaspoons prepared horseradish, or 1 teaspoon ground cumin
Torn mixed salad greens (optional)

1. In a large bowl stir together mashed potatoes, cheese, flour, cilantro, and pepper. Form potato mixture into six patties, each about ¾ inch thick.

2. In a shallow dish beat together egg and water. Place bread crumbs in another shallow dish. Dip potato patties in egg mixture, then in bread crumbs, turning to coat both sides.

3. In a large nonstick skillet heat 1 teaspoon of the oil over medium heat; reduce heat to medium-low. Add four patties to the skillet; cook for 4 minutes or until bottoms are golden brown. Gently turn patties and cook for 4 to 5 minutes more or until golden brown. Remove to a baking sheet. Keep warm in 300°F oven. Cook remaining patties using remaining 1 teaspoon oil.

4. Meanwhile, in a small bowl stir together sour cream and tapenade. Serve hot patties with sour cream mixture. If desired, serve with salad greens on the side.

Per serving: 198 cal., 12 g total fat (4 g sat. fat), 39 mg chol., 527 mg sodium, 18 g carbo., 2 g fiber, 5 g pro.
Daily Values: 5% vit. A, 7% vit. C, 9% calcium, 4% iron

 Stuffing Patties

Be sure to snip the dried cranberries for this recipe so they will distribute evenly throughout the mixture. When shaping the patties, use damp hands for easier handling of the mixture.

Start to Finish: 25 minutes **Makes:** 8 patties

1 egg, beaten
3 cups leftover cooked stuffing or dressing
½ cup snipped dried cranberries
3 tablespoons cooking oil
½ cup canned whole cranberry sauce

1. In a large bowl combine egg, stuffing, and dried cranberries. Form stuffing mixture into eight patties, using about ⅓ cup mixture for each.

2. In a large skillet cook patties in hot oil over medium-high heat for 10 to 12 minutes or until brown and crisp, turning once; add additional oil during cooking if necessary. Serve patties with cranberry sauce.

Per patty: 237 cal., 12 g total fat (2 g sat. fat), 26 mg chol., 421 mg sodium, 29 g carbo., 3 g fiber, 3 g pro.
Daily Values: 8% vit. A, 1% vit. C, 3% calcium, 6% iron

Mashed Potato Patties with Tapenade Cream

Stuffed Bread Pudding

Use a variety of mushrooms—button, cremini, shiitake, and portobello—in this fun side dish. Take it to main-dish status by using a sausage-based stuffing and reducing the servings to four.

Prep: 25 minutes **Bake:** 45 minutes
Stand: 15 minutes **Oven:** 350°F **Makes:** 8 servings

>   2 **cups sliced fresh mushrooms**
>   1 **cup finely chopped onion (1 large)**
>   2 **tablespoons butter or margarine**
>   3 **eggs, lightly beaten**
> 1½ **cups milk**
>   3 **cups leftover cooked stuffing or dressing**
>   1 **cup shredded provolone or mozzarella cheese (4 ounces)**

1. Preheat oven to 350°F. Grease a 1½-quart rectangular baking dish; set aside. In a large skillet cook mushrooms and onion in hot butter over medium-high heat until onion is tender.

2. In a large bowl beat together eggs and milk. Stir in mushroom mixture. Add stuffing and cheese, stirring well to coat. Spoon mixture into prepared baking dish. Press mixture down lightly with the back of a wooden spoon.

3. Bake, uncovered, for 45 to 55 minutes or until the top is puffed and golden brown and a knife inserted near the center comes out clean. Let stand 15 minutes before serving.

Per serving: 267 cal., 16 g total fat (7 g sat. fat), 100 mg chol., 574 mg sodium, 20 g carbo., 1 g fiber, 11 g pro.
Daily Values: 12% vit. A, 3% vit. C, 19% calcium, 8% iron

Sweet Potato Spice Cake

If you use leftover sweet potatoes, be sure they aren't highly seasoned or the flavor of this spice cake could be compromised.

Prep: 30 minutes **Bake:** 30 minutes **Cool:** 2 hours
Oven: 350°F **Makes:** 12 servings

>   1 **package 2-layer-size white or yellow cake mix**
> 1½ **cups leftover mashed cooked sweet potatoes or ½ of a 24-ounce package refrigerated mashed sweet potatoes***
>   3 **eggs**
>   ¾ **cup water**
>   ¼ **cup cooking oil**
>   1 **teaspoon pumpkin pie spice**
>   1 **cup dried cranberries and/or dried tart red cherries**
>   ½ **cup finely chopped pecans, toasted**
>   1 **16-ounce can cream cheese frosting**
>   **Chopped pecans, toasted (see tip, page 63)**

1. Preheat oven to 350°F. Grease and lightly flour two 9×1½-inch round cake pans; set aside.

2. In a large mixing bowl combine cake mix, sweet potatoes, eggs, water, oil, and pumpkin pie spice. Beat with an electric mixer on low speed just until combined. Beat on medium speed for 2 minutes more, scraping the sides of the bowl occasionally. Stir in cranberries and finely chopped pecans. Spread batter into prepared pans.

Stuffed Bread Pudding

3. Bake for 30 to 35 minutes or until a wooden tooth-pick inserted near centers comes out clean. Cool in pans on wire racks for 10 minutes. Remove cake layers from pans; cool thoroughly on wire racks.

4. Place one cake layer on a serving plate. Frost cake top with about ⅓ cup of the cream cheese frosting. Top with second cake layer. Frost cake top and sides with remaining frosting. Sprinkle with additional toasted pecans.

*Note: If desired, substitute 1½ cups mashed, canned sweet potatoes. (One 17.2-ounce can of sweet potatoes will yield 2 cups mashed.)

Per serving: 520 cal., 24 g total fat (5 g sat. fat), 53 mg chol., 393 mg sodium, 76 g carbo., 2 g fiber, 6 g pro.

Daily Values: 130% vit. A, 9% vit. C, 9% calcium, 9% iron

Sweet Potato Cheesecake

 **Sweet Potato Cheesecake**

Whipped cream and caramel-flavored ice cream sauce top this lovely spiced cheesecake.

Prep: 30 minutes **Bake:** 40 minutes **Cool:** 2 hours
Chill: 4 hours **Oven:** 375°F **Makes:** 12 servings

- 1½ **cups finely crushed vanilla wafers (about 45)**
- ½ **cup finely chopped pecans**
- ⅓ **cup butter, melted**
- 3 **8-ounce packages cream cheese, softened**
- 1½ **cups leftover mashed cooked sweet potatoes (see note, above)**
- 1 **cup sugar**
- 2 **tablespoons all-purpose flour**
- 1 **teaspoon vanilla**
- ½ **teaspoon ground cinnamon**
- ¼ **teaspoon ground cloves**
- ¼ **cup half-and-half, light cream, or milk**
- 3 **eggs, lightly beaten**
- ½ **teaspoon finely shredded orange peel (optional)**
  Whipped cream and/or caramel-flavored ice cream topping (optional)

1. Preheat oven to 375°F. For crust, in a medium bowl combine crushed wafers and pecans. Stir in melted butter. Press the crumb mixture on the bottom and about 1 inch up the sides of a 9-inch springform pan; set springform pan on a baking sheet. Set aside.

2. For filling, in a large mixing bowl beat cream cheese, sweet potatoes, sugar, flour, vanilla, cinnamon, and cloves with an electric mixer until well combined. Beat in half-and-half just until smooth. Stir in eggs and if desired, orange peel.

3. Pour filling into crust-lined pan. Bake about 40 minutes or until a 2½-inch area around the outside edge appears set when gently shaken.

4. Cool in pan on wire rack for 15 minutes. Using a small sharp knife, loosen crust from pan sides; cool for 30 minutes. Remove sides of pan. Cool cheesecake completely on rack. Cover and chill at least 4 hours before serving. If desired, top each serving with whipped cream and/or caramel topping.

Per serving: 508 cal., 35 g total fat (18 g sat. fat), 131 mg chol., 304 mg sodium, 44 g carbo., 2 g fiber, 8 g pro.

Daily Values: 149% vit. A, 9% vit. C, 8% calcium, 11% iron

Soup Party

Hot, hearty, and comforting—everyone loves a steaming bowl of soup when the temperatures drop! The aromas of soups and stews simmering on the stove are enough to warm the cold right out of winter. There's no better way to gather with friends for a pre-holiday get-together than over bountiful bowls of these brothy favorites. Make a buffet of choices, combining rich soups, such as Seafood and Corn Chowder or Mashed Potato Soup, with savory delights, such as Pronto Beefy Mushroom Soup or Meatball Stew. Or turn it into a potluck party and have guests bring a pot or two of their own winter favorites. Toss together a leafy green salad, bake some crusty bread, and settle in for a holiday gathering like no other!

Tortellini Chowder, page 137

Meatball Stew

Make an extra batch of this stew and freeze in individual containers for busy nights.

Start to Finish: 30 minutes **Makes:** 6 to 8 servings

- 5 **cups water**
- 1 **14.5-ounce can diced tomatoes, undrained**
- 1 **cup diced carrot (2 medium)**
- 1 **cup sliced celery (2 stalks)**
- 1 **cup chopped onion (1 large)**
- ⅓ **cup quick-cooking barley**
- 3 **beef bouillon cubes or 1 tablespoon instant beef bouillon granules**
- 1 **teaspoon seasoned salt**
- 1 **teaspoon dried basil, crushed**
- 1 **bay leaf**
- 1 **18-ounce package frozen cooked meatballs (about 36 meatballs)**

1. In a large saucepan combine water, undrained tomatoes, carrot, celery, onion, barley, bouillon, seasoned salt, basil, and bay leaf. Bring to boiling over medium heat, stirring occasionally.

2. Add frozen meatballs. Cover and simmer for 5 to 10 minutes or until meatballs are heated through, stirring once or twice. Discard bay leaf.

Per serving: 330 cal., 22 g total fat (9 g sat. fat), 30 mg chol., 1,518 mg sodium, 21 g carbo., 4 g fiber, 13 g pro.
Daily Values: 70% vit. A, 20% vit. C, 9% calcium, 7% iron

 ## Barley Soup with Meatballs

A trio of winter vegetables—squash, carrots, and parsnips—brim in this warming soup.

Start to Finish: 1 hour **Makes:** 6 to 8 servings

Barley Soup with Meatballs

1 recipe Homemade Meatballs
4 slices bacon or peppered bacon
½ cup chopped onion (1 medium)
2 cloves garlic, minced
1 1- to 1½-pound butternut or acorn squash,
   peeled and cut into ¾-inch pieces
   (about 4 cups)
2 medium carrots, cut into ¾-inch pieces
2 medium parsnips, cut into ¾-inch pieces
4 14-ounce cans reduced-sodium chicken
   broth or lower-sodium beef broth
   (about 7 cups)
1 cup apple juice or water
1 teaspoon dried Italian seasoning, dried
   thyme, or dried oregano, crushed
1 cup quick-cooking barley
   Salt and ground black pepper

1. Prepare and bake the Homemade Meatballs. Meanwhile, in a 4-quart Dutch oven cook bacon until crisp. Remove bacon from pan, reserving 1 tablespoon drippings in pan. Drain bacon on paper towels; set aside.

2. Cook onion and garlic in reserved drippings over medium heat until tender. Add squash, carrot, and parsnip; cook for 5 minutes more, stirring occasionally. Add broth, apple juice, and Italian seasoning. Bring to boiling; stir in barley. Reduce heat. Simmer, covered, for 10 to 15 minutes or until barley and vegetables are tender. Add meatballs; heat through. Season to taste with salt and pepper.

3. To serve, ladle into bowls. Crumble cooked bacon and sprinkle over individual servings.

Homemade Meatballs: Preheat oven to 400°F. Line a 15×10×1-inch baking pan with foil; set aside. In a large bowl combine 1 egg, lightly beaten; ½ cup soft French or Italian bread crumbs; ¼ cup finely chopped onion; 2 cloves garlic, minced; 1 teaspoon dried oregano or thyme, crushed; ½ teaspoon salt; and ¼ teaspoon ground black pepper. Add 1 pound lean ground beef; mix well. Shape into 24 meatballs (about 1 tablespoon mixture per meatball). Arrange meatballs in prepared pan. Bake about 15 minutes or until juices run clear. Drain fat. Makes 24 meatballs.

Make-Ahead Directions: Prepare as above, except place cooked bacon in a resealable plastic bag. Quick chill the soup by placing Dutch oven in a sink filled with ice water for 10 minutes, stirring frequently. Transfer soup to a storage container. Cover and refrigerate soup and bacon for up to 3 days. To serve, transfer soup to a 4-quart Dutch oven. Bring soup to boiling; stirring frequently. Serve as above. (Do not freeze the soup.)

Per serving including meatballs: 402 cal., 13 g total fat (5 g sat. fat), 89 mg chol., 1117 mg sodium, 47 g carbo., 7 g fiber, 23 g pro.
Daily Values: 60% vit. A, 25% vit. C, 7% calcium, 18% iron

Pronto Beefy Mushroom Soup

Dress up onion soup mix with fresh mushrooms and onion for a bowl of soup that tastes as if it came from the kitchen of a French bistro. While the soup simmers, you'll have time to heat garlic bread in the oven.

Start to Finish: 15 minutes
Makes: 4 side-dish servings

1 small red or yellow onion, thinly sliced
1 8-ounce package sliced fresh mushrooms
2 tablespoons butter or margarine
1 14-ounce can beef broth
1½ cups water
1 envelope onion-mushroom soup mix or
   beefy onion soup mix
1 to 2 tablespoons dry sherry (optional)

1. In a medium saucepan cook onion and mushrooms in hot butter over medium heat for 5 minutes. Stir in beef broth, water, and dry soup mix. Cook and stir over medium-high heat until bubbly; reduce heat. Simmer, uncovered, for 5 minutes. If desired, stir in sherry.

Per serving: 98 cal., 6 g total fat (4 g sat. fat), 15 mg chol., 1,093 mg sodium, 8 g carbo., 1 g fiber, 3 g pro.
Daily Values: 4% vit. A, 4% vit. C, 1% calcium, 2% iron

 Country French Beef Stew

Dry red wine adds a layer of robust flavor to this classic beef stew. Add some crusty bread and serve with the leftover wine.

Prep: 30 minutes **Cook:** 1 hour 55 minutes
Stand: 1 hour **Makes:** 6 servings

- ½ cup dry navy beans or one 15-ounce can cannellini beans (white kidney beans) or navy beans, rinsed and drained*
- 2 cups water
- ¼ cup all-purpose flour
- ½ teaspoon ground black pepper
- 2 pounds boneless beef chuck pot roast, cut into 1-inch pieces
- 2 tablespoons olive oil
- 1 medium onion, cut into thin wedges
- 3 cloves garlic, minced
- ⅔ cup dry red wine
- 1 14-ounce can beef broth*
- 2 teaspoons dried thyme, crushed, or 2 tablespoons snipped fresh thyme
- 4 medium carrots, cut into ½-inch slices
- 2 medium parsnips, cut into ½-inch slices
- 1 cup chopped tomato
  Salt and ground black pepper
  Snipped fresh parsley (optional)

1. If using dry beans, rinse beans. In a medium saucepan combine the dry beans and the water. Bring to boiling; reduce heat. Simmer, uncovered, for 2 minutes. Remove from heat. Cover and let stand for 1 hour. (Or place dry beans in water in pan. Cover and let soak in a cool place for 6 to 8 hours or overnight.) Drain and rinse beans.

2. Place flour and ½ teaspoon pepper in a plastic bag. Add beef pieces, a few at a time, shaking to coat. In a 4- to 6-quart Dutch oven brown half of the beef in 1 tablespoon of the hot oil; remove beef. Add remaining oil, remaining beef, onion, and garlic to Dutch oven. Cook until beef is brown and onion is tender. Drain fat, if necessary. Remove beef; set aside. Stir in wine, scraping until the brown bits are dissolved. Return beef to Dutch oven. Stir in soaked or canned beans, broth, and dried thyme (if using). Bring to boiling; reduce heat.

3. Simmer, covered, for 1½ hours. Add carrot, parsnip, and tomato. Return to boiling; reduce heat. Simmer, covered, for 25 to 30 minutes more or until beef and vegetables are tender. Stir in fresh thyme (if using). Season to taste with salt and pepper. If desired, garnish with parsley.

*Note: If using canned beans, decrease beef broth to 1 cup.

Per serving: 393 cal., 12 g total fat (3 g sat. fat), 89 mg chol., 478 mg sodium, 28 g carbo., 8 g fiber, 38 g pro.
Daily Values: 142% vit. A, 23% vit. C, 7% calcium, 30% iron

 Clam Chowder

This creamy chowder is a snap to prepare thanks to canned soup and frozen potatoes.

Prep: 15 minutes **Cook:** 15 minutes
Makes: 4 to 6 servings

- 2 10.75-ounce cans condensed cream of celery soup
- 2 cups frozen diced hash brown potatoes with onions and peppers
- 1 8-ounce bottle clam juice
- 1 6.5-ounce can minced clams, undrained
- 2 teaspoons Worcestershire sauce
- 1 teaspoon dried thyme, crushed
- 1 cup half-and-half or light cream
- 3 slices packaged ready-to-serve cooked bacon, chopped
  Ground black pepper (optional)

1. In a large saucepan combine soup, hash browns, clam juice, undrained clams, Worcestershire sauce, and thyme. Bring to boiling; reduce heat. Cover and simmer about 15 minutes or until potatoes are tender, stirring frequently.

2. Stir in half-and-half and heat through. Sprinkle individual servings with bacon. If desired, season to taste with pepper.

Per serving: 459 cal., 17 g total fat (7 g sat. fat), 62 mg chol., 1,693 mg sodium, 57 g carbo., 4 g fiber, 17 g pro.
Daily Values: 17% vit. A, 17% vit. C, 15% calcium, 66% iron

 **Seafood and Corn Chowder**

This impressive soup goes together from start to finish in 35 minutes. If desired, pass bottled hot sauce at the table and serve with your choice of crispy crackers or crusty bread with butter.

Prep: 15 minutes **Cook:** 20 minutes
Makes: 4 or 5 servings

- 1 14-ounce can chicken broth or
  1¾ cups homemade chicken broth
- 1 cup sliced celery (2 stalks)
- 1 cup chopped onion (1 large)
- ½ cup sliced carrot (1 medium)
- 1 14.75-ounce can cream-style corn
- 1 cup whipping cream
- ½ teaspoon snipped fresh thyme or
  ¼ teaspoon dried thyme, crushed
- ⅛ teaspoon ground black pepper
  Few dashes bottled hot pepper sauce
- 10 to 12 ounces cooked or canned lump
  crabmeat and/or peeled, deveined,
  cooked shrimp
  Fresh thyme sprigs (optional)
  Assorted crackers (optional)

1. In a medium saucepan combine broth, celery, onion, and carrot. Bring to boiling; reduce heat. Simmer, covered, about 20 minutes or until vegetables are tender. Cool slightly.

2. Transfer half of the broth mixture to a blender or food processor. Cover and blend or process until smooth. Repeat with remaining cooked mixture. Return mixture to saucepan. Stir in corn, whipping cream, thyme, pepper, and hot pepper sauce. Bring to boiling; reduce heat. Stir in crabmeat and/or shrimp; heat through. If desired, garnish each serving with fresh thyme and serve with assorted crackers.

Per serving: 388 cal., 24 g total fat (14 g sat. fat), 154 mg chol., 948 mg sodium, 27 g carbo., 3 g fiber, 18 g pro.
Daily Values: 73% vit. A, 20% vit. C, 14% calcium, 7% iron

Seafood and Corn Chowder

 Mashed Potato Soup

Start to Finish: 15 minutes **Makes:** 3 servings

- 1 24-ounce package refrigerated
  mashed potatoes
- 1 14-ounce can chicken broth
- ¼ cup sliced green onion (2)
- 2 ounces Swiss, cheddar, or smoked
  Gouda cheese, shredded (½ cup)
  Dairy sour cream (optional)

1. In a medium saucepan combine mashed potatoes, broth, and green onion. Cook over medium-high heat just until mixture reaches boiling, whisking until nearly smooth. Add cheese; whisk until cheese is melted. If desired, serve with sour cream.

Per serving: 355 cal., 19 g total fat (12 g sat. fat), 55 mg chol., 863 mg sodium, 34 g carbo., 4 g fiber, 13 g pro.
Daily Values: 16% vit. A, 47% vit. C, 21% calcium, 11% iron

Potato and Roasted Corn Chowder in Bread Bowls

Yukon gold potatoes are sweeter and creamier than standard baking potatoes, making this chowder truly impressive.

Prep: 25 minutes **Bake:** 20 minutes
Cook: 20 minutes **Oven:** 450°F
Makes: 8 servings

- 1 16-ounce package frozen whole kernel corn
- 1 pound Yukon gold potatoes, peeled and cut into ½-inch cubes
- 2 tablespoons olive oil
- ½ cup thinly sliced leeks
- 2 tablespoons finely chopped shallots
- 4 cups chicken broth
- 1 teaspoon dried marjoram, crushed
- 1 teaspoon kosher salt or salt
- ½ teaspoon ground ginger
- ½ teaspoon ground white pepper
- 3 cups half-and-half or light cream
- 8 individual round loaves of sourdough bread*

1. Preheat oven to 450°F. Thaw frozen corn and pat dry with paper towels. Line a 15×10×1-inch baking pan with foil. Lightly grease foil. Spread corn on half of the prepared pan. In a resealable plastic bag combine potatoes and 1 tablespoon of the oil. Seal and shake well to coat potatoes with oil. Spread potatoes on the other half of prepared pan. Roast, uncovered, for 10 minutes; stir, keeping corn and potatoes separate. Continue to roast for 10 minutes more, stirring once or twice. Remove pan from oven. Set aside.

2. Transfer half of the roasted corn (about ¾ cup) to a food processor or blender. Cover; process or blend corn until pureed (if necessary, add a small amount of chicken broth to help blend mixture).

3. In a 4-quart Dutch oven heat the remaining 1 tablespoon oil over medium-high heat. Add leeks and shallots. Reduce heat to medium. Cook and stir leek mixture for 6 to 8 minutes or until leeks are soft and golden. Add whole corn and pureed corn. Cook and stir for 1 minute. Stir in roasted potatoes, broth,

marjoram, salt, ginger, and white pepper. Bring to boiling; reduce heat. Cover and simmer for 10 to 12 minutes or until potatoes are tender.

4. Add half-and-half. Cook and stir until heated through. Season to taste with additional *salt* and *ground white pepper*.

5. Hollow out sourdough loaves. To serve, spoon chowder into bread bowls.

*Note: Use leftover bread from hollowing out loaves to make bread crumbs for use in other recipes.

Per serving: 588 cal., 15 g total fat (7 g sat. fat), 33 mg chol., 1,342 mg sodium, 94 g carbo., 2 g fiber, 20 g pro.
Daily Values: 10% vit. A, 22% vit. C, 11% calcium, 23% iron

Quick Chicken and Tortellini Soup

From pantry to table in 15 minutes—that is how quickly you can have this creamy soup ready for your friends and family.

Start to Finish: 15 minutes **Makes:** 4 servings

- 2 cups milk
- 1 10.75-ounce can condensed cream of chicken with herbs soup
- 1 10.5-ounce can condensed chicken broth
- 1 9-ounce package refrigerated cheese tortellini
- 1 6-ounce package refrigerated chicken breast strips
- 1 cup purchased shredded carrot or coarsely shredded carrot

1. In a 4-quart Dutch oven whisk together milk, cream of chicken soup, and chicken broth until smooth. Cook over high heat just until boiling, stirring frequently. Stir in tortellini, chicken, and carrot. Reduce heat. Cover and simmer for 5 to 6 minutes or until tortellini is tender, stirring occasionally.

Per serving: 422 cal., 12 g total fat (5 g sat. fat), 78 mg chol., 1,871 mg sodium, 53 g carbo., 4 g fiber, 27 g pro.
Daily Values: 115% vit. A, 3% vit. C, 28% calcium, 9% iron

Tortellini Chowder

Italian-style tortellini combines with Mexican flavors in this hearty chowder. Make it as spicy as you like with green chile and jalapeño peppers.

Prep: 30 minutes **Cook:** 26 minutes
Makes: 6 to 8 servings

- ⅔ cup chopped onion
- ½ cup chopped red sweet pepper
- ⅓ cup chopped fresh green chile pepper,* such as anaheim or poblano
- 1 fresh jalapeño chile pepper,* seeded, if desired, and chopped (about 1 tablespoon)
- 2 tablespoons minced garlic
- 1 tablespoon butter or margarine
- 3 cups chicken broth
- 2 cups cubed peeled potatoes
- 1 teaspoon ground cumin
- ¼ teaspoon salt
- ¼ teaspoon ground black pepper
- ⅛ teaspoon cayenne pepper
- 2 tablespoons all-purpose flour
- 2 tablespoons butter or margarine, melted
- 1 15.25-ounce can whole kernel corn, drained
- 2 cups half-and-half or light cream
- 2 cups refrigerated or frozen spinach tortellini, cooked and drained

1. In a 4- to 6-quart Dutch oven cook onion, sweet pepper, green chile pepper, jalapeño pepper, and garlic in 1 tablespoon butter over medium heat about 5 minutes or until vegetables are tender, but not brown.

2. Carefully stir in broth, potatoes, cumin, salt, black pepper, and cayenne pepper. Bring to boiling; reduce heat. Cover and simmer for 25 to 30 minutes or until potatoes are just tender.

3. In a small bowl stir together flour and 2 tablespoons melted butter; add to soup mixture. Cook and stir over medium heat until thickened and bubbly. Cook and stir for 1 minute more.

4. Reduce heat and add corn, half-and-half, and tortellini. Heat through. Ladle into warm soup bowls.

*Note: Because hot chile peppers contain oils that can burn skin and eyes, avoid direct contact with chiles as much as possible. When working with chile peppers, wear plastic or rubber gloves. If bare hands do touch the chile peppers, wash them well with soap and water.

Per serving: 387 cal., 18 g total fat (11 g sat. fat), 64 mg chol., 979 mg sodium, 47 g carbo., 4 g fiber, 11 g pro.
Daily Values: 22% vit. A, 101% vit. C, 17% calcium, 10% iron

Soups and Stew Toppers

Croutons
Shredded cheese
Chives
Sliced green onion
Chopped roasted red bell peppers
Nuts or seeds
Crumbled hard-boiled eggs
Snipped or chopped fresh herbs
Sour cream or plain yogurt
Capers
Crumbed bacon
Extra virgin olive oil
Pimientos

Tortellini Chowder

New Year's Eve Celebration

Ring in the New Year with style! Host a gathering for family and friends as you reminisce about the past and look forward to the future. While the guests share well-intentioned New Year's resolutions, serve them a feast worthy of this exciting evening. If you're aiming to impress, start with a delectable sampling of Cornmeal Crusted Pork Paté. Follow up with Porcini Rack of Lamb as the main dish; Butternut Risotto as an accompaniment; and beautiful Fig and Fruit Salad to round out the special meal. Or choose one or more of the simple recipes to keep the meal moving smoothly and allow yourself more time to enjoy the festivities. Finish dinner with a sweet something from the Dessert Dazzlers section—whether you go simple or sensational, your dinner guests will be impressed! For a bubbly evening-ender, supply everyone with Champagne or sparkling cider to officially welcome in the coming year.

Fig and Fruit Salad, page 149

Easy Smoked Salmon Pâté

For an elegant looking appetizer, pipe the cream cheese mixture on crackers using a pastry bag.

Prep: 15 minutes
Makes: 1½ cups (twelve 2-tablespoon servings)

- 1 8-ounce package cream cheese, softened
- 1 4-ounce piece smoked salmon (not lox-style), flaked, with skin and bones removed
- ¼ cup chopped red onion
- 1 teaspoon finely shredded lemon peel
- 1 tablespoon lemon juice
- 1 tablespoon snipped fresh dillweed
- 1 tablespoon prepared horseradish
- ¼ teaspoon ground black pepper
  Assorted crackers and/or cucumber slices

1. Cut cream cheese into cubes and place in a food processor. Cover and process with several on/off turns until creamy. Add salmon, onion, lemon peel, lemon juice, dillweed, horseradish, and pepper.

2. Cover and process with several on/off pulses until just combined, scraping down sides as needed. Transfer to serving bowl. Serve with crackers.

Per serving paté: 79 cal., 7 g total fat (4 g sat. fat), 23 mg chol., 134 mg sodium, 1 g carbo., 0 g fiber, 3 g pro.
Daily Values: 5% vit. A, 2% vit. C, 2% calcium, 2% iron

Cornmeal Crusted Pork Pâté

In addition to the pear slices, if you like, serve this crusted pork pâté with a bit of Dijon-style mustard. Add freshness by substituting 1 tablespoon fresh thyme and 1 tablespoon fresh sage for their dried counterparts.

Prep: 1 hour **Bake:** 2 hours **Stand:** 45 minutes
Cool: 1 hour **Chill:** 4 plus 24 hours
Oven: 375°F/400°F **Makes:** 16 servings

- 1 cup finely chopped onion (1 large)
- 1 clove garlic, minced
- 1 tablespoon cooking oil
- 1 egg
- ½ cup milk
- 1 teaspoon dried thyme, crushed
- 1 teaspoon dried leaf sage, crushed
- 1 teaspoon salt
- ¼ teaspoon ground black pepper
- 1 pound lean ground pork
- 1 pound uncooked ground turkey
- 4 ounces thinly sliced salami
- 1 recipe Cornmeal Crust
- 1 egg yolk, lightly beaten
- 1 tablespoon water
  Sliced pears (optional)

1. Preheat oven to 375°F. In a medium skillet cook and stir onion and garlic in hot oil over medium heat until tender; remove from heat and cool slightly. In a large bowl beat egg. Stir in milk, thyme, sage, salt, pepper, and onion mixture. Add pork and turkey; mix well. Divide mixture into thirds. Pat one-third

Cornmeal Crusted Pork Pâté

of the mixture into a 9×5×3-inch loaf pan. Layer with half the salami. Repeat layers; top with remaining pork mixture. Cover with foil.

2. Place loaf pan in a shallow baking pan. Pour hot water around outside of loaf pan to a depth of 1 inch. Bake about 1½ hours or until internal temperature of meat loaf registers 165°F on an instant-read thermometer. Uncover meat loaf and let stand on a wire rack for 15 minutes. Pour off fat. Invert meat loaf onto a rack set in a shallow pan or tray. Pat dry with paper towels. Cover and chill for 4 hours or overnight.

3. Preheat oven to 400°F. Prepare Cornmeal Crust. In a small bowl combine egg yolk and water; set aside. On a lightly floured surface, roll out crust to a 15×12-inch rectangle. Pat the chilled meat loaf with paper towels to remove excess fat. Place the meat loaf in center of the crust. Fold long sides of crust up and over loaf to enclose, trimming excess pastry if necessary. Press sides of crust tightly onto ends of loaf, wrapping it like a package. Brush edges of crust with egg yolk mixture. Fold ends of crust like wrapping a package. Place wrapped loaf on a lightly greased baking sheet. Cut slits in top for steam to escape or use a small leaf-shaped cutter to cut out several leaves from the top. Brush top of crust with egg yolk mixture. If desired, place leaf cutouts on top of loaf and brush top with egg mixture.

4. Bake for 30 to 40 minutes or until golden. Cool on wire rack for 1 hour; loosely cover and chill overnight. Let stand at room temperature for 30 minutes before serving. Slice to serve. If desired, serve with sliced pears.

Cornmeal Crust: In a medium bowl combine 1 cup all-purpose flour, ½ cup yellow cornmeal, and ½ teaspoon salt. Using a pastry blender or two knives, cut in ⅓ cup butter and ¼ cup finely shredded cheddar cheese until mixture resembles coarse crumbs. Sprinkle with 4 to 5 tablespoons cold water, 1 tablespoon at a time, tossing gently until all is moistened. Form into a ball.

Per serving: 215 cal., 13 g total fat (5 g sat. fat), 80 mg chol., 436 mg sodium, 11 g carbo., 1 g fiber, 13 g pro.
Daily Values: 4% vit. A, 1% vit. C, 4% calcium, 7% iron

Easy Shrimp Chowder

Traditionally stewed for hours in an open cauldron, seafood chowders gave hungry fishermen warm, stick-to-your-ribs sustenance. This fast fix-up chowder is ready in minutes and every bit as inviting as its ancestor.

Start to Finish: 20 minutes
Makes: 4 to 6 appetizer servings

- 8 **ounces fresh or frozen small shrimp in shells**
- 1 **10.75-ounce can condensed cream of shrimp soup**
- 1 **cup milk, half-and-half, or light cream**
- ¼ **cup dry sherry, milk, half-and-half, or light cream**
  Snipped fresh parsley (optional)

1. Thaw shrimp, if frozen. Peel and devein shrimp. Rinse shrimp; pat dry with paper towels. Chop shrimp, if desired. Set shrimp aside.

2. In a medium saucepan combine soup, 1 cup milk, and sherry. Bring just to boiling; reduce heat. Simmer, uncovered, for 5 minutes, stirring often.

3. Add shrimp to soup. Return to boiling; reduce heat. Simmer, uncovered, for 1 to 2 minutes more or until shrimp turn opaque. If desired, garnish with parsley.

Per serving: 186 cal., 8 g total fat (2 g sat. fat), 116 mg chol., 687 mg sodium, 10 g carbo., 0 g fiber, 15 g pro.
Daily Values: 5% vit. A, 4% vit. C, 12% calcium, 12% iron

All About Pâté

Whether it's coarsely ground and chunky or silky smooth and easy to spread, pâté is always a special way to start a meal. This appetizer dish is regarded as quite elegant and highly refined—making it an ideal choice when you want to make an impression. Pâtés can be based on a variety of ingredients, including fish, poultry, vegetables, or meats such as pork, veal, ham, or even liver. Seasonings, such as herbs and garlic, are added for delicious accent flavor.

Salmon Pan Chowder

 ## Salmon Pan Chowder

For extra pepper hotness, substitute a dark green poblano chile pepper and a red jalapeño chile pepper for the green sweet pepper and red sweet pepper.

Prep: 25 minutes **Cook:** 28 minutes
Makes: 4 servings

> Nonstick cooking spray
> 1¼ cups white and/or purple pearl onions, peeled
> 1 medium red sweet pepper, cut into ½-inch strips
> 1 medium yellow sweet pepper, cut into ½-inch strips
> 1 medium green sweet pepper, cut into ½-inch strips
> 1 large banana pepper, cut into ¼-inch rings
> 1 14-ounce can vegetable broth or chicken broth
> 1 cup whipping cream
> ½ teaspoon caraway seed, lightly crushed
> ¼ teaspoon salt
> 4 2-ounce skinless, boneless salmon fillets
> Fresh dillweed sprigs

1. Coat a 4-quart Dutch oven with cooking spray; heat pan over medium-high heat. Add onions. Cook and stir, uncovered, over medium-high heat about 7 minutes or until tender. Add red pepper, yellow pepper, green pepper, and banana pepper. Cook and stir for 1 minute more. Carefully add broth. Bring just to boiling; reduce heat. Simmer, uncovered, for 10 minutes. Stir in whipping cream. Return to boiling; reduce heat. Simmer for 10 minutes.

2. Meanwhile, rub caraway seed and salt on both sides of fish. Coat a medium skillet with cooking spray; heat skillet. Cook fillets, uncovered, over medium-high heat for 3 to 4 minutes per side or until fish flakes easily when tested with a fork.

3. To serve, place a salmon fillet in each of four shallow soup bowls. Ladle soup mixture around salmon fillets. Top with dillweed sprigs.

Per serving: 330 cal., 25 g total fat (14 g sat. fat), 112 mg chol.,
601 mg sodium, 15 g carbo., 3 g fiber, 14 g pro.
Daily Values: 46% vit. A, 254% vit. C, 7% calcium, 7% iron

 ## Rib Chops with Baby Squash

This pair of chops is ideal for dinner when the kids are away. Double the recipe and you'll be ready to impress the hungriest quartet.

Prep: 10 minutes **Cook:** 25 minutes
Makes: 2 servings

> 2 pork loin or rib chops, cut 1¼ to 1½ inches thick (about 1½ pounds)
> ¼ teaspoon coarsely ground black pepper
> ⅛ teaspoon salt
> 1 tablespoon cooking oil
> 8 ounces baby summer squash, such as green or yellow pattypan and/or baby zucchini, halved (2 cups); or 2 cups 1-inch slices zucchini and/or yellow summer squash
> ¾ cup half-and-half or light cream
> ½ teaspoon coriander seeds, coarsely crushed

1. Season pork chops with pepper and salt. In a large skillet cook chops in hot oil over medium heat for 18 to 20 minutes or until juices run clear and an instant-read thermometer registers 160°F, turning once. Add squash to skillet for the last 5 minutes of cooking. Remove chops and squash; keep warm.

2. Discard drippings from skillet. Add half-and-half and coriander seeds to skillet, stirring to scrape up browned bits. Bring to boiling; reduce heat. Simmer, uncovered, for 5 to 7 minutes or until sauce is slightly thickened and reduced to about ¼ cup. To serve, place chops and squash on dinner plates; spoon sauce over chops and vegetables.

Per serving: 498 cal., 27 g total fat (11 g sat. fat), 171 mg chol.,
316 mg sodium, 8 g carbo., 2 g fiber, 53 g pro.
Daily Values: 11% vit. A, 37% vit. C, 15% calcium, 12% iron

Apple-Stuffed Pork Chops

Calvados is an apple-flavored spirit produced in the Normandy region of France. Look for it near the brandy at your local wine and spirits store.

Prep: 40 minutes **Bake:** 40 minutes
Oven: 375°F **Makes:** 4 servings

- 1 large cooking apple, peeled if desired, cored, and chopped
- ⅓ cup chopped onion
- 2 teaspoons snipped fresh sage or ½ teaspoon dried sage, crushed
- 1 tablespoon butter or margarine
- ½ ounce white cheddar cheese, shredded (2 tablespoons)
- 4 pork rib chops, pork loin chops, or boneless loin chops, cut 1¼ inches thick (about 3 pounds)
- 1 cup coarse soft crumbs from crusty country bread
- 2 tablespoons butter or margarine, melted
- 2 tablespoons chopped walnuts
- 1 tablespoon snipped fresh Italian (flat-leaf) parsley
- 2 teaspoons finely shredded lemon peel
- 2 tablespoons butter or margarine
- 2 tablespoons all-purpose flour
- ¼ teaspoon salt
  Dash ground black pepper
- 1 cup chicken broth
- ½ cup whipping cream
- 2 tablespoons Calvados or apple juice
- 2 ounces white cheddar cheese, shredded (½ cup)

1. Preheat oven to 375°F. For filling, in a medium skillet cook apple, onion, and sage in 1 tablespoon hot butter over medium heat until tender. Remove from heat. Stir in the 2 tablespoons cheddar cheese; set aside.

2. Trim fat from chops. Make a pocket in each chop by cutting horizontally from the fat side almost to the bone or the opposite side. Divide apple filling

Apple-Stuffed Pork Chops

among pockets in chops. If necessary, secure the openings with wooden toothpicks. Sprinkle chops with *salt* and *ground black pepper*.

3. In a small bowl combine bread crumbs, 2 tablespoons melted butter, walnuts, parsley, and lemon peel.

4. Place chops on a rack in a shallow roasting pan. Top chops with bread crumb mixture. Bake for 40 to 50 minutes or until an instant-read thermometer inserted in center of chops registers 160°F and juices run clear.

5. For sauce, in a medium saucepan melt 2 tablespoons butter. Stir in flour, ¼ teaspoon salt, and dash black pepper. Add chicken broth, whipping cream, and Calvados. Cook and stir over medium heat until thickened and bubbly. Cook and stir for 1 minute more. Stir in ½ cup cheddar cheese until melted and smooth. Serve chops with sauce.

Per serving: 702 cal., 49 g total fat (25 g sat. fat), 157 mg chol., 995 mg sodium, 32 g carbo., 3 g fiber, 30 g pro.
Daily Values: 25% vit. A, 12% vit. C, 24% calcium, 15% iron

2. Remove skillet from heat. Add chicken broth to skillet, scraping up any browned bits in the bottom of the pan. Add drained beans to skillet. Return skillet to heat and bring mixture to boiling. Remove from heat. Coarsely mash bean mixture with a potato masher. Serve chops with bean mixture; top with gremolata.

Gremolata: In a food processor combine ¼ cup fresh Italian (flat-leaf) parsley leaves, 1 tablespoon finely shredded lemon peel, and 3 cloves garlic, quartered. Cover and process with several off/on pulses until finely chopped. (Or finely chop the parsley and garlic; stir together with lemon peel.) Makes about 1 tablespoon.

Per serving: 649 cal., 53 g total fat (22 g sat. fat), 120 mg chol., 732 mg sodium, 16 g carbo., 5 g fiber, 31 g pro.
Daily Values: 6% vit. A, 13% vit. C, 6% calcium, 21% iron

Quick Lamb Chops with Gremolata and White Beans

Gremolata is a sprightly combo of parsley, lemon, and garlic. It is delightful served on these lamb chops but is also perfect on a simple roasted beef or pork.

Start to Finish: 25 minutes **Makes:** 4 servings

- 8 lamb rib or loin chops, cut 1-inch thick
  Salt and ground black pepper
- 1 tablespoon olive oil
- ¾ cup chicken broth
- 1 15-ounce can cannellini beans
  (white kidney beans), rinsed and drained
- 1 recipe Gremolata

1. Trim fat from chops. Sprinkle both sides of chops with salt and pepper. In a 12-inch skillet cook chops, half at a time if necessary, in hot oil over medium heat for 9 to 11 minutes for medium doneness and until an instant-read thermometer registers 160°F, turning once. Transfer chops to a serving plate; cover to keep warm.

Start with a Cocktail

Special occasions call for special drinks— and nothing says "Celebrate!" like these fancy cocktails. You can choose to serve these before, during, or after dinner.

- Stir a spoonful of raspberry liqueur into a glass of white wine or champagne; garnish with a fresh raspberry and a sprig of mint.
- Freeze assorted berries in ice cubes and serve in white or rosé wine.
- Make a quick sangria by crushing some fresh fruit in the bottom of a pitcher. Add ⅔ portion of rosé wine and ⅓ portion of seltzer water.
- Change a Bloody Mary by substituting tequila for vodka. Garnish with a pickled asparagus spear.
- Chill dry sherry and serve on the rocks or with a splash of seltzer or sparkling water.

Porcini Rack of Lamb

A coating of dried porcini (pohr-CHEE-nee) mushrooms lends an intense, woodsy flavor.

Prep: 30 minutes **Roast:** 45 minutes
Stand: 10 minutes **Oven:** 425°/475°F
Makes: 8 servings

    3   large unpeeled shallots
    1½ teaspoons olive oil
    1¼ cups port
    3   tablespoons butter
    2   teaspoons very thinly sliced garlic
    3   tablespoons all-purpose flour
    1   14-ounce can reduced-sodium
        chicken broth
    ¼   cup prepared demi-glace*
    1   teaspoon reduced-sodium soy sauce
    ⅛   teaspoon freshly ground black pepper
    1   ounce dried porcini mushrooms (1 cup)
    1½ teaspoons freshly ground black pepper
    1   teaspoon salt
    3   1¼- to 1-pound racks of lamb, trimmed

1. Preheat oven to 425°F. In a small baking dish place shallots; drizzle with oil. Roast, uncovered, about 30 minutes or until tender; cool. Peel and cut away root and stem of each shallot.

2. Meanwhile, for port sauce, in a small saucepan bring port to boiling; reduce heat. Simmer, uncovered, for 8 to 9 minutes or until reduced to ⅔ cup; remove from pan. In the same saucepan melt 1 tablespoon of the butter; add garlic and cook for 1 minute. Stir in flour; cook and stir about 1 minute more or until light golden brown. Gradually whisk in reduced port, broth, demi-glace, soy sauce, and ⅛ teaspoon pepper. Stir shallots into port mixture. Bring to boiling, stirring constantly; reduce heat. Simmer, uncovered, for 2 minutes; strain through a fine sieve. Discard shallots.

3. In a food processor combine dried porcini, 1½ teaspoons pepper, and salt. Cover and process to a powder. Arrange oven rack to upper third of oven. Increase oven temperature to 475°F. Sprinkle porcini powder onto all meaty sides of lamb. Arrange lamb on a broiler pan, meaty sides up. Roast for 15 to 22 minutes or until an instant-read thermometer inserted in center of lamb registers 135°F.

Porcini Rack of Lamb

4. Transfer lamb to a cutting board. Cover loosely with foil; let stand for 10 minutes. (The temperature of the meat will rise 10° upon standing.) Meanwhile, in a small saucepan heat port sauce over medium heat until hot. Cut up remaining 2 tablespoons butter; whisk into hot sauce. To carve racks, cut slices between rib bones. Serve with port sauce.

***Note:** Prepared demi-glace may be purchased at specialty food stores or from Internet sources, such as www.williams-sonoma.com.

Per serving: 265 cal., 13 g total fat (6 g sat. fat), 71 mg chol., 559 mg sodium, 8 g carbo., 1 g fiber, 20 g pro.
Daily Values: 5% vit. A, 2% vit. C, 2% calcium, 13% iron

 ## Saucy One-Pan Ravioli

Convenient purchased ravioli makes this an easy meal to prepare but don't let that discourage you from serving it to a guest on a special occasion.

Start to Finish: 15 minutes **Makes:** 2 servings

    2   cups cherry tomatoes
    1   clove garlic
    ¾   cup chicken broth
    ¼   teaspoon salt
    ¼   teaspoon ground black pepper

1 9-ounce package refrigerated ravioli
2 tablespoons snipped fresh basil
1 tablespoon snipped fresh
    Italian (flat-leaf) parsley
¼ cup shredded Romano cheese or
    Parmesan cheese (1 ounce)

1. In a blender or food processor combine tomatoes and garlic. Cover and blend or process until smooth. Transfer to a large saucepan. Add broth, salt, and pepper. Bring to boiling.

2. Add ravioli. Return to boiling; reduce heat. Simmer, covered, for 6 to 8 minutes or just until ravioli is tender, stirring gently once or twice. Stir in basil and parsley. Spoon onto plates; sprinkle with cheese.

Per serving: 502 cal., 21 g total fat (11 g sat. fat), 123 mg chol.,
1,346 mg sodium, 56 g carbo., 3 g fiber, 25 g pro.
Daily Values: 31% vit. A, 71% vit. C, 43% calcium, 19% iron

Pumpkin Ravioli with Vodka-Vanilla Sauce

Sensational

Vodka and vanilla in a pasta sauce? Yes! A little bit of vanilla balances any sharpness from the vodka. Don't add too much, or your dish will take on a dessertlike fragrance.

Start to Finish: 40 minutes **Makes:** 4 servings

½ cup canned pumpkin
1 egg yolk
3 tablespoons finely shredded Asiago or
    Parmesan cheese
2 tablespoons fine dry bread crumbs
⅛ teaspoon salt
⅛ teaspoon ground black pepper
    Dash ground nutmeg or ground cinnamon
12 wonton wrappers*
1 egg white, lightly beaten
1 recipe Vodka-Vanilla Sauce
¼ cup chopped hazelnuts (filberts), toasted
    (see tip, page 63)

1. For filling, in a medium bowl stir together pumpkin, egg yolk, cheese, bread crumbs, salt, pepper, and nutmeg.

2. For each ravioli, spoon about 1 tablespoon filling onto center of each wonton wrapper. Brush egg white around edges. Fold diagonally in half to form a triangle; press edges firmly to seal. Cover and set ravioli aside. Prepare Vodka-Vanilla Sauce; keep warm.

3. In a large saucepan bring a large amount of water to boiling. Add ravioli; cook for 3 to 5 minutes or until tender. Using a slotted spoon, lift out ravioli. Drain well.

4. To serve, arrange 3 ravioli on each of four dinner plates. Top with sauce; sprinkle with nuts.

Vodka-Vanilla Sauce: In a small saucepan melt 1 tablespoon butter over medium heat. Add 1 shallot, very finely chopped; cook for 3 to 4 minutes or until tender. Stir in 2 teaspoons all-purpose flour. Add ½ cup reduced-sodium chicken broth and 2 tablespoons vodka. Cook and stir until thickened and bubbly. Cook and stir for 1 minute more. Stir in ¼ cup half-and-half or light cream and ¼ teaspoon vanilla bean paste or vanilla; heat through. Stir in ⅛ teaspoon ground black pepper.

*Note: Look for wonton wrappers in the supermarket produce section.

Per serving: 264 cal., 14 g total fat (5 g sat. fat), 75 mg chol.,
430 mg sodium, 23 g carbo., 2 g fiber, 8 g pro.
Daily Values: 142% vit. A, 4% vit. C, 9% calcium, 12% iron

Pumpkin Ravioli with Vodka-Vanilla Sauce

 **Coconut Rice with Snow Peas**

Coconut milk turns rice into a perfect side dish for Asian entrées or for a simple panfried steak or roasted tenderloin.

Prep: 10 minutes **Cook:** 20 minutes
Stand: 5 minutes **Makes:** 4 servings

- ¾ cup water
- ⅔ cup unsweetened canned coconut milk
- ½ cup uncooked long grain rice
- ¼ teaspoon salt
- 1½ cups 2-inch bias-sliced fresh snow peas or fresh asparagus pieces

1. In a medium saucepan combine water, coconut milk, uncooked rice, and salt. Bring to boiling; reduce heat. Simmer, covered, for 15 minutes.

2. Place pea pods on top of rice. Cover and cook about 5 minutes more or until rice and vegetables are nearly tender; there still may be some liquid. Remove from heat; let stand, covered, for 5 minutes. Season to taste with additional salt.

Per serving: 168 cal., 8 g total fat (7 g sat. fat), 0 mg chol., 158 mg sodium, 22 g carbo., 1 g fiber, 3 g pro.
Daily Values: 5% vit. A, 24% vit. C, 2% calcium, 11% iron

 **Butternut Risotto**

Saffron, said to be the world's most expensive spice, adds a subtle yellow-orange color to this creamy dish. Buy saffron in small quantities (a little goes a long way) and use within six months for maximum flavor.

Prep: 20 minutes **Cook:** 25 minutes
Makes: 8 to 10 servings

- 5 cups reduced-sodium chicken broth
- 3 cloves garlic, minced
- 2 tablespoons olive oil
- 1 pound butternut squash, peeled, seeded, and cut into ¼- to ½-inch cubes (about 3 cups)
- 1½ cups uncooked arborio rice
- ¼ teaspoon thread saffron, crushed, or ground turmeric

- 2 tablespoons butter or margarine
- 2 tablespoons finely shredded Parmesan cheese
- ⅛ teaspoon ground black pepper
  Finely shredded Parmesan cheese (optional)

1. In a medium saucepan bring broth to boiling. Cover and reduce heat until broth just simmers. Meanwhile, in a large nonstick skillet cook and stir garlic in hot oil over medium heat for 15 seconds. Add squash and rice; cook and stir for 1 minute more.

2. Slowly and carefully add ½ cup of the hot broth and saffron to rice mixture, stirring constantly. Continue to cook and stir over medium heat until all of the broth is absorbed. Continue adding broth, ½ cup at a time, stirring constantly until broth is absorbed, but mixture is creamy. (This should take about 25 minutes total.) Remove from heat; stir in butter, the 2 tablespoons cheese, and pepper. Spoon into a serving bowl. If desired, sprinkle with additional finely shredded Parmesan cheese.

Per serving: 183 cal., 7 g total fat (3 g sat. fat), 10 mg chol., 440 mg sodium, 27 g carbo., 1 g fiber, 5 g pro.
Daily Values: 85% vit. A, 19% vit. C, 4% calcium, 11% iron

 **Fruit Bowl with Star Anise**

Sugar syrup is flavored with wine and star anise (a star-shaped pod from China with a hint of licorice flavor). Look for star anise in the spice section.

Prep: 20 minutes **Chill:** 2 hours **Makes:** 6 servings

- ½ cup water
- ⅓ cup sugar
- 3 pods star anise
- ½ cup white Zinfandel wine or apple juice
- 6 cups assorted fresh fruit*
  Fresh mint leaves (optional)

1. In a small saucepan bring water, sugar, and star anise to boiling, stirring occasionally; reduce heat. Simmer, uncovered, for 8 to 10 minutes or until mixture is slightly thickened and syrupy. Remove from heat. Immediately stir in wine.

2. In a large bowl combine desired fruit. Add syrup; toss to coat. Cover and chill for 2 hours or until cold. Discard star anise. If desired, garnish with mint.

*Note: Combine at least three of the following in the fruit bowl: pineapple chunks, blueberries, raspberries, peeled and sliced pears, diced mango, quartered strawberries, cubed cantaloupe, and/or cubed honeydew melon.

Per serving: 142 cal., 0 g total fat (0 g sat. fat), 0 mg chol., 5 mg sodium, 32 g carbo., 5 g fiber, 1 g pro.
Daily Values: 1% vit. A, 28% vit. C, 3% calcium, 6% iron

Fig and Fruit Salad

Tender leaves of spinach and toasted walnuts—tossed with a walnut oil and rice vinegar dressing—become the backdrop for this beautiful salad. Figs, oranges, and goat cheese are arranged on top of the salad.

Start to Finish: 25 minutes **Makes:** 5 servings

- 3 **tablespoons rice vinegar**
- 3 **tablespoons walnut oil**
- 1 **small clove garlic, minced**
- 2 **tablespoons snipped fresh mint**
- ½ **teaspoon salt**
- ⅛ **teaspoon ground black pepper**
- 5 **cups torn fresh spinach**
- 10 **dried Calmyrna (light or golden) figs**
- 2 **oranges and/or blood oranges, peeled and sliced crosswise**
- 3 **ounces semisoft goat cheese (chèvre) rolled in cracked black pepper or herbs and cut into ½-inch-thick slices (optional)**
- ⅓ **cup walnuts, toasted (see tip, page 63)**

1. For dressing, in a blender or food processor combine vinegar, oil, garlic, mint, salt, and pepper. Cover and blend or process until nearly smooth.

2. Place spinach in a large bowl. Drizzle with dressing; toss gently to coat. Divide spinach mixture among five salad bowls or plates. Cut about half of the figs in half. Arrange remaining whole figs, fig

Fig and Fruit Salad

halves, and orange slices with spinach mixture. If desired, top salads with goat cheese slices. Sprinkle with walnuts.

Per serving: 198 cal., 14 g total fat (1 g sat. fat), 0 mg chol., 273 mg sodium, 19 g carbo., 6 g fiber, 3 g pro.
Daily Values: 36% vit. A, 62% vit. C, 8% calcium, 18% iron

Divine Dessert—Fast!

After all the time you spend on a fabulous dinner, you might be searching for something sweet that won't take all night to prepare. Try one of these tasty treats:

- Strawberry ice cream topped with crushed mint cookies
- Vanilla ice cream topped with fresh raspberries and a splash of raspberry liqueur
- Pound cake topped with thawed frozen strawberries in their juices
- Peach ice cream topped with crumbled amaretti cookies
- Angel food cake drizzled with chocolate ice cream topping
- Purchased puff pastry shells, split, and filled with pudding and fresh fruit

Gingerbread House Creations

Two stunning gingerbread houses debut on the following pages. One starts with a packaged dough; the other is a bit more involved—but the beautiful results are worth the investment of time and effort. You will find tips and suggestions for colors and shapes, but use whatever decorating style appeals to you. If you have children or grandchildren, spend an afternoon with them making Easy Gingerbread House cookies. The true fun comes from time spent together giggling and licking icing from your fingers. Take pictures to send to loved ones to show the creativity of your little kitchen helpers. For a more formal and intricate house, try your hand at the ornate Victorian Gingerbread House. Decorated in hues of dusty pink, white, burgundy, and forest green, it would be an eye-catching centerpiece for your holiday table.

Victorian Gingerbread House, page 152

Victorian Gingerbread House

If you like, use any leftover gingerbread dough to make cutouts of trees to decorate and prop up next to the house.

Prep: 15 hours **Bake:** 8 minutes per batch
Stand: 3 hours plus overnight **Oven:** 375°F

3 recipes Gingerbread Dough
2 recipes Royal Icing

Special supplies you will need:
  1 set patterns, enlarged and laminated
     Parchment paper
     Paste food coloring (rose, red, forest or
       juniper green, lemon yellow)
     Disposable pastry bags with couplers and
       tips (ribbon, very small round, and star)
     Small artist's brush
     Decorating sugars (yellow, rainbow, white)
     Candy pebbles
     Straight pins
     Flat 1-inch round pastel wafer candies
       (6 packages Necco wafers)
     Jumbo edible confetti (3 containers confetti)
     Creme-filled pirouette cookies

1. Prepare three recipes Gingerbread Dough. Using a floured rolling pin, roll one portion of dough at a time on a 15×12-inch piece of parchment paper until ⅛ to ¼ inch thick. Place patterns 1 inch apart on dough; cut around patterns with a sharp knife. Remove excess dough. Place parchment paper on a large baking sheet.

2. Bake cookie pieces in a 375°F oven for 8 to 10 minutes or until edges are browned. While pieces are still very warm, place patterns on cookies and trim excess gingerbread as necessary. Return pieces to oven for about 3 minutes or until dry and well browned on edges. Remove the parchment paper with cookie pieces from baking sheet and cool on a wire rack. Remove cookie pieces from parchment. Repeat cutting and baking with all pattern pieces, following directions on patterns. If desired, use a sharp metal pick on cookie pieces to etch outlines of window shapes as guides for decorating. All pieces may be allowed to dry overnight if humidity is low to make more firm.

3. To decorate, prepare two recipes Royal Icing. Keep all icing well covered with plastic wrap when not using. Tint about 2 cups of the icing a pale rose color. Place in a disposable pastry bag fitted with a coupler. (Do not snip end of decorating bag until ready to use. This keeps icing from drying out). Tint about ⅔ cup icing a red color and ⅔ cup icing a dark forest green color. Place these colors in pastry bags with couplers. Tint about ¾ cup icing lemon yellow and add enough drops of water to make the icing thin (like syrup).

4. For the two side sections of the house that will have windows and rose pink siding, you will decorate only the 3 exterior walls of each section (6 walls total). Use a small artist's brush to paint thinned yellow icing where windows will be. Sprinkle windows generously with yellow decorating sugar. Let dry 1 minute before shaking off excess sugar. Fit the rose-colored icing pastry bag with a ribbon tip. For each of the walls, beginning at bottom edge of wall, pipe crosswise rows of pink icing until all of wall (except for windows) is covered. Next finish window trim. Pipe trim around outer edges of windows using red and/or green icing and small round or star tips. Place some white icing in a decorating bag fitted with a small round tip. Pipe white icing trim inside colored trim for window details. For stained glass trim, paint ¾ inch of the tops of windows with thinned yellow icing. Sprinkle with rainbow decorating sugar. Let dry 1 minute before shaking off excess sugar. For the wall with no windows pipe a chimney using white icing and a star tip. Press candy pebbles into icing. Let dry completely for 2 hours or more.

5. Meanwhile, work on the middle section of the house. Decorate only the front and back of this section. Paint windows with thinned yellow icing and coat with yellow decorating sugar, as directed above. Paint the rest of these walls with thinned yellow icing. Sprinkle walls generously with white decorating sugar. Let dry 1 minute before shaking off excess decorating sugar. Outline the windows and doors as desired, using white, red, and green icings, as directed above. Let dry 1 to 2 hours.

6. To assemble, use glass tumblers to hold the walls in place while working. First, assemble the two end sections that have pink siding. For each section, hold the front wall in place with tumblers and attach a side wall, piping a line of white icing with a star tip

Victorian Gingerbread House (rear view)

where the two edges meet. Press them together and hold in place with tumblers. Repeat with the other side wall and the back wall. (Note: The interior side walls will not be decorated.) Let these sections dry while assembling the middle section of the house. Hold the front wall of middle section in place with tumblers while attaching the side walls with lines of icing where they meet. Attach the back wall. Hold in place with tumblers until all sections are dry, about 1 hour. Place all three sections on the gingerbread floor piece, placing the left side section square with the front left corner of the gingerbread floor. Place the other two sections back about 1½ inches from the left side section, but flush with each other. Pipe some white icing on the adjoining walls and press sections together to join. Where the front section comes forward an area of interior wall will be exposed. Now is the time to add rows of pink frosting with a ribbon tip to that area for a finished look. You also may want to add lines of pink icing trim wherever gingerbread is exposed at corners of the house.

7. Working on one section at a time, add roof pieces to top, applying more lines of white icing using a star tip. Use straight pins inserted into gingerbread to keep the steep roof pieces in place until they dry, about 1 hour. For the center section, join the four side roof pieces using lines of white icing. Allow to dry a few minutes before adding the square roof top. Carefully remove straight pins when dry. When roof pieces are dry they may be covered with shingles. Spread or pipe some white icing along bottom of a roof piece. Starting at the bottom, add rows of shingles (Necco wafers) to the roof, overlapping next row over the previous row. Add more icing and rows of shingles until all roof sections are covered. If desired, you may add some pirouette cookies to roof peaks, using some icing. (Tip: For a finished look pipe some icing trim along all unfinished edges of roof pieces.)

8. To make front porch, you will need to cut 7 pirouette cookies to desired height of porch roof (about 3½ inches). Hold porch roof pieces in place to check their placement. Pipe a line of white icing along the back edge of the front porch roof piece. Press onto house front and use pirouette cookies to hold them in place. A dab of icing on top and bottom of the cookies will hold them in place. Attach the side porch roof piece in the same way.

9. To finish, if desired, embellish your house with Christmas trims by piping on green wreaths and garlands and red balls using green and red icing and a small round tip. Pipe a Christmas tree in the front lower window of the left section with white icing and a star tip. Decorate with tiny swirls of pink icing using a small round tip and sprinkle with decorating sugar.

10. If desired, make your own "gingerbread" trims using piped white icing. Place a piece of waxed paper on top of the three filigree and two railing patterns (page 156). Using a decorating bag filled with white Royal Icing and fitted with a small round tip, pipe a lace pattern for the porch and eave filigree. (Use a combination of stripes and swirls. The more your design overlaps and intersects, the stronger it will be.) Pipe straight lines over the pattern for the railings. Move wax paper and continue process for as many filigree and railing pieces as are needed. (Make double what you will need as they are very fragile.) Allow your designs to dry, undisturbed for several hours. To use them, gently peel the dry designs from the waxed paper. Pipe a small amount of icing where you want to apply the designs and gently press into place.

Gingerbread Dough: In a large mixing bowl beat ¼ cup shortening with an electric mixer on medium to high speed for 30 seconds. Add ¾ cup sugar, 1 teaspoon baking powder, 1 teaspoon ground ginger, ½ teaspoon baking soda, ½ teaspoon ground cinnamon, ½ teaspoon ground cloves, and ¼ teaspoon salt; beat until combined. Beat in ⅓ cup molasses, 1 egg, and 1 tablespoon vinegar. Beat in as much of 2½ cups flour as you can with the mixer. Stir in any remaining flour with a wooden spoon. Divide dough in half. Cover each portion with plastic wrap and chill for 3 hours or until dough is easy to handle.

Royal Icing: In a medium bowl combine 3 tablespoons meringue powder, ⅓ cup plus 2 tablespoons warm water, one 16-ounce package powdered sugar, 1 teaspoon vanilla, and ½ teaspoon cream of tartar. Beat with an electric mixer on low speed until combined; beat on high speed for 7 to 10 minutes or until very stiff. When not using, keep icing covered with plastic wrap and refrigerate to prevent drying.

Easy Gingerbread House Cookies

Prep: 1 hour **Bake:** 8 minutes per batch
Oven: 375°F **Makes:** five or six 6-inch cookies

1 16.5-ounce package refrigerated gingerbread cookie dough or one 18-ounce package refrigerated sugar cookie dough
¼ cup all-purpose flour
1 tube each purchased white, red, and green decorating icing
   Colored decorating sugars and/or sprinkles
   Waffle-shaped pretzels or pretzel sticks

1. Preheat oven to 375°F. In a large bowl place the cookie dough and flour. Stir with a wooden spoon or gently mix with hands until combined. On a lightly floured surface, roll out half of the dough at a time until ¼ inch thick. Use a 6-inch house-shape cookie cutter to cut out shapes or use a small knife to cut out house shapes of your own design. Arrange cutouts 3 inches apart on an ungreased cookie sheet. (If desired, use a small knife to cut door or window shapes in dough.) Bake for 8 to 10 minutes or until edges are lightly browned. Cool on cookie sheet for 2 minutes; transfer to wire racks and let cool.

2. Use tubes of decorating icing to decorate cooled cookies. Sprinkle colored sugars and/or sprinkles over the icing while still moist. Attach waffle-shape pretzels with some of the icing for windows.

Per serving: 494 cal., 21 g total fat (6 g sat. fat), 44 mg chol., 418 mg sodium, 70 g carbo., 0 g fiber, 4 g pro.
Daily Values: 1% vit. A, 14% iron

Easy Gingerbread House Cookies

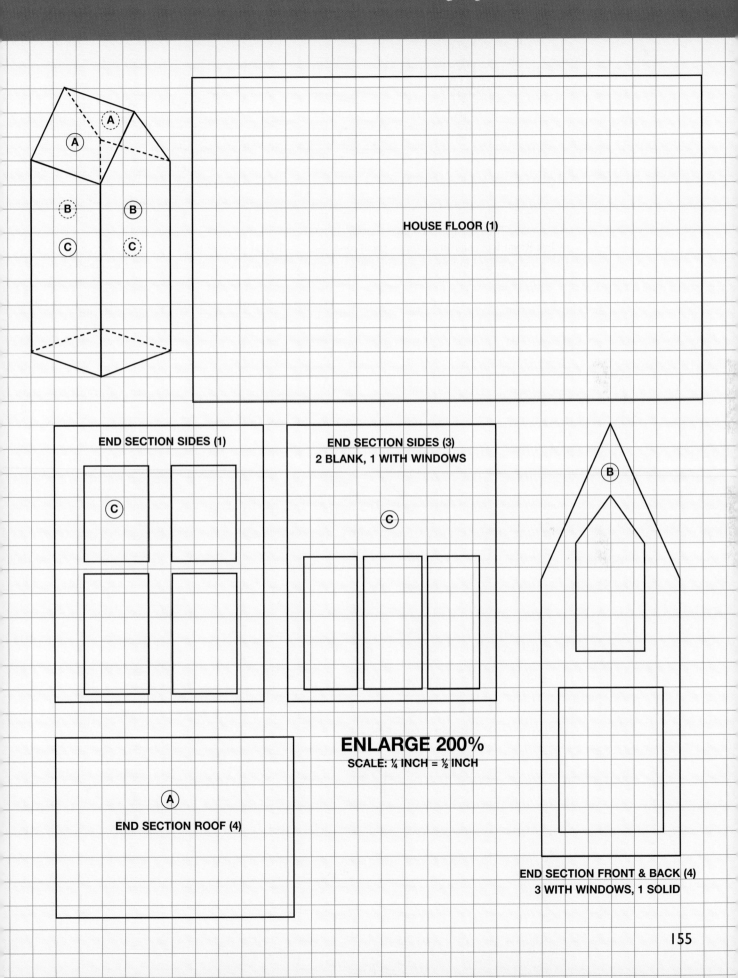

HOUSE FLOOR (1)

END SECTION SIDES (1)

C

END SECTION SIDES (3)
2 BLANK, 1 WITH WINDOWS

C

B

ENLARGE 200%
SCALE: ¼ INCH = ½ INCH

A

END SECTION ROOF (4)

END SECTION FRONT & BACK (4)
3 WITH WINDOWS, 1 SOLID

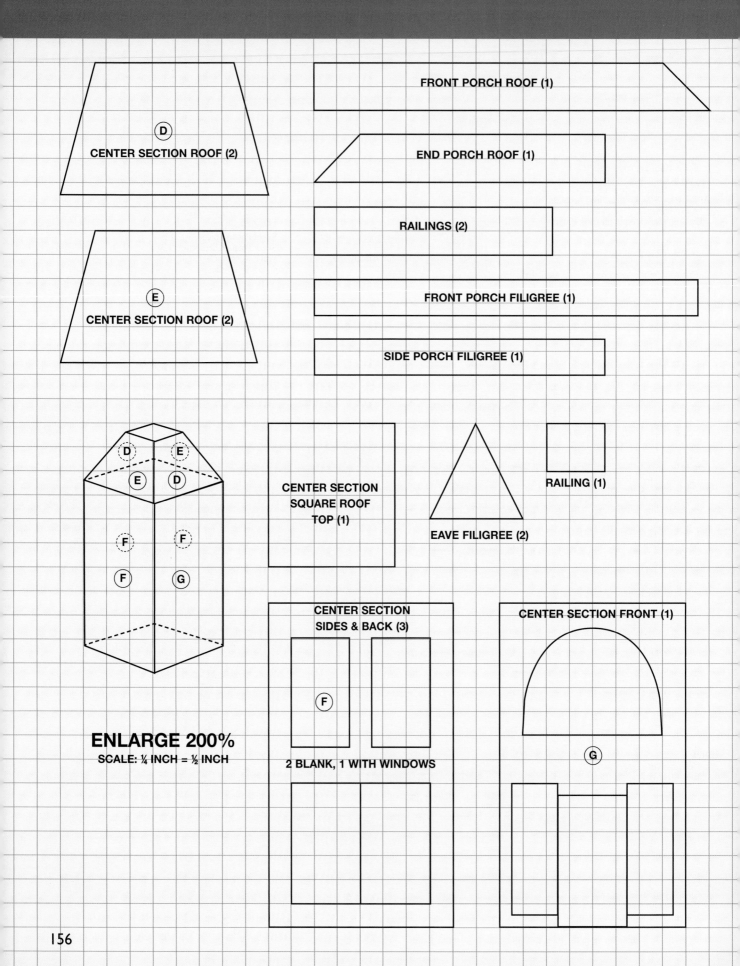

CENTER SECTION ROOF (2) — D

FRONT PORCH ROOF (1)

END PORCH ROOF (1)

RAILINGS (2)

FRONT PORCH FILIGREE (1)

SIDE PORCH FILIGREE (1)

CENTER SECTION ROOF (2) — E

CENTER SECTION
SQUARE ROOF
TOP (1)

RAILING (1)

EAVE FILIGREE (2)

CENTER SECTION
SIDES & BACK (3)

2 BLANK, 1 WITH WINDOWS

CENTER SECTION FRONT (1)

ENLARGE 200%
SCALE: ¼ INCH = ½ INCH